THE AGE OF THE POETS

THE AGE OF THE POETS

AND OTHER WRITINGS ON TWENTIETH-CENTURY POETRY AND PROSE

———————◆———————

ALAIN BADIOU

Edited and Translated by
Bruno Bosteels

With an Introduction by
Emily Apter and
Bruno Bosteels

VERSO
London • New York

Liberté · Égalité · Fraternité
RÉPUBLIQUE FRANÇAISE

This book is supported by the Institut francais
as part of the Burgess programme
www.frenchbooknews.com

First published by Verso 2014
Translation © Bruno Bosteels 2014
Introduction © Emily Apter and Bruno Bosteels 2014
Parts of the introduction were previously published as
'Forcing the Truth' in Bruno Bosteels, *Badiou and Politics*
(Durham, NC: Duke University Press, 2011) and in Emily Apter,
'Laws of the '70s: Badiou's Revolutionary Untimeliness',
Cardozo Law Review 29.5 (April 2008)

1 3 5 7 9 10 8 6 4 2

Verso
UK: 6 Meard Street, London W1F 0EG
US: 20 Jay Street, Suite 1010, Brooklyn, NY 11201
www.versobooks.com

Verso is the imprint of New Left Books

ISBN-13: 978-1-78168-569-3 (PB)
ISBN-13: 978-1-78168-570-9 (HB)
eISBN-13: 978-1-78168-571-6 (US)
eISBN-13: 978-1-78168-710-9 (UK)

British Library Cataloguing in Publication Data
A catalogue record for this book is available from the British Library

Library of Congress Cataloging-in-Publication Data
A catalog record for this book is available from the Library of Congress

Typeset in Sabon by MJ & N Gavan, Truro, Cornwall
Printed in the US by Maple Press

CONTENTS

II. On Prose

INTRODUCTION

I

The texts collected in this volume correspond to Alain Badiou's work from the past fifty years on poetry and novelistic prose. Almost all of these texts – essays, prefaces, talks and reviews not yet included in previous books – are translated here for the first time. Some proved nearly impossible to locate, while others have yet to be published even in French. Taken together, they provide the reader with a broad vista onto a much underappreciated aspect of Badiou's oeuvre, which includes not only four novels of his own hand but also a relentless and longstanding engagement with modern literature that starts in 1965 with 'The Autonomy of the Aesthetic Process' and continues all the way to his most recent talk on 'Poetry and Communism' in the spring of 2014 at the Sorbonne.

Two great polemics run through these texts. The first and most recent polemic, which is the principal impetus behind the writings from the 1990s on the so-called 'age of the poets', takes aim at those ways of thinking of the link between poetry and philosophy that we can find in Martin Heidegger's writings as well as in the critical work from French readers of Heidegger's thinking such as the late Philippe Lacoue-Labarthe. The second and much older polemic, hearkening back to the late 1960s, refers to the 'novelistic effect' in a critical rejoinder to the way in which literature is situated in relation to the epistemological break between science and ideology that we have come to associate with the canonical work of Louis Althusser, as well as that of disciples of his such as Pierre Macherey. Thus, in addition to providing the interested reader with a systematic account of Badiou's own take on the role of literature in and for philosophy, *The Age of the Poets and Other Writings on Twentieth-Century Poetry and Prose* also represents a theoretical settling of accounts with the mostly parallel yet similarly dominant strands of contemporary thought that are Heideggerianism and Althusserianism.

In both cases, moreover, the stakes are far from being limited to the age-old rivalry between philosophy and poetry – a jealous rivalry that was old already for the Ancients, as seen most notably and predictably in Plato's *Republic*. Rather, the uncomfortable rapport, or non-rapport, between poets and philosophers is at the same time rife with ideological tensions, hidden obstacles, and as-yet-unfulfilled promises. Philosophy and poetry, in other words, are secretly triangulated by politics. Thus, it is fitting that the first half of this collection should open with the title-essay 'The Age of the Poets', only to conclude, via Wallace Stevens and Pier Paolo Pasolini, with a return to the question of the essential link between poetry and communism in light of the unique internationalist experience of the civil war in Spain that brought together the likes of César Vallejo, Pablo Neruda, Paul Éluard and Nâzim Hikmet. Thus, also, if Nazism inevitably casts its long and ominous shadow over the polemic with Heidegger's readings of Friedrich Hölderlin or Georg Trakl, or with the same master's silent non-response to Paul Celan, by contrast, in the second part of this collection, the theoretical detour through Althusserian Marxism will be taken to task slowly but surely in order to raise anew the question of the egalitarian political destiny of narrative prose, following a requiem for the old Marxism, among writers as diverse as Severo Sarduy, Natacha Michel and Pierre Guyotat.

Some thirty years ago, in *Peut-on penser la politique?*, Badiou already proposed a similar rule of thumb that is also applicable to *The Age of the Poets*: 'For those of us who, like me, accept that literature can name a real to which politics remains closed, there is room here to open a literary polemic.'[1] Speaking of what he would later come to name, borrowing an expression from Mallarmé's poetry, the 'obscure disaster' of the 'death' of Soviet communism, Badiou admits:

---

1 Alain Badiou, *Peut-on penser la politique?* (Paris: Seuil, 1985), p. 31. Badiou also briefly revisits the comparison between Solzhenitsyn and Shalamov in his *Ethics: An Essay on the Understanding of Evil*, trans. Peter Hallward (London: Verso, 2002), pp. 11–12. A detailed account of Badiou's previously published readings of poetry and prose would have to include the following: the long analysis of Mallarmé's poetry as an instance of the structural dialectic, in *Theory of the Subject*, trans. Bruno Bosteels (London: Continuum, 2009), pp. 51–110; the meditations on Mallarmé and Hölderlin in *Being and Event*, trans. Oliver Feltham (London: Continuum 2005), pp. 191–8, 255–61; *On Beckett*, trans. Alberto Toscano and Nina Power (London: Clinamen, 2003); Chapters 4–6 in *Conditions*, trans. Steven Corcoran (London: Continuum, 2008), pp. 35–90; most of *Handbook of Inaesthetics*, trans. Alberto Toscano (Stanford, CA: Stanford University Press, 2004); the readings of Saint-John Perse, Paul Celan, Fernando Pessoa, Bertolt Brecht, Osip Mandelstam and others scattered throughout *The Century*, trans. Alberto Toscano (London: Polity, 2007); the sections on Paul Valéry and Jean-Jacques Rousseau's treatment of love in *The New Heloise*, in *Logics of Worlds*, trans. Alberto Toscano (London: Continuum, 2009), pp. 367–9, 455–9. And, of course, Badiou's ongoing Wednesday seminars rarely fail to invoke the poets and novelists of our time, especially in the recently published *Images du temps présent, 2001–2004*, which is part of Badiou, *Le Séminaire* (Paris: Fayard, 2014). For a critical analysis of some of the operations and shortcomings in Badiou's take on literature, see the essays by Pierre Macherey, Gabriel Riera and Jean-Michel Rabaté in *Alain Badiou: Philosophy and Its Conditions* (Albany, NY: SUNY Press, 2005), pp. 61–115; Jean-Jacques Lecercle, *Badiou and Deleuze Read Literature* (Edinburgh: Edinburgh University Press, 2012); Quentin Meillassoux, 'Badiou et Mallarmé: l'événement et le peut-être', in *Autour d'Alain Badiou*, ed. Isabelle Vodoz and Fabien Tarby (Paris: Germina, 2011), pp. 103–25; and Jacques Rancière, 'The Poet at the Philosopher's: Mallarmé and Badiou', in *The Politics of Literature* (London: Polity, 2011), pp. 183–203.

Subjectively, it is well known that it is in the prophetic
resource of art that the Russian horror has finally managed
to come to light for the Western conscience. The simple
stating of the facts by Victor Serge, David Rousset, and
many others, did not suffice for this. Only the genius of
Alexander Solzhenitsyn has completely shaken the regime
of blind certitudes.[2]

However, promptly proceeding to contrast the Christic,
nationalistic and staunchly antidemocratic ideology of
The Gulag Archipelago with the ethical simplicity of a
few principles and the universality of an unshaken will
in Varlam Shalamov's short stories collected in *Kolyma:
Stories of Life in the Camps*, Badiou warns against the
naive glorification of literary evidence in and of itself:
'We should not pick the wrong writer, when it is art that
governs the possibility of political thought. No matter
how great Solzhenitsyn is, his grandeur mirrors the dark
grandeur in which Stalin consummated the red disaster.'[3]
A genuine assessment of the disastrous failures and no
less disastrous defeats of twentieth-century communism is
still before us. Shalamov's prose, like Brecht's poetry, can
help us understand the enormous scale of this task, which
requires nothing less than the complete reinvention of a
new time for politics, without nostalgia or renegacy: 'All
of *Kolyma*, in the very name of the victims, calls for them
not to settle for political innocence. It is this non-innocence
that must be invented, elsewhere than in pure reaction. To
end with the horror demands the advancement of a politics
that integrates that which its absence has cost.'[4]

2

As for the polemic with Heidegger, this should not be mis-
understood as if to suggest that the age of the poets were

2 Badiou, *Peut-on penser la politique?*, pp. 30–1.
3 Ibid., p. 34.
4 Ibid., p. 39.

merely an invention of the thinker from Todtnauberg. Such an era or historic moment in the development of modern poetry did actually take place long before the essays on Hölderlin, Rilke or Trakl were published in Heidegger's *Poetry, Language, Thought* or *On the Way to Language*. As Badiou writes in *Manifesto for Philosophy*: 'The fact is that there really was an age of the poets, in the time of the sutured escheat of philosophy.'[5] Heidegger only succeeded in giving this historic moment the quasi-sacred aura of an ontological destiny: 'The existence of the poets gave to Heidegger's thinking, something without which it would have been aporetic and hopeless, a ground of historicity, actuality, apt to confer upon it – once the mirage of a political historicity had been concretized and dissolved in the Nazi horror – what was to be its unique, real occurrence.'[6]

Badiou certainly admits the greatness of Heidegger's thinking. He opens *Being and Event* by referring to the author of *Being and Time* as 'the last universally recognizable philosopher'.[7] Heidegger is greeted as the one responsible for raising again the quintessential philosophical question of being qua being: 'Our epoch can be said to have been stamped and signed, in philosophy, by the return of the question of being. This is why it is dominated by Heidegger.'[8] In Heidegger's interpretations of poetry, therefore, it is not the ontological question as such that is the issue of polemics, but rather the particular – poeticizing – orientation thereof, summarized in the prophetic answer to the question: 'What are poets for in times of distress?' In fact, Badiou's own philosophy of the event is inaugurated by a refusal to pursue the themes of the end or the times of distress according to the hermeneutico-historical path that takes its inspiration from Heidegger's thinking about poetry.

5 Alain Badiou, *Manifesto for Philosophy*, trans. Norman Madarasz (Albany, NY: State University of New York Press, 1999), p. 70 (translation modified).
6 Ibid., p. 74.
7 Badiou, *Being and Event*, p. 1.
8 Alain Badiou, *Deleuze: The Clamor of Being*, trans. Louise Burchill (Minneapolis, MN: University of Minnesota Press, 2000), p. 19.

This refusal, together with the accompanying search for an alternative ontological orientation – that is, the clearing of a path away from poetry and towards mathematics – really constitutes the first founding gesture of Badiou's renewed Platonism. On one hand, the aim is to substitute an axiomatic ontology of subtraction for the hermeneutic ontology of presence and the retreat of presence, or of the enigma and unconcealment of meaning or sense; on the other hand, the project consists in interrupting, through a consistent pursuit of the matheme, the suture of philosophy onto the poem, by taking one further step in the unfolding of the intrinsic power of each of the four generic procedures of truth that are science, politics, art and love.

Suture, in Badiou's philosophy, has at least two different meanings, neither of which should be confused with how Jacques-Alain Miller in his early days defined the concept in classic texts written for the Lacano-Althusserian journal *Cahiers pour l'analyse*, a definition that was subsequently popularized both in the direction of film theory, around the journal *Screen*, and in the political theory of figures such as the late Ernesto Laclau and Chantal Mouffe, above all in *Hegemony and Socialist Strategy*. For Badiou, suture in the first place describes the way in which the discourse of ontology, as the science of being qua being, is linked onto being through the void. This is how the concept appears in *Being and Event*: 'I term *void* of a situation this suture to its being.'[9] From within a given situation, we can think of the sheer multiplicity of being only through the void of this situation. Suture thus has a first, productive meaning in *Being and Event*, as that which enables the discourse of ontology. But this meta-ontological use of the concept has almost nothing to do with the second meaning of suture, advanced in *Manifesto of Philosophy* to describe the way in which modern philosophy, particularly after Hegel, has tended to abdicate and delegate its own powers of thought to just one of its four conditions – first to science, with positivism, and then to politics, with revolutionary Marxism.

9 Badiou, *Being and Event*, p. 55.

Marxism, in fact, combines both sutures in the claim to ground revolutionary politics in the science of History. The age of the poets, then, intervenes in this process by remitting the task of philosophy, or of post-metaphysical thinking, to the speech of the poets as a way to stay clear of both the scientific positivity of the object and the political sense or meaning of History: 'In thrall in the West to science, in the East to politics, philosophy has attempted in western Europe at least to serve the other Master, the poem. Philosophy's current situation is that of a harlequin serving three masters.'[10]

The treatment of the poetico-hermeneutic tradition in *Being and Event* and *Manifesto for Philosophy*, which is continued in the texts on the age of the poets in this volume, can nonetheless lead to a number of misunderstandings. It presumes, first of all, that one accepts the description, which is supposed to be consensual, of hermeneutics (here used as a name for Heidegger's legacy) as a thinking of near-sacred presence. This description, however, is extremely surprising insofar as it hides the extent to which hermeneutic ontology, too, claims to be a thinking of the event. If we simply accept Badiou's opposition between subtraction and presence, it thus becomes extremely difficult to grasp in what sense the event of being, in the Heideggerian legacy, serves precisely to deconstruct rather than restore and resacralize the metaphysics of presence. This potential debate is obscured not only because hermeneutic thinking is voided of its event-like potential, but also – and this is the second reason why there might be a misunderstanding involved – because the ontology of presence is identified exclusively with the operation that sutures philosophy to the poem. 'What we must recall from Heidegger', Badiou writes, 'is the idea that, in times of distress, thought is foremost on the way to speech',[11] so that the only possible answer to

---

10   Badiou, *Manifesto for Philosophy*, p. 67 (translation modified).

11   Alain Badiou, *Briefings on Existence: A Short Treatise on Transitory Ontology*, trans. Norman Madarasz (Albany, NY: SUNY Press, 2006), p. 108.

the hermeneutic tradition necessarily passes through a de-suturing of philosophy from the poem: 'For this reason, the fundamental criticism of Heidegger can only be the following one: the age of the poets is finished; it is necessary *also* to de-suture philosophy from its poetic condition.'[12]

This partial and potentially misleading reading of hermeneutic ontology explains why, in the wake of the publication of *Being and Event* and *Manifesto for Philosophy*, the debate with the Heideggerian tradition became fixated on the question of the 'age of the poets', as in this collection's title essay, which was first presented as a talk for the seminar organized by Jacques Rancière on *The Politics of Poets: What are Poets for in Times of Distress?*[13] Witness, for example, the few public exchanges that took place, sometimes hidden away in a footnote, with Jean-Luc Nancy and Philippe Lacoue-Labarthe. The latter summarizes the debate, or rather reopens it, by stating that the problem cannot be reduced to a suturing of philosophy to the poem, since the true question at issue is rather some kind of political re-suturing of the artistic suture – that is, the aestheticization of politics of which Walter Benjamin had already spoken: 'There is, if you want, some kind of misunderstanding, which bears on poetry, for sure, but also on politics – or at the very least on a determinate type of politics, even a style, to which the philosophy from which Badiou seeks to demarcate himself is not foreign.'[14] At the same time, Lacoue-Labarthe's answer puts into question the link between art, philosophy and politics from the point of view not so much of the poem, but of what he calls the mytheme, in the sense of an immanent putting-to-work of the collective. Of

12 Badiou, *Manifesto for Philosophy*, p. 74 (translation modified).
13 Alain Badiou, 'L'Âge des poètes', in Jacques Rancière, ed., *La politique des poètes: Pourquoi des poètes en temps de détresse?* (Paris: Albin Michel, 1992), pp. 21–38.
14 Philippe Lacoue-Labarthe, 'Poésie, philosophie, politique', in Rancière, *La politique des poètes*, p. 47. See also Philippe Lacoue-Labarthe, *Heidegger and the Politics of Poetry*, ed. and trans. Jeff Fort (Urbana, IL: University of Illinois Press, 2007).

such mythic or fictive putting-to-work or self-fashioning we all know only too well the disastrous consequences in what Lacoue-Labarthe and Nancy, in *The Nazi Myth*, call 'national-aestheticism'.[15] To this disastrous outcome, the same authors claim, we can then barely begin to oppose, on one hand, the idea of a becoming-prose of poetry – that is, the interruption of myth – and, on the other, the retreat of the political, which is at once a new treatment of that which withdraws, or of that which never took place to begin with – for instance, the idea of sovereignty – as the condition both of the possibility and the radical impossibility of politics as such.

By contrast, as far as the clear ontological alternative is concerned between the paths of presence and subtraction, or, in terms of the conditions of philosophy, between the poem and the matheme, these decisions, which are absolutely fundamental to Badiou's philosophy, seem to carry no weight at all in the eyes of someone like Nancy, who is otherwise ideally placed to judge the questions of art and the event according to Heidegger. In his beautiful book *The Sense of the World*, for instance, Nancy comes to a point where he is able to find in Badiou's mathematical ontology of subtraction what he considers to be 'certain formulations that are strictly equivalent to those to which a deconstruction of onto-theology leads', with the difference between the two paths being reduced, by way of 'a carefully arranged lexical transcription', to a mere question of styles or modes, whether 'a more pathos-laden mode (Heidegger) or in a cooler mode (Badiou)'.[16] Despite

---

15 Philippe Lacoue-Labarthe and Jean-Luc Nancy, *Le mythe nazi* (La Tour d'Aigues: Éditions de l'Aube, 1991), available in English as 'The Nazi Myth', trans. Brian Holmes, *Critical Inquiry* 16 (Winter 1990), pp. 291–312.

16 Jean-Luc Nancy, *The Sense of the World*, trans. Jeffrey S. Librett (Minneapolis, MN: University of Minnesota Press, 1997), p. 175 n. 19. As Nancy explains with regard to the subject who decides in the face of the event, according to Badiou, 'One is, at bottom, on a Heideggerian register, that of "*Das Ereignis trägt die Wahrheit = die Wahrheit durchragt das Ereignis*" (the event carries truth = truths juts out through the event), where the verb *durchragen* would call for a long gloss. It is "jutting across", and

Badiou's affirmation of a trenchant rupture, some of the
subtlest readers of the ontology of presence, in turning to
this author, thus find nothing if not one more endeavour in
the general deconstruction of metaphysics.

With regard to Heidegger, in other words, it is a matter
not so much of defining a thought of the event in opposition to the oblique approach of presence as of opposing two
clearly distinct ideas – or two different orientations – of the
event itself. Furthermore, the space for this harsh and often
hushed polemic cannot be reduced to the problems relative
to the age of the poets, during which philosophy – in its
Heideggerian closure and repetition – ends up sutured to
the enigma of being proffered by the poetic word. To the
contrary, the polemic extends to other conditions as well.
Thus, an updated confrontation with the Heideggerian
path of deconstruction should also bear on the efforts to
delimit what the condition of politics, or of the political,
holds for us today, after the critique both of its immanent
presentation by the people, masses or multitude and of its
external representation by the machinery of the state. In
this regard, a discussion of the collective project surrounding the seminars *Rejouer le politique* and *Le retrait du
politique* (partially translated as *Retreating the Political*),
organized at the Centre for the Philosophical Study of the
Political at the École Normale Supérieure in rue d'Ulm in
the early 1980s by Nancy and Lacoue-Labarthe – a project
in which Badiou participated with the two conferences
that were later published in *Peut-on penser la politique?* –
would lead to a wholly different outlook, irreducible to
the opposition between poem and matheme, or between
presence and subtraction, in order to serve up an answer
to the deconstruction of metaphysics in the footsteps of
Heidegger and Derrida.[17]

---

thus also "piercing" and almost "tearing" ("incising" in Badiou's vocabulary). Any thought that privileges truth, that takes on *the style of truth*,
dedicates itself to the tension of an internal tornness, whether it does so in a
more pathos-laden mode (Heidegger) or in a cooler mode (Badiou)' (ibid.).

17 See the two collections of papers produced during the seminar

3

'It is only possible to think the singularity of a thought by *evacuating time*', proposes Badiou in *Metapolitics*, paraphrasing Sylvain Lazarus's argument in his 1996 book *Anthropology of the Name*.[18] Why must time be evacuated? In order, it would seem, for the singularity of 'the possible' to be inserted as a caesura into the sequence of political time. This is not a caesura featured as openness or clearing, but as actualization of the generic multiple; as subtraction of event from situation, or as escape from the regime of the one. 'What name can thinking give to its own immemorial attempt to subtract being from the grip of the one?' Badiou asks in his essay 'The Question of Being Today', which discusses Heidegger. Too many thinkers exceed the framework of the destiny of Western metaphysics for Heidegger's philosophical apparatus to be the only path to follow, according to Badiou.

> Can we learn to mobilize those figures who so obviously exempt themselves from Heidegger's destinal apparatus? Figures such as the magnificent Lucretius, in whom the power of the poem, far from maintaining the Open in the midst of epochal distress, tries instead to subtract thinking from every return of the gods and firmly establish it within the certitude of the multiple?[19]

The naming of the possible prescription, if one extrapolates here, has everything to do with the possibility of

---

on the political organized at the École Normale Supérieure by Lacoue-Labarthe and Nancy: *Rejouer le politique* (Paris: Galilée, 1981) and *Le retrait du politique* (Paris: Galilée, 1983); in English, a selection can be found in *Retreating the Political*, ed. and trans. Simon Sparks (New York: Routledge, 1997).

18 Alain Badiou, *Metapolitics*, trans. Jason Barker (London: Verso, 2005), p. 33. See also Sylvain Lazarus, *Anthropologie du nom* (Paris: Seuil, 1996).

19 Alain Badiou, 'The Question of Being Today', in *Theoretical Writings*, ed. and trans. Ray Brassier and Alberto Toscano (London: Continuum, 2006), p. 43.

bringing a truth or prescription into existence, of making it happen in political time. This idea of the name of the event as a subtracted 'possible' or 'thinkability' is what allows political time to be re-sequenced. For Badiou, this rarely happens without recourse to the immanent capacities not just of the language of poetry but of the novel's narrative prose as well.

The Century already actively enlists poetry to re-time the political. Badiou tries to imagine how the twentieth century would articulate its movement in its own language, subjectivizing itself as century-think. Two poems allow us to hear the century 'speak', so to speak. The first poem is by Saint-John Perse, a privileged turn-of-the-century Francophone diplomat from Guadeloupe; the second by Paul Celan, a Romanian-born polyglot Heideggerian Jewish translator who survived a labour camp during World War II and committed suicide in 1967. 'Anabasis' is their common title – a trope signifying an errant path, an unedited return or *égarement*. For Badiou, anabasis becomes the name for a 'small century' interrupted on the eve of May '68 – a poetic span leading from Perse's 'fraternal axiom' (the 'I' which becomes 'we' in the voyage out, the sacrifice of identitarian security) to Celan's 'ensemble' or 'together' (the set of 'we' that escapes 'I', the spectre haunting the 1970s in the form of a group subject, a set or category excluded from its own terms). This timing of anabasis is a suspended revolutionary temporality, a mini-century in need of subtraction from the global period of Restoration that began in the 1980s, themselves timed according to competitive individualism and the regime of profit.

Against the long century of so-called totalitarianism, poetry thus contributes to what we might name another fractional time-signature – Badiou's short or mini-century that threatens to be eclipsed by the Heideggerian appropriation of the age of the poets: a temporality that is *of* the 1970s insofar as it coincides with Badiou's Maoist turn, and his rejection, from then on, of all systems of 'capitalo-parliamentarianism' that represent themselves through 'the subjective law of "democracy"'.[20] The Badiou century reopens the revolutionary sequence of the Commune or group subject and is identifiable with a heightened sense of time itself. The spaces and sensations of time that collect around iconic dates are compressed, accelerated, and rendered trans-historical. As Dominique Lecourt puts it, writing about May '68 in France, 'In our theoretical rear-view mirror we saw 1936, 1871, 1848 and 1793 march past in speeded-up motion. We rediscovered France, "classical country of the class struggle", as the old Marx had written. Some doctrinaires were predicting the Commune for the end of June!'[21] Badiou's century, shaped by the writers with whom he shared literary and activist trajectories (Natacha Michel, Pierre Guyotat, Henry Bauchau, the 'Red Hawks' Guy Lardreau and Christian Jambet), is marked by Althusserianism, Maoism, anti-imperialism, *Anti-Oedipus*, worker strikes, new social movements, sexual liberation, and the initial organizing of *les sans-papiers* and *les sans-abri*. This century continues in the refusal to surrender to post–Berlin Wall ideologies of capitalist triumphalism and neoliberal consensus, and in what we might call Badiou's 'post-Maoism' – an uncompleted political sequence that exceeds the period normally assigned to French Maoism, the so-called 'red years' of 1966–76.[22]

---

20 Badiou, quoted in Peter Hallward, *Badiou: A Subject to Truth* (Minneapolis, MN: University of Minnesota Press, 2003), p. 45.

21 Dominique Lecourt, *The Mediocracy: French Philosophy since 1968*, trans. Gregory Elliott (London: Verso, 2001), p. 28.

22 Badiou's main texts from this period are *Théorie de la contradiction* (Paris: François Maspero, 1975); *De l'idéologie* (Paris: François Maspero, 1976); and *Le noyau rationnel de la dialectique hégélienne* (Paris: François Maspero, 1977). These texts have recently been reissued in French under the title *Les années rouges* (Paris: Les Prairies Ordinaires, 2012). For a more detailed account of Badiou's post-Maoism, see Chapters 3 and 4 in Bruno Bosteels, *Badiou and Politics* (Durham, NC: Duke University Press).

4

In the earliest stages of this Maoist sequence, long before he would engage in polemical struggles with the Heideggerian legacy over the age of the poets, Badiou began his career as a philosopher by tackling the theory of science and ideology of his mentor Althusser from the point of view of literary art. Thus, after achieving considerable critical acclaim with *Almagestes* (1964) and *Portulans* (1967), two avant-garde novels or anti-novels that promptly drew praise from Sartre, Badiou's first publication was 'The Autonomy of the Aesthetic Process'.[23] Completed in June 1965 as part of a seminar presented under the aegis of Althusser and published the following year in a special issue of the *Cahiers Marxistes-Léninistes* on 'Art, Language, and Class Struggle', edited by members of the Union des Jeunesses Communistes (Marxiste-Léniniste) at the École Normale Supérieure in rue d'Ulm, the essay also shows Badiou taking his distance from the discussions about art and ideology as they were taking shape at the time – that is, in the immediate wake of the 1965 publication of *For Marx* and *Reading Capital*, most notably in an essay from the same year by Pierre Macherey devoted to Lenin's famous literary criticism on Leo Tolstoy.

Anticipating what would soon become his core proposal in *A Theory of Literary Production*, Macherey follows Althusser in arguing for art and literature's special status in comparison to other ideological forms. While clearly unable to produce the kind of knowledge associated with science, art also cannot be equated with the purely imaginary effects of ideology. Macherey and Althusser 'solve' this enigma of the specific difference of artistic production by positing *within* art a relation of internal distancing, or redoubling, with regard to its own ideological nature.

In his 1966 'Letter on Art in Reply to André Daspre', for instance, Althusser tries to answer the question of whether

---

23   Alain Badiou, 'L'autonomie du processus esthétique', *Cahiers Marxistes-Léninistes* 12–13 (1966), pp. 77–89.

art is just like any ideological form, such as religion, or else participates somehow in a different kind of activity that would come closer to scientific knowledge, without ever achieving its proper status. 'Art (I mean authentic art, not works of an average or mediocre level)', writes Althusser, adding a significant parenthetical qualification, 'does not give us a *knowledge* in the *strict sense*, it therefore does not replace knowledge (in the modern sense: scientific knowledge), but what it gives us does nevertheless maintain a certain *specific relationship* with knowledge. This relationship is not one of identity but one of difference.'[24] Art would take its place somewhere between science and ideology. Its specific difference would consist in the fact that what it produces is not quite on the order of scientific knowledge or cognition, but also does not produce merely an effect of ideological (mis)recognition. Thus, firstly, Althusser shifts the attention away from the question of knowledge towards one of perception and sensation. Secondly, he adds a certain reflective twist by arguing that art, while not escaping the effects of ideology entirely, nonetheless shows us the functioning of normal ideological operations. Finally, in order further to explain the nature of this 'showing', he has recourse to the notions of 'retreat' and 'internal distantiation':

> What art makes us *see*, and therefore gives us in the form of '*seeing*', '*perceiving*' and '*feeling*' (which is not the form of *knowing*), is the *ideology* from which it is born, in which it bathes, from which it detaches itself as art, and to which it alludes ... Balzac and Solzhenitsyn give us a 'view' of the ideology to which their work alludes and with which it is constantly fed, a view which presupposes a *retreat*, an *internal distantiation* from the very ideology from which their novels emerged. They make us 'perceive' (but not know) in some sense *from the inside*, by an *internal distance*, the very ideology in which they are held.[25]

---

24 Louis Althusser, 'Letter on Art in Reply to André Daspre', in *Lenin and Philosophy, and Other Essays*, trans. Ben Brewster (London: New Left Books, 1971), p. 222.
25 Ibid., pp. 222–3.

Art, in a sense, 'shows' the functioning of ideology, rendering its operations visible and breaking the spontaneous effects of closure, recognition and misrecognition that are characteristic of ideology in general. 'Art, or at least literature, because it naturally scorns the credulous view of the world, establishes myth and illusion as *visible objects*', Macherey similarly concludes his commentary on Lenin and Tolstoy. 'By means of the text it becomes possible to escape from the domain of spontaneous ideology, to escape from the false consciousness of self, of history, and of time.'[26]

Incidentally, one principle seems to be a crucial component of this legacy of Althusser's structuralism, which as a result at once becomes a version of poststructuralism: the principle of the uneven development of any given structure, which appears as though dislocated from within, due to a series of gaps that are never the effect of purely external contingencies but instead signal the structure's own immanent deadlock. Althusser's favourite term for such gaps is *décalages*, typically translated in English as 'dislocations' or as 'discrepancies'.[27] A lot of later work by post-Althusserians continues to rely on the presence of such discrepancies within the social orders, political phenomena and artistic scenes that they are famous for analysing. Rancière, for example, may not label these discrepancies *décalages*, preferring instead to speak of the effects of an *écart* – a 'gap' or 'breach'.[28] But the analysis of a structure's

---

26   Pierre Macherey, 'Lenin, Critic of Tolstoy', in *A Theory of Literary Production*, trans. Geoffrey Wall (London: Routledge & Kegan Paul, 1978), pp. 132–3. See also Althusser, 'Letter on Art in Reply to André Daspre', p. 222.

27   See, for example, Louis Althusser, 'Rousseau: The Social Contract', in his *Politics and History: Montesquieu, Rousseau, Marx*, trans. Ben Brewster (London: Verso, 2007), pp. 111–60.

28   In *Disagreement*, for example, Rancière will describe the process of all political action in terms of the gap that separates a given social identity from itself. But the opening up of such a space is possible only if the policing of identities is at least momentarily interrupted in an act of political subjectivization, which Rancière compares to the art of literature as the opening up of a rupture, a breach, or an interval, in the order between things and words: 'The modern political animal is first a literary animal,

internal excess that separates it from itself can nonetheless be said to express the lasting debt that contemporary thought owes to Althusser's legacy. We might say that later thinkers only generalize the notion of the internal distantiation that for Althusser is characteristic of art's relation to the ideological forms of its time. If Rancière's thought refuses to accept the label of philosophy, for example, it is because it is a thinking of the essential gap, discrepancy and impropriety at the heart of every identity, property and propriety, including disciplinary ones. As soon as we take away the minimal distance or retreat, though, art and politics offer nothing more than redistributions of the sensible. Moreover, the subversive or transformative effects of internal distancing are by no means self-evident. This distance might also provide us with the false assurance of not being part of the game, all the while serving as the guarantee of our obeying its every rule.

Badiou, for his part, problematizes Althusser and Macherey's principal thesis about the internal displacement of ideology in art, all the while making his own secondary and apparently contradictory thesis concerning the autonomy of art's form-giving processes. For Macherey,

> it could be said that the work has an ideological content, but that it endows this content with a specific form. Even if this form is itself ideological, there is an internal displacement of ideology by virtue of this *redoubling*; this is not ideology contemplating itself, but the mirror-effect which exposes its insufficiency, revealing differences and discordances, or a significant incongruity.[29]

---

caught in the circuit of a literariness that undoes the relationships between the order of words and the order of bodies that determine the place of each.' Jacques Rancière, *Disagreement: Politics and Philosophy*, trans. Julie Rose (Minneapolis, MN: University of Minnesota Press, 1999), p. 37. For a detailed comparison between Badiou and Rancière on the question of literature, see Jacques-David Ebguy, 'Le travail de la vérité, la vérité au travail: usages de la littérature chez Alain Badiou et Jacques Rancière', in *Les Philosophes Lecteurs*, special issue of *Fabula: Littérature Histoire Théorie* 1 (February 2006).

29   Macherey, 'Lenin, Critic of Tolstoy', p. 133.

Focusing his attention on the very process of this elaboration of a specifically aesthetic form irreducible to the ideological content on which it is supposed to work, Badiou goes a step further by arguing that, far from 'redoubling' and 'demystifying' ideology as if in a broken mirror, art only ever 'turns' or 'reverts' already aestheticized elements into a kind of self-sufficient reality. Thus, instead of a *redoublement* as in Macherey and Althusser, Badiou speaks of a *retournement* as the key to the autonomy of the aesthetic process. Finally, the pertinent unit for this kind of analysis is no longer the unique work of art, let alone the genial artist-creator, but rather what Badiou calls an aesthetic mode of production. The example he chooses to elaborate is the novel, or the novelistic mode of production. In fact, Badiou envisaged elaborating his first published essay into a whole monograph on *L'effet romanesque* ('The Novelistic Effect'), which was to be published in the same 'Théorie' book series edited by Althusser in which, in 1966, Macherey's *A Theory of Literary Production* would appear – perhaps taking the wind out of Badiou's sails.[30]

Read today, this early beginning of Badiou's work as a philosopher raises a number of fascinating questions not only about what his philosophy has actually become, but also – and perhaps even more – about what it might have become and did not. First, there is the question concerning the place of truth in art: by refusing to phrase the problem of art's status in terms of the passage from the real to the work, does Badiou, in 'The Autonomy of the Aesthetic Process', lay the groundwork for his later thesis that art is one of the generic processes or procedures for producing truth? How, then, does the later notion of truth as developed in *Being and Event* relate – if at all – to the science/ideology dyad? Second, concerning the relation of aesthetic theory to history, or of the synchronic to the diachronic, as Badiou says at the very end of 'The Autonomy

---

30 On Badiou's project for a book-length study on *l'effet romanesque*, 'the novelistic effect', see Louis Althusser's allusion in his *Lettres à Franca (1961–1973)* (Paris: Stock/IMEC, 1998), p. 691.

of the Aesthetic Process': to what extent has the later focus on the philosophical treatment of individual art forms such as dance, theatre, poetry or film – discussed in *Handbook of Inaesthetics*, for example – overshadowed his earlier interest in the genealogical analysis of aesthetic modes of production such as the novel? Finally, a question that reaches beyond Badiou's mode of philosophizing but certainly affects all the work of fellow ex-Althusserians such as Rancière who increasingly move away from the political and towards the aesthetic regime of art: how can we understand the historicity of the formulation of the relation between art and ideology in these terms? Could we not say that the demystifying promise of an internal distancing, privileged within art, has since the late 1960s, and especially since the neoliberal Restoration beginning in the 1970s, turned out to be the very model of ideology's smooth functioning?[31]

5

Even if, for the time being, the answers to these questions about the autonomy of the aesthetic mode of production are anyone's guess, Badiou subsequently revisited some of the same problems addressed in his first publication on the prose novel, particularly in a little-known series of book reviews about the novelistic production of his friend and fellow Maoist militant Natacha Michel, a co-founder, with Badiou and Lazarus, of Organisation Politique.

Michel's novelistic mise-en-scènes, like those of Badiou, capture the out-of-sync experience of space and time that registers the event. As in Badiou's literary work, we find a mix of political passion, love and sexuality, and violent recrimination characteristic of *gauchiste* culture in the late

---

31   See Bruno Bosteels, 'Reviewing Rancière, or, the Persistence of Discrepancies', *Radical Philosophy* 170 (2011), pp. 25–31 – subsequently expanded for Documenta 13 in Bruno Bosteels, *Some Highly Speculative Remarks on Art and Ideology* (Ostfildern: Hatje Cantz, 2012).

1960s and 1970s. From her *La Chine européenne* (1975) to the more recent *Circulaire à toute ma vie humaine* (2005), Michel chronicles the destinies of brilliant '68 theorist-philosophers, some of whom retain fidelity to the engagements of militant times, while others have joined the ranks of what Dominique Lecourt calls the *piètres penseurs*, or 'mediocrats', such as André Glucksmann, Bernard-Henri Lévy, Luc Ferry and Alain Renaut, who march to the rhythm of technocratic neoliberalism or, like the new moralist André Comte-Sponville, embrace new spiritualisms and privatized credos of love. *Circulaire ...* chronicles these post-'68 political transvaluations. Its protagonists include Thomas Féroé, a new-age spiritualist with a cult following; Simon Jude, a Marxist philosopher whose courses once inspired fear in his disciples but who, over the years, has given in to the American-style academic temptations of soft politics and high lecture fees; and Sébastien Lechevalier, a militant who refuses to renounce his principles, but who recognizes with anguish that he is out of step with the times. Into this mix is thrown a young woman called Nour who discovers a cache of radical tracts spanning the years from 1966 to 1972, and suddenly realizes that '[l]ife hadn't always been what she had known ... Apparently life could be changed, and human beings, it seemed, devoted their whole existence to it. Where were they? What had they become? Why didn't she see them anymore? Or were they somewhere still, disguised or visible, and she hadn't recognized them?'[32] When Nour's pursuer, an old Maoist turned famous biologist, comes across the same memorabilia, he too experiences the shock of anachronism on seeing terms like 'factory struggle', 'revisionism', 'exploitative boss', or 'GPCR' (Great Proletarian Cultural Revolution). This re-timed anachronism opens up the possibility of a non-foreclosed revolutionary sequence, sprung from reactionary periodicity into an intergenerational, future-oriented duration.

---

32 Natacha Michel, *Circulaire à toute ma vie humaine* (Paris: Seuil, 2004), p. 147.

In her own theoretical reflections, Natacha Michel also shares with Badiou an ongoing obsession with the fate of the novel in the wake of frequently repeated declarations of its imminent crisis or death. Against the *piètres penseurs* and the self-styled writer–curators or *écrivains–artistes*, she proposes the figure of the *écrivain pensif*, or thinking-writer: 'I believe that literature thinks. But in its own way and without rivalry, because it thinks with its muses. What inspires it is its truth and its meditation.'[33] Like Badiou, Michel has an unwavering faith in the capacity of narrative prose to constitute a form of thought in its own right. This faith runs counter to the twin diagnostics about the novel that we can find, on one hand, in the theory of what Sartre was the first to call *l'écriture blanche* – that is, the 'white', 'blank' or 'neutral' writing that was to become associated with a certain French Heideggerianism found in the prose of Maurice Blanchot or the poetry of Michel Deguy, and later commented upon by Roland Barthes in *Writing Degree Zero*; and, on the other hand, what can be described as the 'applied structuralism' of formal experimentation in the style of Oulipo writers such as Georges Perec. Thus, in a long interview from 1983 published in the newsletter of Organisation Politique, Michel and Badiou reject both of these options out of hand.

Explicitly returning to some of his concepts from 'The Autonomy of the Aesthetic Process', Badiou proposes: 'Let us compare prose to a productive force and the novel to a mode of production.'[34] In that case, what would be the shifting relation between novel and prose? Sure, the modern novel may have died a difficult death somewhere between Proust and Joyce. But the productive force of novelistic prose has not for this reason completely withered away. 'There has been an uneven development in the withering, rather than a stopping point', claims Michel. 'It is the unified mode of the novel that has waned. But there persists

33   Natacha Michel, *L'écrivain pensif* (Paris: Verdier, 1998), p. 16.

34   Alain Badiou, 'Et la littérature (1)', *Le Perroquet: Quinzomadaire d'opinion* 19/20 (21 January 1983), p. 1.

perhaps a dispersion in its capacities.'[35] Natacha Michel's wager consists in affirming the immanent resources of language for solving the problem of form. Neither neutral nor constructivist, neither blank nor simply structural, the novelistic effect stems from the fictionalization or fabulation of an entire world based on a minimal anecdote. Narration (*récit*), story or history (*histoire* in French can mean both, oscillating between what Badiou calls 'the little story', *la petite histoire*, and 'History at large', *la grande Histoire*) and world-making (*le faire-monde*) are thus the three component parts that, according to Natacha Michel, might inaugurate a second modernity for the novel, after Proust and Joyce.

6

No discussion of Badiou's take on poetry and narrative prose would be complete without taking into account his own creative production. Here we find what may be the most radical instances of experiments in literary timing and untimeliness. *L'Écharpe rouge* (*The Red Scarf*), a *romanopéra*, or operatic novel, is perhaps the most relevant work from this point of view. Published in 1979 and staged in 1984 by Badiou's close friend Antoine Vitez, with music by Georges Aperghis accompanying Badiou's libretto, it captures the 1970s as an experiment in turning Mao's credo of 'one divides into two' into narrative-theatrical praxis. Documented in real time, in all their messiness and ill-synchronized procession, the politics of class struggle, sectarian infighting, colliding epistemes, and violent disagreements over strategy and tactics find expression in a declamatory mode that often comes dangerously close to casuistry in its slide between the registers of theology, law and politics.

L'Écharpe rouge occupies the mid-point in a literary career that spans Badiou's first novel, *Almagestes*,

---

35   Natacha Michel, in 'Et la littérature (1)', *Le Perroquet: Quinzo-ma-daire d'opinion* 19/20 (21 January 1983), p. 2.

published in 1964, and the *Ahmed* tetralogy of the 1990s.[36] Most recently, in 1997, *Calme bloc ici-bas* appeared, a novel whose title reprises the first half of the same famous line from Mallarmé's poem 'The Tomb of Edgar Allan Poe' from which Badiou had previously drawn the expression 'of an obscure disaster': 'Calme bloc ici-bas d'un désastre obscur.'[37] *Ahmed le subtil* invites being read through the lens of *Cyrano de Bergerac,* insofar as it arguably rewrites the tradition of French national theatre from an Algerian immigrant's point of view. Badiou takes on the full repertoire of Edmond de Rostand's stock pyrotechnic devices: the tirade, the rapid-fire verbal duel, wordplay that breaks syntax down into a defamiliarizing array of spaces and abstracted particles of diction. *Ahmed le subtil* is radical comedy, with Ahmed playing communists, reactionaries, syndicalists and extreme-left militants off against one another. He is a protean figure, with no fixed position of his own, but in the end he rights the 'situation' – there is a grand resolution in which all sides come together to form an ironically harmonious celebration of a new political compact.

In contrast to the *Ahmed* plays, Badiou's early novel *Almagestes* is more genuinely utopian. The title refers to the Latin translation of the Arabic title of Ptolemy's famous astronomical treatise, and is lifted from a verse of

---

36   On the *Ahmed* tetralogy, see Alain Badiou, *Rhapsody for the Theatre,* trans. Bruno Bosteels (London: Verso, 2013), pp. 139–66. For an overview of Badiou's production as a novelist, see Cécile Winter, 'Les romans d'Alain Badiou', in *Autour d'Alain Badiou,* eds Isabelle Vodoz and Fabien Tarby (Paris: Germina, 2011), pp. 353–76. In the same volume, see also the critical rejoinders to Badiou's take on the novel and poetry, respectively, Natacha Michel, 'Badiou en fer à cheval, ou: L'écrivain craintif et le philosophe' and Judith Balso, 'Atalante et Hippomène', in *Autour d'Alain Badiou,* pp. 181–210. Finally, it should be noted that whereas Badiou never wrote any poetry (other than a supplementary stanza of his own invention added to one of Mallarmé's sonnets in *Theory of the Subject*), in addition to his novels he also wrote a short story, inspired by his role as a human rights observer for the trial of Régis Debray in Bolivia. See 'L'autorisation', *Les Temps Modernes* 258 (November 1967), pp. 761–89.

37   Alain Badiou, *Calme bloc ici-bas* (Paris: P.O.L, 1997).

Saint-John Perse's poem *Exile*, which Badiou uses as an epigraph: 'almagestes, portulans et bestiaires'.[38] *Almagestes* sits in apposition to nautical maps and bestiaries, suggesting new taxonomies and new worlds. It is probably no exaggeration to say that the ambition of this precocious work stretches as far as the redesign of the universe – from the paths of stars to planetary alignments. Sporting a photo on the back cover of a young, flute-playing Badiou, *Almagestes* reads like a documentary of the revolutionary carnival that fomented the conditions of May '68. It is a Babelian threnody of Marxism, existentialism and structuralism that doubles as a diagram of the evental site, or void of the situation. The book comes equipped with a map resembling a situationist plan of Paris plotted on the *dérive* (streets commemorating heroes of the left – Danton, Fabre, Hugo, Guesde – offer escape from the larger avenues named after military figures and colonies). A set of instructions at the back provides the key to computing the actions of the characters. The cast is drawn from the student milieu, with each personage symbolizing a mathematical formula. 'FD = C' is the equation signifying how much Fréville's affection for Dastaing disturbs Chantal. B (Bérard) is the integer of subjective neutrality, an X-factor of transferential alterity. Throughout the book, the coda tells us, self-properties and thing-properties will be exchanged. Characters will shift status as subject and object, and engage in word-sharing, thereby precluding all claims to exclusionary, proprietary identity. This de-totalized ontology is complemented by a nonlinear diegesis loosely structured around the quest for a new Babel, an explosive and prophetic cipher of truth:

The First Truth
The general purpose of this story [*récit*] is the attainment of an *equilibrium point* between the theme of the epoch (of

---

38 Alain Badiou, *Almagestes* (Paris: Seuil, 1964), p. 7. Following the programme set out in Saint-John Perse's verse, *Almagestes* is thus followed by a second novel titled *Portulans* (Paris: Seuil, 1967). Yet, in a rare case of unfulfilled promises, a third novel supposed to complete the series under the title *Bestiaires* never saw the light of day.

action) and the book's rhetorical aesthetic. It is an exercise in innumerable, more or less arbitrary rules, dissolved by the sheer evidence of its practical fusion. Having reached this point, *Almagestes* liquidates its subject (the expressive baroque) by submitting it to the test of human violence.[39]

An obscure programme, to be sure, but one that becomes more accessible through dialogue. The characters expend great energy on parsing revolutionary slogans ('We must mobilize the masses, and right now!' ... 'We'll never do anything with these radico-bigoted chickens') and fighting over terms. The choice of 'salaried class' over 'ensemble of the salaried', or 'proletariat' over 'victims of neo-capitalism' is no mere exercise in theoretical hair-splitting, but a matter of political truth or death. 'The reflection on language', says Badiou in his prolegomena, 'is substantial, not just theoretical.'[40]

Almagestes and *Portulans* serve as preludes to *L'Écharpe rouge*, which is above all an experiment in political retiming that involves imagining a post-revolutionary possible world. Hypotheticals are arraigned and subjected to critical reflection in the spirit of a key question posed by Badiou: 'What becomes of the poor worker after the Revolution?' *L'Écharpe rouge*, we might say, responds to this question proleptically, by imagining a sequence in which the Paris Commune of 1871 is elided with that brief moment in May '68 when the fragile coalition between workers and students gave rise to the hope of a life-changing general strike. The sequence also splices together episodes from the Cultural Revolution: sessions of self-criticism, endless arguments over revisionism, stagings of 'one divides into two', and the meting out of justice (as when Antoine 'takes out' Gaston as he savours a gourmet meal, to the background chant: 'It's the final struggle / Let's group, and tomorrow, the International / will be the generic form of the human'). Badiou's aim here seems to

---

39 Badiou, *Almagestes*, p. 310.
40 Ibid., p. 9.

be the revival of the historical novel in the genealogy of
Hugo, Stendhal and Zola. It shares with Hugo's *Quatre-
vingt-treize* a taste for the political frieze, big panoramic
scenes, larger-than-life characters who retain traits of real
historical figures, polyphonic voices, giant blocks of prose,
the mélange of styles (classical, romantic and modern), and
a plot highlighting the singularity of the egalitarian revolution. And just as Hugo un-times 1793, treating the date
as a baptismal fount for a futural event, so Badiou's operatic novel a-synchronizes the Commune of 1871 with his
chorus of workers from every period and nation – some in
nineteenth-century smocks, others in caps worn during the
October Revolution, still others in the twentieth-century
uniform of worker blue.

Badiou's political functionalizing of the outmoded and
the anachronistic, like his efforts to represent the psychic
disarray of epistemological rupture, still owes much to
his former master Althusser, specifically to his mandate of
a belated return to Marx. As is well-known, Althusser's
renewal of Marxist theory as an antihumanism involved
playing off late Marx against early Marx, thereby creating
a space for the expression of delayed materialism, or non-
Hegelian dialectics:

> Althusser's stroke of genius consisted in endeavouring
> to collect the payout in aid of a renovated Marxism. He
> baptized historical materialism the 'science of history'
> and, basing himself on Gaston Bachelard, revealed to our
> astounded eyes the famous 'epistemological break' that
> definitively separated Marx from his own youth from
> 1845 onwards! ... He sought a non-Hegelian concept of
> the social totality, which repudiated the reigning econo-
> mism; he invited reconsideration of the type of causality
> governing social phenomena, and opened up original lines
> of investigation in anthropology and sociology, as well as
> linguistic theory.[41]

---

41 Lecourt, *The Mediocracy*, pp. 18–19. For a more systematic
account of Badiou's rapport with Althusserianism, see Chapters 1 and 2 in
Bosteels, *Badiou and Politics*.

The stakes of alternative models of causality and dialectics are especially apparent in *L'Écharpe rouge*. As in *Almagestes*, the jumble of scenes and mix of forms (airs, ariosos and recitatives) exaggerates the sense that time is out of joint or dislocated. The action is loosely organized around factional struggles between capitalists, Maoists, Communists, and *gauchistes* of varying stripes. The genre is epic, in the mould of Brechtian epic theatre, and constructed around impassioned speeches, ideological disputations, tirades and tribunals. The effect here resembles what Roland Barthes ascribed to Brecht's verbal realism – his art of the *secousse* or shake-up, his revelation of the political in the noise emitted by signs when their naturalized word order is broken up and they fall out of the logosphere. Staccato Brechtian inflections are fully present in Badiou's text. A vast cast of characters enters and exits; some are identified by proper name, others by generic status and occupation: 'Worker', 'Immigrant', 'Youth', 'Comrade', 'Soldier', 'Cop', 'Peasant', 'Teacher'. The opera-novel is written in argot-inflected French seasoned with *immigré* dialect and a local patois of Badiou's own invention.

Like *Almagestes*, *L'Écharpe rouge* maps an imagined world of post-historical revolutionary time that, in the tradition of Atlantis or More's Utopia, is both here and nowhere. Shaded according to liberated and non-liberated zones, this is a cartography in which the French hexagon merges with the land-masses of its former colonial territories. There is a capital city more or less where Paris might be, a tropical south-west, an orientalized interior corridor, a Midi of port towns, and a Massif Central dominated by mining and steel production. In this hypothetical France, history is as unhinged as geography. A revolutionary event has occurred, but its name and outcome remain uncertain. In the early scenes we are introduced to Antoine, a *pur et dur*, and Claire, the radicalized daughter of a corporate magnate. Antoine professes love for Claire, but she refuses his invitation to conduct political education campaigns for the people on the island: 'What would I do in this tunnel of principles next to you who needs nothing else?' They argue about politics, she aligning herself with the 'ordinary worker', he exhorting her to transcend the ordinary by becoming an 'exceptional citizen'.[42] Their exchange sets the programme insofar as it takes up Badiou's conviction that the 'worker' is the fulcrum of the ongoing egalitarian revolution. From the 1980s on, Badiou and his comrades in the Organisation Politique would indeed insist that the term 'worker' was being unduly displaced by *immigré* and *clandestin*. In 2005, the Organisation Politique launched the rallying cry: '*Immigré*, no, worker yes.' Peter Hallward reminds us that, for Badiou, '"workers" means something almost as broad as "people", insofar as they cannot be reduced to units of capital'.[43] He cites Badiou's article of 1991 from *La Distance Politique*: 'The word "workers" is a condition of freedom of thought.'[44]

The melodrama of *L'Écharpe rouge* grows precisely out of this crisis of who lays legitimate claim to the worker. Claire's brother Simon represents 'Marxist-Leninist Maoism' and the objectives of the Cultural Revolution, while Vestral, an insurgent modelled on Che Guevara who has been captured by Simon, represents *autonomia*, an alliance of worker-campesinos wedded to a rigorist refusal of party. Similar scissions shape the civil war on the Island as Communist Islanders face off against nativist *autogestionnaires* who categorically reject the influence of superstates and the jurisdiction of central committees. These conditions of political impasse and civil disorder prompt Claire to long for 'a time before when a transparent world existed that fused discipline with revolt'.[45] What Claire desires is a new dispensation of justice that will effect an evental break, even at the risk of her own purging. *L'Écharpe rouge* culminates in a trial, with Antoine and

---

42 Badiou, *L'Écharpe rouge* (Paris: François Maspero, 1979), p. 11.
43 Hallward, *Badiou: A Subject to Truth*, p. 231.
44 Ibid., p. 232.
45 Badiou, *L'Écharpe rouge*, p. 209.

Claire pronounced guilty of counter-revolution. At this point, one could say, Brechtian operatic militancy takes over: the stage is turned over to feminist militants who issue statutes, authorize executions, enact revolutionary subjectivization (justice, courage), and proclaim a new century, christened an 'epoché of forests', a kind of grassed commons.[46] The situation is far from utopian – rival models of partyless politics are *not* reconciled, the circle of the 'Commune without party' is *not* squared – but it renders thinkable the terms of a new *nomos*, a world of new names, laws and axioms. As one of the high points of Badiou's novelistic prose, *L'Écharpe rouge*'s ceaseless replaying of scission and revisionism *is* the form of the *nomos* in its embryonic state: non-dialectical, intervallic, historically compressed, out of step with the times, and futural.

In short, common to Badiou's own novels and all the texts in *The Age of the Poets*, whether they deal with the status of the poem after Heidegger or the fate of novelistic prose after Proust and Joyce, is the belief in literature as a form of thought in its own right: literature as a thought-practice, or a practised thinking, a poem-thought or novel-thought, not limited to the conceptual realm alone but traversing the sensual, corporeal, linguistic, visual and rhetorical all at once. Herein lies Badiou's fundamental optimism with regard to the capacities of language: ultimately, poetry and prose after the age of the poets testify to the possibility and even the necessity that we do not remain silent about that of which we cannot speak.

Emily Apter and Bruno Bosteels

---

46   Ibid., p. 245.

I. On Poetry

1

THE AGE OF THE POETS

I first introduced the idea of an 'age of the poets' in 1989.[1] In spite of the word 'poets', the category 'age of the poets' is not immanent to poetry. It is not the poets who declared the age that was theirs. Some of them – but this concerns a trait which signals rather the closure of the age in question – undoubtedly adopted the *pose* of 'modern poet', as the prophet withdrawn from his own time, the one who proffers the crucial aphorisms that trace the destitute time of thinking. But it is not this 'pre-Socratic' pretence I have in mind.

In spite of the word 'age', the category in question is not historicist. It does not pretend to offer a periodization of the different sequences of poetry. It is true that I – vaguely – situate this age between the Paris Commune and the aftermath of World War II, between 1870 and 1960, or between Arthur Rimbaud and Paul Celan, with Friedrich Hölderlin being more of an angelical announcer. But this determination remains external to the category itself.

Finally, it is also not an aesthetic category, or one belonging to the judgment of taste. I am not saying that

1 Alain Badiou, 'The Age of the Poets', in *Manifesto for Philosophy*, trans. Norman Madarasz (Albany: SUNY Press, 1999), pp. 69–77.

the 'great poets' of the period in question are the poets who best exemplify the age of the poets. My own taste also includes Victor Hugo, Gerard Manley Hopkins and T. S. Eliot, whom I do not inscribe as poets of the age in question, unlike Stéphane Mallarmé, Arthur Rimbaud, Georg Trakl, Osip Mandelstam or Celan, whom I do inscribe as such, and whom I also love as pure poets, albeit no doubt from another angle.

The age of the poets is a *philosophical* category. It organizes a particular way of conceiving the knot tying the poem to philosophy, which is such that this knot becomes *visible* from the point of view of philosophy itself. 'Age' refers to an epochal situation of philosophy; and 'poets' refers to the poem as condition, since the earliest times, of philosophy.

I call 'age of the poets' the moment proper to the history of philosophy in which the latter is sutured – that is to say, delegated or subjected to a single one of its conditions.[2] In essence, it is a question of the sutures to

- the scientific condition, in the different avatars of positivism and the doctrine of progress;
- the political condition, in the different avatars of revolutionary political philosophy;
- a mixture of the two, which is reflected in Marxism as 'scientific socialism' – that is, the superposition of a science of History and a political voluntarism whose philosophical projection has been dialectical materialism.

In these conditions, inherited from the nineteenth century, the poem *can* assume within thinking the operations left vacant by philosophy when its suture obliterates or paralyses it.

It should be clear that, for me, poetry always constitutes a place of thought or, to be more precise, a procedure of truth – or generic procedure.[3] 'Age of the poets' by no

---

2 See the chapter 'Sutures' in *Manifesto for Philosophy*, pp. 61–7.
3 On the notion of generic procedure, see *Manifesto for Philosophy*

means designates the 'entrance into thought' of the poem, no more than the 'end' of the age of the poets – an end which I declare a necessity – would mean a repudiation of 'thinking' poetry. I simply want to say the following: in a situation in which philosophy is sutured either onto science or onto politics, certain poets, or rather certain poems, come to occupy the place where ordinarily the properly philosophical strategies of thought are declared.

The centre of gravity of this occupation in my view is the following: the poems of the age of the poets are those in which the poetic saying not only constitutes a form of thought and instructs a truth, but also finds itself constrained to *think this thought*. In this sense, Mallarmé is emblematic, since we all know that he declares, as an assessment of his great intellectual crisis in the 1860s, that his thinking has thought itself.

However, to think the thought of the poem cannot be a reflection, since the poem offers itself only in its act. To think the thought of the poem supposes that the poem *itself* takes a stance with regard to the question 'What is thinking?' And what is thinking in conditions in which the poem must establish this question on the basis of its own resources?

The poem then finds itself unwillingly – I mean without this position stemming from a calculation or a rivalry – in a kind of breach, which is also an overlap, with philosophy, whose originary vocation is precisely to think the time of thought, or to think the epoch as site of compossibility of the different generic procedures (poem, matheme, politics and love[4]).

I will simply say that the age of the poets is signalled by the intrapoetic putting into work of certain *maxims of thought*, nodal points of the poem in which the thinking

---

and, above all, Alain Badiou, *Being and Event*, trans. Oliver Feltham (London: Continuum, 2005).

4 On the four conditions of truth, see *Manifesto for Philosophy*, pp. 33–9.

that it is indicates itself as relation or incision of thought 'in general'.

Examples of such maxims are legion, and I obviously sample only a few of them.

Rimbaud, as early as in the historic and intellectual pro-gramme that he assigns to the poem in his letters to Paul Demeny and to Georges Izambard, declares the expira-tion of the cogito as the investigative matrix of all possible thought: 'It is wrong to say: I think. One ought to say: People think me.'[5] This deposing of thought in the ano-nymity of a trajectory authorizes its appropriation by the poem as dictation of being.

When Mallarmé concludes his testamentary work with the maxim 'every thought emits a dice throw', the 'every' comes to outweigh the singularity of the poem, by the foundational connection it establishes between thought, chance, and number.

In the 'heavy-handed' poetry of Trakl, which Martin Heidegger fallaciously pushes in the direction of a sacrali-zation of presence, the operations which indicate the 'salvific' thought – hence the effect-less effect of a truth – are not discernible except at the most profound level of experience, which is certainly linked to suffering, to pain, to blood, but which the poem delivers with a strange neutral pain. The axiom of the poem is the essential link between dereliction and the power of truth. See, in 'Gródek', the following: 'Tonight a mighty anguish feeds the hot flame of spirit.'[6] But this suffering, this bloody loss, is material, related to work – it does not metaphorize any moral or sacred presence. Thought resides in the silence of labour:

---

5   Arthur Rimbaud, 'To Georges Izambard (May 13, 1871)', in *Complete Works, Selected Letters: A Bilingual Edition*, trans. Wallace Fowlie, updated and revised by Seth Whidden (Chicago: The University of Chicago Press, 2005), p. 371.

6   Georg Trakl, 'Gródek', in *Song of the Departed: Selected Poems of Georg Trakl*, trans. Robert Firmage (Port Townsend: Copper Canyon Press, 2012), p. 183.

But muter humanity calmly bleeds in a dark cave,
Assembles the redeeming head out of hard metals. ('To the
Muted')[7]

Trakl holds that a thought always stands under the *visible*
imperative of death, and that its labour is as taciturn as
this imperative.

In the guise of his heteronym in the position of mastery,
Alberto Caeiro, Fernando Pessoa multiplies the maxims.[8]
Their tension, which is both paradoxical and serene, is the
result of the fact that, for Caeiro, the essence of thought is
to abolish thought. We could evoke Mallarmé who, after
having announced that his thought has thought itself, adds
'I am utterly dead',[9] if it did not quickly turn out that Caeiro
is anything but a poet of death. Non-thought is rather, for
him, the living wisdom of thought itself, and in particular
of philosophy in its entirety: 'There's enough metaphysics in not thinking about anything' (*The Keeper of Flocks*,
poem 5).[10] The word 'metaphysics' indicates quite well
the relation of breaching/overlapping that forms the knot
between the poem and philosophy. Caeiro implicitly seems
to understand that the error of (philosophical) metaphysics has been to establish itself in the affirmative reflection
of thought. The poem restores the 'thing' to its un-thought.
As he says even more radically (poem 34): 'Nothing thinks
about anything.' Is it then a question of nihilism? Not at
all. The thought of which the poem declares the abolition in non-thought qua *true* metaphysics is the thought

---

7 Georg Trakl, 'To the Muted', in *The Last Gold of Expired Stars: Complete Poems 1908–1914*, trans. Jim Doss and Werner Schmitt (Sykesville, MD: Loch Raven Press, 2010), p. 135.

8 On heteronymy as an operator of thought, see Judith Balso, *Pessoa, the Metaphysical Courier*, trans. Drew Burk (New York: Atropos Press, 2011).

9 Stéphane Mallarmé, Letter to Henri Cazalis (14 May 1867), in *Selected Letters of Stéphane Mallarmé*, ed. and trans. Rosemary Lloyd (Chicago: The University of Chicago Press, 1988), p. 74.

10 Fernando Pessoa, *The Complete Poems of Alberto Caeiro*, trans. Chris Daniels (Exeter: Shearmans Books, 2007), p. 21. Badiou uses the French translation by Armand Guibert.

subjected to the cogito. For it is conscious reflection that constitutes a monadic, or closed obstacle, to the evidence of being, to presence as such – evidence whose well-nigh constant poetic sign, for Caeiro as for many other poets of the age of the poets, is the Earth:

> If I think about these things
> I'll stop seeing trees and plants
> And stop seeing the Earth
> For only seeing my thoughts ...
> (*The Keeper of Flocks*, Poem 34)[11]

Being does not give itself in the thought of being, for all thinking of being is in reality only the thinking of a thought. Being gives itself in the immediacy of a test; it is what I feel in the unreflective element of this probing experience that works as proof:

> I try to say what I feel
> Without thinking about things I feel.
> I try to lean words on the idea
> And not need a corridor
> From thought to words.
> (Poem 46)[12]

What is an Idea in this context? The Idea is properly the thought that is not a thought of thought: thought sub-tracted from the mediation of the cogito. Thought becomes a corridor as soon as it establishes itself only in relation to itself. For the poem as thought, it is a matter of *not* borrowing the path of this corridor, and thus of enduring directly a speech which is such that, between thought as Idea and the Earth, we do not have the time of thought's closure onto itself.

Hence the almost untenable imperative under which the poem operates: 'wholly being only my exterior' (Poem 14).[13] Thinking, such as Caeiro's poem states the maxim

---

11   Pessoa, *The Complete Poems of Alberto Caeiro*, p. 56.
12   Ibid., p. 68.
13   Ibid., p. 36.

of thought, is the insurrection of an outside without interiority.

In the guise of his 'modern' heteronym, Alvaro de Campos, Pessoa apparently says almost the exact opposite. Campos indeed exalts absolute interiority, the salvific correlate of an outside structured by the noise of a machinic desire. However, here too negation comes to strike thought. Not because we would need the law of non-thought, as Caeiro claims, but because it is indispensable to *think of nothing*. Between Caeiro, the master, and his most loyal disciple, Campos, there is the distance that is almost nil between the nothing of thought and the thought of nothing. Here is a poem from 6 July 1935, the year of Pessoa's death:

> To think about nothing
> Is to fully possess the soul.
> To think about nothing
> Is to intimately live
> Life's ebb and flow.[14]

However, in all these cases, Caeiro and Campos seek to distribute the connection between thinking and the void. Every maxim of thought is a *localization of the void*. For Caeiro, the void is interiority, which delivers the event of a pure, untotalizable outside. For the late Campos, the void is exteriority, which delivers the event of a pure, unqualifiable inside.

For Mandelstam – at least the Mandelstam of the great poems of the 1920s – poetry initiates thought *as thought of the century*. To be more precise, the poem asks what are the conditions of a thought that embraces in all its effects the seism of 1917. The polemic of the poem is aimed against everything that would pretend to make sense of these effects, against any presupposition of a sense or meaning of History that the song would have the task of

14 Fernando Pessoa, 'I've been thinking about nothing at all', *Fernando Pessoa & Co: Selected Poems*, trans. Richard Zenith (New York: Grove Press, 1998), p. 210.

celebrating. To the contrary, the poem-thought demands of its subject that it proceed from turmoil as its base, from the innocence of being properly lost in the century. I quote Mandelstam (a poem from 1 January 1924):

> Oh clay life! Oh you, dying century!
> I'm afraid that no one can know you
> without that helpless smile,
> mark, emblem of the man who has lost
>   himself.[15]

Thought has as its condition that, at the very place where the fury of the time demands the hero, as the dispenser of plenitude, there comes to be the one who operates according to an essential insufficiency of self for self, which is such that it is impossible to represent it as a fixed point or origin of the poetic word. In 'Whoever Finds a Horseshoe', Mandelstam, speaking of the coins that the past bequeaths to us, indicates the present of the century as a breaching of the past that can only be discerned as a subtraction from itself:

> Their time tried to bite them through, here are the
>   teethmarks.
> Time cuts me down like a clipped coin
> and I'm no longer sufficient unto myself.[16]

This effect of the incision of thought cut down by the time of the century, this withdrawal of plenitude, remits the poem to a kind of terrestrial anonymity, a petrification which is not without evoking Caeiro's 'thing':

> What I am saying, now, is not being said by me,
> it's dug from the earth, like grains of petrified wheat.[17]

15 Osip Emilevich Mandelstam, 'January 1, 1924', *Complete Poetry*, trans. Burton Raffel and Alla Burago (Albany: SUNY Press, 1973), p. 138 (translation modified). Badiou quotes from the French translation by Tatiana Roy.

16 Mandelstam, *Complete Poetry*, p. 133.

17 Ibid.

Thus, for Mandelstam, the thought of the poem's thought is the defection of a place of incision, of dislocation, of insufficiency, from where proceeds an anonymous and disoriented speech. There the time of the century can be stated, precisely because it is the century that is declared full, centred, self-sufficient, oriented. Contrary to what the historical century declares, the poem resides in the weakness of sense, and in the non-contemporaneity of this sense with the real contemporary. This sheds light on why Mandelstam, in another poem from 1924, comes to exclaim: 'I was never anyone's contemporary, no.'[18] The thought of its time is the thought of a weak point disassembled from this time itself. (But suddenly I think that here we should name Gennady Aygui, the Chuvash poet, for example: 'Let us ask ourselves where, in which writing, there is most sleep'[19]).

We could then say that Celan, who is like a fraternal inversion of Mandelstam, takes the imperative of the weakness of sense all the way to the point of breakdown of song, because in the intimacy of song there still remains something like an excessive deposit of sense. For Celan, the clear and unblinded thought supposes the breakage of the poem as aesthetic ethos, the immanent annulment of numerous or rhythmic thought (I quote from *Zeitgehöft*):

> If one who
> smashed the canticles
> were now to speak to the staff
> his and everyone's
> blinding
> would be revoked.[20]

---

18 Mandelstam, *Complete Poetry*, p. 139.

19 Gennady Aygui, 'Sleep-and-Poetry (Notes)', in *Veronica's Book with Notes on Sleep-and-Poetry*, trans. Peter France (Edinburgh: Polygon, 1989), p. 86. Badiou quotes the French translation by Léon Robel.

20 Paul Celan, *Poems of Paul Celan*, trans. Michael Hamburger (New York: Persea Books, 2002), p. 323. Badiou quotes the French translation by Martine Broda.

If the canticle's song is broken, if the poem is relieved of
the poem, if we accept the narrowest cut of a single deadly
mark (and I recognize in this 'narrow cut' the breaching,
the subtraction of Mandelstam), a mark without aura or
echo, then a *new* meaning arrives, at the heights of the
defection from all presence:

> There also comes a meaning
> down the narrowest cut,
> it is breached
> by the deadliest of our
> standing marks.[21]

I read Celan as saying that, yes, the poem demands to be
relieved of the poem – but Caeiro had already written:
'I write the prose of my verses' – or else that the poem-
thought arrived at the breaking of its support, of its song,
demands to be reopened onto the pure dimension of its
meaning or sense. This can also be said as follows: the age
of the poets is closed.

With regard to this terminal point, we are entitled to
ask whether, of all these jurisdictions of the poem about
thought, of all these maxims of thought that illuminate the
poem, we might retain and fixate a few that would bring
them together.

First of all, no doubt, there is the will to have a method.
These poets set up the method of the poem qua poem. The
(philosophical) discourse on method is followed by the
poems of method. 'We assert you, method!' says Rimbaud,
or again: 'impatient to find the place and the formula'.[22]
Indeed the poem establishes guidelines for thought, proposing singular *operations* for it. 'Operation' here is opposed
to the romantic theme of the meditation, or of contempla-
tion: the patriarchal and prophetic figure of which Hugo
is the emblem, which can still be heard in Paul Claudel,

---

21   Paul Celan, *Selections*, trans. Pierre Joris (Berkeley: University of
California Press, 2005), p. 142.

22   Rimbaud, 'Morning of Drunkenness', in *Complete Works*, p. 323;
and 'Vagabonds', in *Complete Works*, p. 331.

of course, but also, muted, ordered and abstract, in Paul Valéry or Rainer Maria Rilke. To grasp the age of the poets would require first of all that one establish an inventory of the operations active in the poem. For these are the operations that, from within the poem, legislate about and against the sutures of philosophy.

I will only mention three: counter-romanticism, detotalization, and the diagonal.

1) The poets of the age of the poets have all been forced to subtract the poem, in its role as thought, from its romantic definition. This subtraction takes the form of a series of prohibitions, which aim to *centre* the poem on a tacit concept rather than on the power of the image. Poetry is that place, Mallarmé will say,

> where the true poet's broad and humble gesture must
> keep them from dreams, those enemies of his trust.[23]

Similarly Rimbaud, with that touch of promptitude and fury that is characteristic of him:

> Ah! dreaming is shameful
> Since it is pure loss![24]

Caeiro, Mandelstam and Celan share this prohibitive vocation of the poem as the counter-image, the affirmative interruption, of the dream. But, by a paradox which is that of poetry itself, defined as a thinking of the sensible as such, the vector of an image almost always carries the prohibition that strikes the image. This image, which is rather the imaged subtraction of the image, is that of the earth. Rimbaud again:

---

23   Stéphane Mallarmé, 'Funerary Toast', in *Collected Poems and Other Verse*, trans. E. H. Blackmore and A. M. Blackmore (Oxford: Oxford University Press, 2006), p. 51.
24   Rimbaud, 'Comedy of Thirst', in *Complete Works*, p. 179.

> If I have any taste, it is for hardly
> Anything but earth and stones.[25]

This earth is by no means the nostalgic sheltering, the appropriation of the origin, or the great natural Mother. It is the naked place of the poem's address, 'space, its own peer, whether it fail or grow' (Mallarmé).[26] It is that which is *not* sacred or sacralizable, which turns away from complacency with the dream and the image in order to entrust the poem to the rigorous laws of metaphor. Again from Mandelstam – for whom air and sea are, in different operations, equally essential ('Whoever Finds a Horseshoe'):

> They stood on the uncomfortable ground
> too, as on a donkey's spine
> ...
> No word is better than another word,
> the earth honks with metaphor
> ...
> Air kneaded thick as earth –
> you can't leave it, and it's hard to get in.[27]

Subtracted from presentation, as the place of regulated metaphorical exchanges, this ungrateful earth of the poets does violence to all nostalgia.

2) Against the supposition of a Great Whole – a supposition from which even someone like Charles Baudelaire never fully escapes – the poets of the age of the poets think detotalization, the separate, irreconcilable multiplicity. They impose on themselves the rule of a principle of inconsistency. Caeiro is in this regard the most conceptual, the most 'prosaic':

---

25 Rimbaud, 'Alchemy of the Word', *A Season in Hell*, in *Complete Works*, p. 291.
26 Mallarmé, 'When the shade threatened ...', in *Collected Poems*, p. 67.
27 Mandelstam, 'Whoever Finds a Horseshoe', in *Complete Poetry*, p. 132.

And a real and true wholeness
Is a sickness of our thought.
Nature is parts without a whole.[28]

But it is without a doubt Celan who offers the maxim
to which the philosopher has nothing to add, the central
maxim of all intervening thought in the conditions that are
our own:

Lean yourself
On the inconsistencies.[29]

A whole poetic tradition, emerging out of epic and great
lyric, proposes to *cross* in ordered fashion the strata of signification, to unfold, as story or initiation, an order that
would appease the chaos and console the lamentation. The
poets of the age of the poets would much rather draw a
line in language that would trace a diagonal stroke through
whatever classification one imagines for it, to produce a
short-circuit in the circulation of linguistic energy. It is
principally not a question of attempting paradoxical comparative approximations, as in Paul Éluard's famous 'the
earth is blue like an orange'. Such attempts are only the
secondary rhetoric of the diagonal operation. It is a question of a statement of the poem *wagering* that a nomination
may come and interrupt signification, and from the point
of this interruption for a *localizable* thought to establish
itself, without any pretence to totality, but capable of being
loyal to its own inauguration. I am thinking for example
of the opening lines of Trakl's poem 'Psalm' (and I like to
think that this title is also that of a poem by Celan): 'It is a
light, which the wind has blown out.'[30] The 'it is' or 'there
is', which is so frequent in Trakl, is never anything but the
'there is' of a lack, for the sole benefit of a breath of air.
And is this not exactly our site of thinking, in which no

---

28   Pessoa, *The Collected Poems of Alberto Caeiro*, p. 70.
29   Paul Celan, *Selected Poems and Prose*, trans. John Felstiner (New
York: W. W. Norton, 2001), p. 34 (translation modified).
30   Trakl, 'Psalm', in *Song of the Departed*, p. 61.

light is nameable any more except inasmuch as the wind of History has forever extinguished it?

But there is also this poem from 1937, in which Mandelstam begins precisely – this is the rule of interruption – by saying 'No comparisons: everyone alive is incomparable' – and which, echoing Rimbaud, continues by saying 'I'd drift down an arc of journeys that never began'.[31]

That there could be a light without light, or that one could navigate without ever having left: such are the acts by which the poem, naming a disappearance, suspends the game of sense and makes a diagonal of being and its annulment. The poetic diagonal declares that a faithful thought, thus capable of truth, makes a hole in whatever knowledge is concentrated in significations. It cuts the threads, for another circulation of the current of thought. This sectioning off, though, is not a negation – it is not a labour of the negative. On the contrary, the diagonal is always affirmative: it says 'I' or 'there is'.

Obviously there would be many more operations to list. But, as far as philosophy is concerned – that philosophy which beyond its sutures we can place again under the condition of the poem as much as of the matheme, politics, and love – there are finally two principal kinds of gesture by which the poem points towards its own thought.

First, against the reduction of thought to knowledge, whereby knowledge exposes being in the figure of the object, the poetry of these poets activates a de-objectification.

What is an object? It is what disposes the multiple of being in relation to meaning or signification. The age of the poets animates a polemic against meaning, thus targeting objectivity, which is being as *captive* of meaning, and proposing to us the figure without figure, or the unfigurable figure, of a subject without object. Caeiro says this with his habitual clarity:

---

31 Mandelstam, *Complete Poetry*, p. 266.

Things don't have meaning: they only have existence.
Things are the only hidden meaning of things.[32]

Let us understand that, for Caeiro, the 'thing' is by no means an object. The thing is the multiple-existent as such, subtracted from every regime of the One. Consequently, the entire poem is destined to place us in this subtraction, to extract us from the pressure of sense, so that the restrictive paradigm of the object is succeeded by the pure dispersion of existence.

This is also the meaning that I think we should give in Celan's poetics to the unstable multiplicity of that which is the most fixed, the most illuminating, which Plato even makes into the very metaphor of the One: the sun. Thus, in *Zeitgehöft*:

> There are two suns, you hear,
> Two,
> Not one –
> Yes and?[33]

Or, in 'Erratic', a poem from the collection *Die Niemandsrose*:

> Near all
> Dispersed
> Suns, soul,
> You were, in the ether.[34]

Here we see how the address aimed at the subject as other, at the 'you' on whom Celan bases his hope in language, supposes the dispersal of the one, the dissipation of the recourse to this one that might put some order in objectivity. The soul finds its ether only if it is withdrawn from any objective correlate and is linked only to inconsistency.

---

32 Pessoa, *The Collected Poems of Alberto Caeiro*, p. 61.
33 Paul Celan, *Zeitgehöft: Späte Gedichte aus dem Nachlaß* (Frankfurt am Main: Suhrkamp, 1976), p. 56.
34 Paul Celan, 'Erratisch', in *Die Niemandsrose* (Frankfurt am Main: S. Fischer Verlag, 1964), p. 53.

Second, against the apology for the sense or meaning of History, the poetry of the age of the poets organizes a *disorientation* in thought. We already saw that this disorienting operation was at the heart of the thought of the century in Mandelstam. But also, or already, in Rimbaud, so concerned with History, we find the absolute gap, which is totally disorienting, between on one hand the active and wilful hatred of the established order, of existing society, the idea of radical revolution; and, on the other, a kind of stagnation, an impossible departure, or ineluctable restoration. As if, as soon as it became barely visible, the violent orientation of sense turned out to be illusory and unpracticable:

> ... Industrialists, princes, senates,
> Perish! Power, justice, history, down with you!
> That is our due. Blood! Blood! Golden flame!
>
> All to war, to vengeance and to terror,
> My Spirit! Let us turn about in the Biting Jaws: Ah!
> Vanish,
> Republics of the world! Of emperors,
> Regiments, colonists, peoples, enough!
>
> ... I am here! I am still here![35]

The 'I am still here' runs counter to the 'enough!' of revolutionary profanation, and revokes the meaning that negation teaches us. Just as, in *A Season in Hell*, the 'you cannot get away' cancels the anticipation of a departure that would dispense an orientation of life.[36]

There are certainly different poetic operations that put under erasure the presumption of a sense that gives meaning and orientation to History. To disorient thought itself, Trakl opposes to it this absolutely disruptive figure that is death: not the care or the chagrin of death, not the subjective effect of death, but death itself, the corpse of the

---

35 Rimbaud, 'What does it matter for us, my heart', *Complete Works*, p. 215.

36 Rimbaud, *A Season in Hell*, in *Complete Works*, p. 269.

young man on the surface of the visible (an image we may associate with Rimbaud's 'A Sleeper in the Valley'). Trakl's means are pictorial: it is a matter of capturing death in the intense networks of materiality. Colours are the emblem of this depthless visibility: gold, blue, green-black, the blood of the prey, the green river come to present the dead as the latent centre of a given space. There is a slowness in the appearing of death in the place of these colours, colours which cut out a segment of time and bring it to a halt. Trakl's poem disorients us with a pure present of material death, as if death found its point of the real in space rather than in time. Disorientation, for Trakl, is a loss of time in the slow and sweet trials of death. Let us give way to this loss by listening to 'Elis 2':

> A gentle glockenspiel sings in Elis' breast
> At evening,
> When his head sinks into the black pillow.
>
> A blue prey
> Bleeds softly in the thornbush.
>
> A brown tree stands in isolation there;
> Its blue fruits have fallen from it.
>
> Signs and stars
> Sink softly in the evening pond.
>
> Beyond the hill it has turned winter.
>
> At night
> Blue doves drink up the icy sweat
> That flows from Elis' crystal brow
>
> Along the black walls
> Forever drones the lonely wind of God.[37]

Notice how such a poem is radically *non-addressed*. No reader is supposed or marked in the forms and colours

---

37   Trakl, 'Elis 2', in *Song of the Departed*, p. 95.

that frame an evasive and elongated figure of death. Disorientation is taken to the point where *our* place is nowhere attested to. Thought is assigned its residence, without any vision, in the pure 'there is' in which the sole advent, in the lonely wind, is that of a cadaver.

De-objectification and disorientation concentrate whatever this poetry opposes to the sutures of philosophy, a poetry that dissolves the objectivity of science – which captivates the positivisms – into pure multiplicity, and disorients History – which fascinates revolutionary thought. The age of the poets bequeaths to us, in order to liberate philosophy, the imperative of a clarification without totality, a thinking of what is at once dispersed and unseparated, an inhospitable and cold reason, for want of either object or orientation. To the coldness that de-objectifies and disorients, the poem even restores a subjective tonality, which is like the winter 'colour' of the subject without object. Mallarmé is the winter poet par excellence:

> Let the cold with its scythe-like silence run,
> I shall not howl out any void lament, not one
> if this so white frolic on earth's bare face
> denies the honor of some feigned vista to any place.[38]

But Celan, when he encounters the silence of the masters, which is precisely the sutured abdication of philosophy, also names at once the inseparate, the clear and the cold, as thought which is imparted to us in thought:

> Before the
> masters en-
> silencing us,
> in the undifferentiated, attesting
> itself: the clammy
> brightness.[39]

---

38 Mallarmé, 'My old tomes closed upon the name Paphos ...', in *Collected Poems*, p. 81.
39 Celan, *Selections*, p. 143.

These poets have detected everything that the infinite *weight* of the situations contains, in terms of its being, as latent void: the void that the event alone summons, even if it is the event of the poem itself. This void is ubiquitous in Mallarmé, 'on the empty room's credences', the 'blank paper' ...[40] But it is everywhere, and even in Mandelstam, no doubt more concerned than the others – except for Rimbaud – with *filling* it. Look at this poem from 1910, in which the whole movement goes from absence to emptiness, mediated by the wild torment of the world:

> The sail stretches its delicate ears,
> staring eyes go empty
> and a silent choir of midnight birds
> sails over the soundlessness.
>
> I'm as poor as nature
> and as simple as the sky,
> my freedom is as ghostly
> as the singing of midnight birds.
>
> I see a stagnant moon
> and a sky deader than canvas:
> oh emptiness, I accept
> your morbid wild world![41]

The poem's aim is to find, for this void latent under the weight of the world, the supernumerary grace of a name. And the only norm of thought, that which the poem thinks, is to remain faithful to this name, even as the weight of being, which for a moment has been suspended, comes back, returns always.

A poem from the age of the poets is to go with the void, in the midst of gravity, under the emblem of a name. Celan, to conclude:

---

40 Mallarmé, 'With her pure nails offering their onyx high', in *Collected Poems*, p. 69; and 'Sea Breeze', in *Collected Poems*, p. 25.

41 Mandelstam, *Complete Poetry*, p. 38.

It is the weight holding back the void
that would
accompany you.
Like you, it has no name. Perhaps
you two are one and the same. Perhaps
one day you also will call
me so.[42]

42   Celan, *Poems of Paul Celan*, p. 163.

WHAT DOES THE POEM THINK?

Today in France we have an amazing number of truly remarkable poets, and one of them made the headlines this morning.[1] But who knows it? Who reads them? Who memorizes them?

Poetry, alas, is receding from us. The cultural account is oblivious to poetry. This is because poetry can hardly stand the demand for clarity, the passive audience, the simple message. The poem is an exercise in intransigence. It is without mediation, and thus also without mediatization. The poem remains rebellious – defeated in advance – to the democracy of audience ratings and polls.

Indeed, the poem does not belong to the order of communication. The poem has nothing to communicate. It is only a saying, a declaration, which draws its authority only from itself.

Let us listen to Rimbaud:

> Ah! dust of the willows shaken by a wing!
> The roses of the reeds devoured long ago![2]

---

1 *Translator's note*: Badiou is referring to the poet Jacques Roubaud.
2 Arthur Rimbaud, 'Memory', in *Complete Works*, p. 209.

Who is speaking? Of what world is the nomination here being arranged? With what or for what are we thus being asked to share in an exclamation? Nothing in these words is communicable, nothing is previously destined; for it is not certain that any opinion can be assembled on the basis of the statement that reeds have their roses, or that a poetic wing comes from within language to disseminate the dust of the willows.

The singularity of what is being declared here does not correspond to any of the possible figures of interest. The action of the poem cannot be general, nor constitute the conviviality of an audience. The poem offers itself as a thing of language, which one encounters each time as an event. About the poem, Mallarmé says: 'It takes place all by itself, finished, existing.'[3] This 'all by itself' of the poem is its peremptory rising in language. This is why the poem neither communicates nor enters into general circulation. A purity folded onto itself, the poem awaits us without anxiety, in the abruptness of its closed manifestation, as a fan that only our gaze unfolds. The poem says:

> Understand how, by ingenious deceit,
> to keep one wing within your hand.[4]

It is always an 'ingenious deceit' that links us to the encounter of the poem, for no sooner have we encountered and unfolded it than we act as if it had been forever destined for us. And in this way, guarded by that wing in our hand, we regain confidence in the native innocence of words.

Withdrawn and reserved, the modern poem is haunted by a central silence. A pure silence, devoid of anything sacred, it interrupts the general racket. It lodges silence in the central framework of language and, from there, skews it towards an unprecedented affirmation. This silence is an

---

3 Stéphane Mallarmé, 'Restricted Action', in *Divagations*, trans. Barbara Johnson (Cambridge: Harvard University Press, 2007), p. 190 (translation modified).

4 Mallarmé, 'Fan (Belonging to Madame Mallarmé)', in *Collected Poems*, p. 57 (translation modified).

operation. And the poem, in this sense, says the opposite of Wittgenstein. It says: I create silence in order to say that which is impossible to say in the shared language of consensus, to separate it from the world so that it may be said, and always re-said for the first time.

This is why the poem demands in its own words an operation of silence. Therein lies an imperative of reserve. About poetry we may say:

> as she is poising to caress,
> neither old wood nor old edition,
> but instrumental featheriness –
> being the silence's musician.[5]

'The silence's musician': as reserved and withdrawn speech, the poem belongs to what Mallarmé named 'restricted action'.[6] And already Mallarmé opposed it to another use of language, which governs us today: the language of communication and of reality, the language of the disarray of images, always mediated and mediatized. The language that Mallarmé called 'universal reporting'.[7]

Yes, the poem is first and foremost this unique fragment of speech all by itself subtracted from the universal reportage. The poem is a halting point. It stops language in its tracks and prohibits its squandering in the vast commerce that is the world today. Against the obscenity of 'everything to be seen' and 'everything to be said', the showing, polling, and commenting of everything, the poem is the guardian of the decency of the saying. Or of what Jacques Lacan called the ethics of well-saying.

In this sense, the poem is a delicacy of language against language; it is a delicate *touching* of the resources of language. Now, our age, Mallarmé has already observed, acts in all things rather indelicately: 'They act indelicately … to let loose waves of vast human incomprehension.'[8]

---

5 Mallarmé, 'Saint', in *Collected Poems*, p. 49.
6 Mallarmé, 'Restricted Action', in *Divagations*, pp. 215–19.
7 Mallarmé, 'Crisis of Verse', in *Divagations*, p. 210.
8 Mallarmé, 'The Mystery in Letters', in *Divagations*, p. 232.

Let us say: the poem is language itself, exposing itself in solitary exception to the ruckus that takes the place of understanding.

What can we say then about the poem and understanding? Musician of its own silence, proven guardian of *our* own delicacy, is the poem something by which a form of knowledge is organized? Which one?

On this point the modern interpreters of poetry present us with a major dispute. Some of them hold that the poem is nothing more than what I already said: the touching of language, the exploration at the limits of language's affirmative capacities.

These interpreters explore the poem's form; they painstakingly delimit what is poetry and what is prose. They explain the metre and the rhythm. The poem is thus language grasped in its intimate cadence; language come into its own under the law of its scansion, or its breathing. The poem, we might say, is then *the number or rhythm of an action* within language. This morning Jacques Roubaud added that this rhythmic action of language takes place in memory.

Neither Rimbaud nor Mallarmé ignored this assignation of the poem to the link between act and rhythm – the first when he underscored that 'in Greece, verses and lyres *give rhythm to Action*', and the second, when he declares that the poet 'yields the initiative to words, through the clash of their ordered inequalities; they light each other up through reciprocal reflections like a virtual swooping of fire across precious stones.'[9]

In this view, the poem can certainly be a form of thought; but it is, more originarily, the song of thought – or, still Rimbaud, 'a thought sung *and* understood by the singer.'[10]

Others, by contrast, hold that the poem is destined to keep us in the opening of being, to keep the visible qua

---

9   Rimbaud, 'To Paul Demeny (15 May 1871)', in *Complete Works*, p. 374; and Mallarmé, 'Crisis of Verse', in *Divagations*, p. 208.

10   Rimbaud, 'To Paul Demeny (15 May 1871)'.

visible; or again, to sustain for thinking the disclosure of that which comes to us, or presents itself to us. Of course, this is Martin Heidegger's thinking. But it is also, in a completely different register, that of the poet Yves Bonnefoy, when he writes that 'the chance of poetry to come is that it is on the verge of knowing whatever presence is capable of opening.'[11]

The coming into its own of language in the numbered breath of its cadence, in the song that it contains; or destiny of pure presence in thought: such is the interlacing of the contemporary dispute with regard to the poem.

The observation that I would like to make to inscribe myself in this dispute is rather banal: the poem, or the great poem, lets itself be *translated*. Admittedly, the loss is immense and irreversible. Song, rhythms, cadence, sounds, stanzas are almost always abolished in one fell swoop. And yet, I claim that the *voice* of the poet, the singularity of his or her musician's silence, remains, even in the midst of the loss of almost all the music.

When I read the following in Georg Trakl – 'It is a light, which the wind has blown out'[12] – I know that there has been a deposition of original language and its breath. But I recognize the limpid and sad paradox of a light that subsists beyond the absence of sparkle.

And when, by the same Trakl, I read:

> A blue prey
> Bleeds softly in the thornbush.
>
> A brown tree stands in isolation there;
> Its blue fruits have fallen from it.
>
> Signs and stars
> Sink softly in the evening pond.[13]

---

11 Yves Bonnefoy, 'L'acte et le lieu de la poésie', in *L'improbable et autres essais* (Paris: Gallimard, 1992), p. 133.

12 Trakl, 'Psalm', in *Song of the Departed*, p. 61.

13 Trakl, 'Elis 2', in *Song of the Departed*, p. 95.

– here, too, the slow emblematic coming of death, the painting, or figuration, of these browns and these blues which encircle and expose the blood and the stars: all this is bestowed on me as evidence that only the poem institutes.

And so what is it that passes in this way from one language to another? What remains in spite of the linguistic ruin of almost everything – if not a form of thought?

Let us say that what the poem thinks is what endures victoriously the test of a mutilated, or forgotten, rhythm.

I say 'thought' and not a form of 'knowledge'. Why? We must reserve the word 'knowledge' for that which is supported by an object, the object of knowledge. The delimitation of knowledge supposes that the real comes to experience in the form of the object.

Now – this point is crucial – the poem does not aim, nor suppose, nor describe, any object, or any objectivity. If I say:

> as on some spar lowly in station
> plummeting with the caravel
> constantly frolicked through the swell
> a bird of new intoxication
> which cried in a drab monotone
> though the helm never swerved aside
> a bearing that could be no guide
> night and despair and precious stone.[14]

– what is here apparently narrated, in a peremptory use of the imperfect, and allows for no discussion, is certainly not the objectivity of the discovery of new lands by Vasco da Gama. And the messenger, 'a bird of new intoxication', does not have, nor will it ever have, the figure of an object whose experience one might be able to share.

The poem has neither an anecdote nor a referential object. It declares from beginning to end its own universe.

Not only does the poem have no object, but a large part of its *operation* aims precisely to deny the object, to

---

14   Mallarmé, 'For the sole task of travelling', in *Collected Poems*, p. 213.

ensure that thought no longer stands in a relation to the object. The poem aims for thought to declare what there is by *deposing* every supposed object. Such is the core of the poetic experience as an experience of thought: to give access to an affirmation of being that is not arranged as the apprehension of an object.

The poem generally manages to do so by two contrary operations, which I will call subtraction and dissemination.

Subtraction is what assembles the poem with the direct aim of a withdrawal of the object; the poem is a negative machine, which states being, or the idea, at the very point where the object has vanished.

This is the logic of Mallarmé: where objective reality – for example, the setting sun – starts to disappear, to give rise to what Mallarmé calls 'the pure notion'.[15] It is a form of pure thinking, de-objectified or disenchanted with the object – a form of thinking henceforth *separated* from any given object. The emblem of this notion is often the star, or the constellation, which resides 'on some vacant and higher surface', which is 'cold with neglect and disuse'.[16]

The operation of the poem seeks to pass from an objective tumult, the solar certainty, 'blaze of fame, blood in foam, gold, storm and stress', to an inscription which *gives* nothing, which is inhuman and pure, 'a fixed septet of scintillations', which has the withdrawn and abstract appearance of the mathematical number, that constellation which enumerates 'the successive impact starrily of a full reckoning in the making.'[17]

Such is the subtractive operation of the poem, which submits the object to the test of its lack.

Dissemination, for its part, seeks to dissolve the object by way of its infinite metaphorical distribution. And so, as

---

15 Mallarmé, Letter to Henri Cazalis (14 May 1867), in *Selected Letters of Stéphane Mallarmé*, ed. and trans. Rosemary Lloyd (Chicago: The University of Chicago Press, 1988), p. 74.

16 Mallarmé, 'A Dice Throw', in *Collected Poems*, p. 181.

17 Mallarmé, 'The fine suicide fled victoriously', in *Collected Poems*, p. 69; 'With her pure nails offering their onyx high', in *Collected Poems*, p. 71; and 'A Dice Throw'.

soon as it is mentioned the object emigrates elsewhere in
the realm of sense, is de-objectified by becoming something
other than what it is. The object loses its objectivity, not as
the effect of a lack but as the effect of an excess: an excessive equivalence with other objects. This time the poem
leads the object astray into pure multiplicity.

Rimbaud excels in the operation of dissemination –
not only because he sees 'frankly a mosque in place of a
factory'; not only because life itself, the subject, is other
and multiple, as with 'this gentleman' who 'does not know
what he is doing. He is an angel', and this family which
is 'a litter of dogs';[18] but also, and even more so, because
the poem's wish is the incessant migration into heterogeneous phenomena. The poem, at the farthest remove from
the *foundation* of objectivity, sets about to make it literally
founder or *melt*:

> But can one melt where the guideless cloud melts
> – Oh! Favored by what is cool!
> And expire in these damp violets
> Whose dawns fill these forests?[19]

Thus the object is caught and abolished either in the poetic
hunger of its subtraction, or in the poetic thirst of its
dissemination.

Mallarmé will say:

> Satisfied by no fruits here, my starvation
> Finds equal savor in their learned deprivation.[20]

The fruit, subtracted, nonetheless appeases the hunger as
an expression of a subject without object.

And Rimbaud, concluding 'Comedy of Thirst', will
spread this thirst all over nature:

---

18   Rimbaud, *A Season in Hell*, in *Complete Works*, p. 288 and
pp. 292–5.

19   Rimbaud, 'Comedy of Thirst', in *Complete Works*, p. 179.

20   Mallarmé, 'My old tomes closed upon the name Paphos'.

The pigeons fluttering in the field
The game, which runs and sees in the dark,
The water animals, the animal enslaved,
The last butterflies! ... are also thirsty.[21]

Here Rimbaud makes thirst into the dispersed vacancy of every subject, as well as of every object.

The poem brings to language the following: what is an experience without object? A pure affirmation, which constitutes a universe that nothing assures either in its right to be or even its probability?

The thought of the poem does not begin until after a complete de-objectification of presence. This is why we can say that, at the farthest remove from knowledge, the poem is exemplarily a thought that is obtained in the retreat, or the defection, of everything that supports the faculty to know. And no doubt this is why the poem has always *disconcerted* philosophy.

I have often mentioned the proceedings initiated by Plato against painting and poetry. However, if we follow in detail the arguments of Book X of the *Republic*, one is struck by the subjective complication, the embarrassment, of this gesture that excludes the poets from the city-state.

Plato clearly oscillates between an excessive, almost overblown conviction and an evident weakness with regard to the poetic temptation. The stakes are apparently enormous, and this should put us on alert. Plato does not hesitate to write that 'the city whose principle we have organized is the best one, and especially, I think, because of the measures taken in the matter of poetry.'[22] All the same, this is an astounding sentence! The fate of the political depending on the fate of the poem! The poem here is recognized as having an almost boundless power.

Later, all kinds of concessions and half-regrets expose the temptation, and offer the poet a path of civic

---

21 Rimbaud, 'Comedy of Thirst'.
22 Plato, *The Republic*, trans. Paul Shorey (Cambridge, MA: Harvard University Press, 1969), 595a (translation modified).

incorporation. Plato recognizes that it is only in the 'hard' way or 'by force', *bía*, that one can let go of the poem. He admits that the defenders of poetry may 'plead her cause in prose without metre'[23] – whereby prose is summoned to come to the aid of the poem, which is a point that would require a long commentary of its own.

These oscillations allow us to say that the poem, for philosophy, is exactly the equivalent of a *symptom*. This symptom, like all symptoms, insists. And here we are without doubt at the most secret point of Plato's text. We might think that Plato links the condemnation of poetry to his own speculative and political endeavours, that he *invents* the conflict between the philosopher and the poet. But that is not what he says. To the contrary, he evokes an older, almost immemorial conflict: *palaia tis diaphora philosophia te kai poiètikè* ('ancient is the discord between philosophy and poetry'). What does this antiquity of the conflict refer to?

The thesis of imitation – the interior and illusory character of mimetics – is not, in my eyes, the most fruitful clue for us. What mimetic hallmark might we possibly perceive when Rimbaud mysteriously declares:

> O seasons, O castles
> What soul is without flaws?[24]

Because it is delinked from the object, the poem, in fact, does not install any imitative regime. It is even the epitome of a nomination without imitation. Mallarmé goes so far as to say, in the poem itself, that it is nature that is incapable of imitating the poem. Thus the Faun, asking himself if the wind and the water bear the trace of his sensory memory, ends up abandoning this quest by observing that wind and water are unequal in power to what the flute alone is capable of:

---

23 Plato, *Republic*, 607d and 607e.
24 Rimbaud, 'O seasons, O castles', in *Complete Works*, p. 211.

the cool dawn's struggles, not a sound
of water but my flute's outpourings murmurs round
the thicket steeped in music; and the one stir of air
my dual pipes are swiftly shedding everywhere
and then dispersing in a sonorous arid sleet,
is, over the horizon that no ripples pleat,
the visible, serene and artificial sigh
of inspiration reascending to the sky.[25]

The poem imitates all the less in that it is rather by imitation that the real disposition of objects fails.

What Plato says above all is that the poem ruins discursivity. In Greek: *dianoia*. What is opposed philosophically to the poem is not the dialectic, not the intuition of ideas, but *dianoia* – discursive thought that proceeds by putting arguments in a chain, the paradigm for which is mathematics.

Plato explicitly recalls that, against the poem, the remedies found are 'measuring, numbering, and weighing'.[26] In the background of this conflict, we find these two extremes of language: the poem, which aims at presence without object; and mathematics, which ciphers the Idea.

Plato lets the geometers come in through the principal entrance so that the poets may leave the premises via the back stairs.

Now, I tell myself the following: what is disconcerting to philosophy, what makes the poem into a symptom of philosophy, is not illusion or imitation. It is that the poem might well be a form of thinking without knowledge, or even: a properly incalculable thought.

Dianoia is the thought that passes through, the thought that is the traversing of the thinkable.

The poem does not traverse. It is integrally affirmative – it stands still on the threshold of what it is, withdrawing or dispersing the objects that overburden it.

But is this movement not *also* that of the dialectic, when the latter arrives at the supreme principle of all that is?

25 Mallarmé, 'A Faun in the Afternoon', in *Collected Poems*, p. 41.
26 Plato, *Republic*, 602d.

Plato certainly guarantees the *grip* of thought on being by the intercession of knowledge and objects of knowledge. The idea is the intelligible exposure of the experience of the object, of objective experience *in its entirety*. For there are, as we know, ideas of hair, of horse and of mud, just as there are ideas of movement, of quiet repose and of justice.

But beyond all the ideas of object, beyond ideal objectivity, there is the good, or the One, which is not an Idea, which is even, according to Plato's expression, beyond substance, beyond the ideal being-there.

This One, this good, are they not subtracted from intelligible objectivity? And is it not impossible to know them, if it is even possible to *think* them? And, to talk about them, must we not use the metaphor of the sun, the myth of the dead returned to earth – in short, the resources of the poem? Finally, in order to *surpass* the donation of being based on the disposition of objects, the *dianoia* is insufficient. We must rely on the great de-objectifying operations of the poem: subtraction and dissemination. On the principle of what is, insofar as it is, the argumentative traversing comes to founder.

It could well be, therefore, that the poem disconcerts philosophy insofar as the poem's operations *rival* those of philosophy. It could well be that the philosopher has always been a jealous rival of the poet. Or, to put it differently: the poem is a thought in its very act, which therefore has no need to be also the thought of thought. Now, philosophy establishes itself in the desire to think thought. But it is always uncertain whether the thought in action, the sensible thought, is not more real than the thought of thought.

Between the thought that cuts short and the thought that takes, or wastes, the time to think itself: such would be *the ancient discord* evoked by Plato. This rivalry would shed light on the symptom, the painful separation, the violence and the temptation.

But the poem is scarcely more tender. It is not tender

towards *dianoia*: 'You mathematicians expired', Mallarmé says abruptly. And it is not tender towards philosophy either: 'Philosophers', grumbles Rimbaud, 'you are of your West.'[27]

Let us posit that this quarrel is the very essence of the relation between philosophy and poetry. Let us not wish for an end of this quarrel, for that would always mean either that philosophy gives in on argumentation or that the poem reconstitutes the object.

Now, to give up on the rational mathematical paradigm is deadly for philosophy, which is not just envious of the poem. And a return to objectivity leads only to a didactic and extenuated poetry – poetry led astray into philosophy.

Yes, the relation between philosophy and poetry must remain, as Plato says, *mégas o agôn*, 'a great battle'. So let us do battle, divided, torn, unreconciled. Let us do battle for the conflicted respite, we philosophers, forever torn between the norm of literal transparency of mathematics and the norm of singularity and presence of the poem. Let us do battle by recognizing the *common task*, which is to think that which was unthinkable, to say that which was impossible to say. Or again, Mallarmé's imperative, which I think is shared even in the antagonism between philosophy and poetry: 'Over there, wherever it is, denying the ineffable, which lies.'[28]

---

27   Mallarmé, 'Igitur', in *Selected Poetry and Prose*, ed. Mary Ann Caws (New York: New Directions, 1982), p. 92; and Rimbaud, 'The Impossible', in *Complete Works*, p. 299.

28   Mallarmé, 'Music and Letters', in *Divagations*, p. 194.

THE PHILOSOPHICAL STATUS OF
THE POEM AFTER HEIDEGGER

When Parmenides places his poem under the invocation of the goddess and begins with the image of a horse-riding initiation, we must confess that this is not, or not yet, philosophy. For any truth that accepts its dependence with regard to revelation and narration is still caught in mystery, and philosophy's whole being consists in wanting to tear apart mystery's veil.

In Parmenides the poetic form is essential, as with the poem's authority it keeps discourse in proximity to the sacred. Now philosophy cannot begin except by a desacralization: it installs a discursive regime that is its own, purely earthly legitimation. Philosophy demands that the mysterious and sacred authority of proffered profundity be interrupted by the secularism of argumentation.

Besides, it is on this very issue that Parmenides serves as a kind of pre-commencement of philosophy – when, with regard to the question of non-being, he sketches out a reasoning from the absurd. This latent recourse to an autonomous rule of consistency is, within the poem, an interruption of the collusion that the poem organizes between truth and the sacred authority of the image or the story.

It is essential to notice that the support for this interruption can only be of the order of the matheme, if by this we understand the discursive singularities of mathematics. Apagogic reasoning is without a doubt the most significant matrix of an argumentation that supports itself with nothing but the imperative of consistency, and turns out to be incompatible with any legitimation by way of storytelling, or by the (initiated or sacred) status of the subject of the enunciation. The matheme, here, is that which, making the speaker disappear, emptying its place of any and all mysterious validation, exposes the argumentation to the test of its autonomy, and thus to the critical or dialogical examination of its pertinence.

Philosophy began in Greece because there alone the matheme enabled the interruption of the sacral exercise of validation by way of the story (by the mytheme, Philippe Lacoue-Labarthe would say). Parmenides is the proper name for the pre-moment of this interruption, which is still internal to the sacred story and its poetic capture.

We know only too well that Plato, for his part, names the reflection of this interruption, pushed all the way to the point of the systematic suspicion of anything reminiscent of the poem. Plato proposes to us a complete analysis of the gesture of interruption that constitutes the possibility of philosophy. Insofar as the imitative capture of the poem is concerned – its seduction without a concept, its legitimation without an idea – we must set it aside, ban it from the space in which the royalty of the philosopher operates. This is a painful and interminable rupture (look at Book X of the *Republic*), but what is at stake is the very *existence* of philosophy, and not just its style alone.

The support that mathematics provides for the desacralization, or de-poeticization, of truth, must be explicitly sanctioned: pedagogically by the crucial place reserved for arithmetic and geometry in political education, and ontologically by their intelligible dignity, which functions as the vestibule to the final deployments of the dialectic.

For Aristotle, who is as unpoetic as possible in the

technique of his exposition (Plato by contrast, as he himself recognizes, is at all moments sensitive to the charm of that which he excludes), the poem is nothing more than a particular object offered up to the arrangements of knowledge, while at the same time mathematics loses all the attributes of ontological dignity that Plato granted to it. 'Poetics' is a regional discipline of philosophical activity. With Aristotle, the foundational dispute is finished, and philosophy, stabilized in connection to its parts, no longer returns dramatically to that which conditions it.

Thus, as early as with the Greeks, *three possible regimes for the link between poetry and philosophy* have been found and named.

1. The first, which I will call Parmenidean, organizes the *fusion* between the poem's subjective authority and the validity of those statements held to be philosophical. Even when certain 'mathematical' interruptions figure under the heading of this fusion, they are ultimately subordinated to the sacred aura of proffered speech, to its 'profound' value and its enunciating legitimacy. Imagery, language's equivocity, and metaphor all escort and authorize the speaking of truth. Authenticity resides in the flesh of language.

2. The second, which I will call Platonic, organizes the *distance* between the poem and philosophy. The former is held in the gap that separates a dissolving fascination, a diagonal seduction, from truth; and the latter must exclude the possibility that whatever it treats could be treated by the poem *in its stead*. The effort to extricate oneself from the prestige of poetic metaphor is such that it demands that one find support in that which, in language, stands as its opposite – that is, the literal univocity of mathematics. Philosophy cannot establish itself except in the contrast between poem and matheme, which are its primordial conditions (the poem, of which it must interrupt the authority, and the matheme, of which it

must promote the dignity). We might also say that the Platonic relation to the poem is a (negative) relation of *condition*, which implies that there are other conditions (the matheme, politics, love).

3. The third, which we will call Aristotelian, organizes the *inclusion* of the knowledge of the poem into philosophy, itself represented as the Knowledge of knowledges. The poem is no longer thought according to the drama of its distance or its intimate proximity, it is caught *in the category of the object*, in what, having been defined and reflected as such, delimits within philosophy a regional discipline. This regionality of the poem founds what will become aesthetics.

We might also say: the three possible relations of philosophy (as thought) to the poem are the *identifying rivalry*, the *argumentative distance* and the *aesthetic regionality*. In the first case, philosophy envies the poem; in the second it excludes it; and in the third it classifies it.

With regard to this triple disposition, what is the essence of the procedure of Heidegger's thinking? I will schematize it according to three component parts:

1. Heidegger has very legitimately re-established the autonomous function of the thought of the poem. Or, to be more precise, he has sought to determine the place – a place itself withdrawn or concealed – from where to perceive the common destiny of the conceptions of the thinker and the utterances of the poet. We can say that this tracing of a community of destiny is opposed most of all to the third type of relationship – the one subsumed under an aesthetics of inclusion. Heidegger has subtracted the poem from philosophical *knowledge*, in order to render it onto *truth*. In doing so, he has founded a radical critique of all aesthetics, of all regional philosophical determination of the poem. This foundation is acquired as a pertinent feature of modernity (its non-Aristotelian character).

2. Heidegger has shown the limits of a relation of condition, which would shed light only on the separation
between the poem and the philosophical argument. In
fine particular analyses, he has established that during
a long period, starting with Hölderlin, the poem serves
as the relay of philosophy on a number of essential
themes, principally because philosophy during this
whole period is the captive either of science (positivism) or of politics (Marxism). It is its captive just as
we said that for Parmenides it was still a captive of the
poem: with regard to these particular conditions of its
existence, philosophy does not create enough room
to establish its own law. I have proposed to call this
period the 'age of the poets'. Let us say that, by invest-
ing this age with unprecedented philosophical means,
Heidegger has shown that it was not always possible
or just to establish a distance from the poem by way
of the Platonic procedure of the ban. Philosophy is
sometimes bound to expose itself to the poem in far
more perilous ways: it must think for itself the *operations* by which the poem takes note of a truth of its
time (for the period in question, the principal truth
that has been poetically taken charge of is the destitu-
tion of the category of objectivity as the obligatory
form of ontological presentation). Whence the poetically crucial theme of presence, albeit for instance
in Mallarmé, in its inverted form, the isolation or
subtraction.

3. Unfortunately, in this historical set-up, and more
particularly in its evaluation of the Greek origin of
philosophy, Heidegger has only been able to *revert* to
the judgment of interruption, and to restore, under
subtle and varied philosophical names, the sacral
authority of poetic proffering – and the idea that the
authentic lies in the flesh of words. There is a profound unity between, on one hand, the recourse to
Parmenides and Heraclitus considered as the delimitation of a site of the presencing of being prior to its

oblivion; and, on the other hand, the heavy-handed and fallacious recourse to the sacred in the most questionable of the poetic analyses, especially those of Trakl. The Heideggerian miscomprehension of the true nature of the Platonic gesture, with at its heart the miscomprehension of the mathematical sense of the Idea (which is precisely that which, by denaturalizing it, exposes thought to the retreat of being), entails that in the place of the invention of a *fourth relation* between philosophy and poetry, which would be neither fusional nor distanced nor aesthetic, Heidegger prophesies in the void a reactivation of the sacred within the undecipherable coupling of the saying of the poets and the thinking of the thinkers.

From Heidegger we will retain the devaluation of all philosophical aesthetics and the critical limitations of the effects of the Platonic procedure of exclusion. By contrast, we will contest whether, in the conditions that would be those of the end of philosophy, it is once again necessary to suture this end to the poem's authority-without-arguments. Philosophy continues – insofar as the positivisms have been exhausted and the Marxisms are worn out, but also insofar as poetry itself, in its contemporary force, enjoins us to relieve it of any identifying rivalry with philosophy – to undo the false coupling of the poem's speech and the philosopher's thought. For this pair of speech and thought, oblivious to the ontological subtraction inaugurated by the inscription of the matheme, is in fact formed by the preaching of the end of philosophy and the romantic myth of authenticity.

The fact that philosophy continues liberates the poem – the poem as singular operation of truth. What will the poem be after Heidegger – the poem after the age of the poets, the post-romantic poem? As I said before, this is something the poets will tell us, for unsuturing philosophy and poetry, taking leave of Heidegger without reverting to aesthetics, also means thinking otherwise the provenance of the poem, thinking it in its *operative distance*, and not in its myth.

Just two indications:

1. When Mallarmé writes: 'The moment of the Notion of an object is thus the moment of the reflection of its pure present in itself or its present purity',[1] what programme is he tracing for the poem, if the latter is attached to the *production* of the Notion? It would be a matter of determining by which operations internal to language one can make a 'present purity' *rise up* – that is, the separation, the isolation, the coldness, of that which is present only insofar as it no longer disposes of any link with reality to ensure its self-presence. We could hold that poetry is the thought of the presence of the present, and that it is precisely for this reason that it is in no way a rival for philosophy, for which the stakes are the compossibility of its time, and not pure presence. Only the poem would accumulate the means to think out-of-place, or beyond every place, 'on some vacant and higher surface', that part of the present that cannot be reduced to its reality but summons the eternity of its presence: 'A constellation, cold with neglect and disuse.'[2] A presence which, far from contradicting the matheme, also implies 'the one and only Number that cannot be any other'.[3]

2. When Celan tells us:

    > Wurfscheibe, mit
    > Vorgesichten besternt,
    > Wirf dich
    > Aus dir hinaus,[4]

---

1   *Translator's note*: See Stéphane Mallarmé, 'Notes de 1869', *Œuvres complètes* (Paris: Gallimard, 1945), p. 853.

2   *Translator's note*: See Mallarmé, 'A Dice Throw', in *Collected Poems*, p. 181.

3   *Translator's note*: See ibid, pp. 166–7.

4   *Translator's note*: See Paul Celan, *Lichtzwang* (Frankfurt am Main: Suhrkamp, 1970), p. 49.

which we could translate as follows:

> Discus, with
> Foreseeings starred,
> Throw yourself
> Out of yourself[5]

– what is the heart of this intimation? We can understand it as follows: when the situation is saturated by its own norm, when the calculation of itself is inscribed in it without respite, when there is no more void between knowing and foreseeing, then one must *poetically* be ready to be outside of oneself. For the naming of an event, in the sense in which I talk about it – namely, the undecidable supplementation that must be named in order to occur to a faithful being, thus to a truth – this nomination is *always* poetic: to name a supplement, a chance, an incalculable event, we must delve into the void of sense, into the lack of established significations, at the risk of language. We thus must poeticize, and the poetic name of the event is that which launches us outside of ourselves, through the burning hoop of foreseeings.

The poem liberated from philosophical poeticizing, no doubt, will always have been both of these thoughts, or both of these gifts: the presence of the present in the traversing of realities, and the name of the event in the leap outside of calculable interests.

---

5 *Translator's note*: Badiou uses the French translation of his brother and famous Celan scholar Bertrand Badiou and Jean-Claude Rambach. For the English version, see Reginald Gibbons, 'Poetry and Self-Making', in *Poets Teaching Poets: Self and the World*, ed. Gregory Orr and Ellen Bryant Voigt (Ann Arbor: University of Michigan Press, 1996), pp. 190–1.

4

PHILOSOPHY AND POETRY FROM THE VANTAGE POINT OF THE UNNAMEABLE

Let us pose the question that the very place in which I write this – the journal *Po&sie* – compares to an assault: does the radical critique of poetry, in Book X of the *Republic*, manifest the singular limits of the Platonist philosophy of the Idea? Or is it, on the contrary, a constitutive gesture of philosophy itself, philosophy 'as such', which would thus manifest the latter's incompatibility with the poem?

In order not to turn this into a tasteless discussion – in order not in turn to violate the violent assault – we must come to grasp that the Platonic gesture with regard to the poem is not, in the eyes of Plato, secondary or polemical. It is really crucial. Plato does not hesitate to declare: 'The city whose principle we have organized is the best one, and especially, I think, because of the measures taken in the matter of poetry.'[1]

We absolutely must keep intact the trenchant nature of this extraordinary statement, which tells us without any prevarication that what measures the principle of politics is properly speaking the exclusion of the poem – or

---

1 *Translator's note*: See Plato, *The Republic*, trans. Paul Shorey (Cambridge: Harvard University Press, 1969), 595a (translation modified).

at least the exclusion of what Plato names the 'imitative dimension' of the poetic. The destiny of true politics stands or falls with the firmness of one's attitude with regard to the poem.

Now, what is true politics, the well-founded *politeia*? It is philosophy itself, insofar as it assures thought's grasp on collective existence, on the gathered multiplicity of human beings. Let us say that the *politeia* is the collective arrived at its immanent truth; or again, the collective that is commensurable with thought.

If we follow Plato, we thus must posit the following: the city-state, which is the name of humanity in its gathering, is *thinkable* only insofar as its concept is sheltered from the poem. It is necessary to shelter the collective subjectivity from the powerful charm of the poem in order for the city-state to expose itself to thought. Or again: as long as it is 'poeticized', the collective subjectivity is also subtracted from thought and remains heterogeneous to it.

The usual interpretation – largely authorized by Plato's own text – holds that the poem, situated as it is at a double distance from the Idea (secondary imitation of that first imitation that is the sensible), prohibits all access to the supreme principle, the one on which it depends that the truth of the collective arrives at its own transparency. The protocol for banning the poets would depend on the imitative nature of poetry. It would be one and the same thing to prohibit poetry and to criticize mimesis.

Now, I do not think that this interpretation captures the *violence* of Plato's text – a violence that Plato admits is also directed against himself, against the uncontrollable power that the poem has over his own soul. The reasonable critique of imitation does not entirely legitimize why it would be necessary to *wrest* the effects of such a power from oneself.

Let us propose that mimesis is not the real problem. If the poetic utterance must be interrupted in order to render the city-state thinkable, this requires, as if prior to the problem of mimesis, a more fundamental misunderstanding. It seems as though, between thought as thought in philosophy and in the poem, there were a much more radical and ancient quarrel than the one that concerns images and imitation.

It is to this ancient and profound quarrel that Plato alludes, I believe, when he writes: *palaia tis diaphora philosophia te kai poiètikè*: 'There is from old a quarrel between philosophy and poetry.'[2]

The antiquity of this quarrel obviously concerns thinking, the identification of thought. What is it, in thinking, that poetry is opposed to? It is not directly opposed to the intellect, to the *nous*, or to the intuition of Ideas. It is not opposed to the dialectic, as supreme form of the intelligible. Plato is crystal clear on this point: what poetry prohibits is discursive thinking, *dianoia*. About the poem, Plato says that 'he who lends an ear to it must be on guard fearing for the polity of his soul.'[3] *Dianoia* is the thinking that traverses, the thinking that binds and seduces. The poem, for its part, is affirmation and delectation; it does not traverse anything, it holds still on the threshold. The poem is not a rule-bound trespassing but an offering, a proposition without a law.

For this reason Plato will say that the true recourse against the poem is 'measuring, numbering and weighing'.[4] And that the antipoetic part of the soul is 'the work that reasons and calculates', *tou logistikou ergon*.[5] He will also say that, in the theatrical poem, what triumphs is the principle of pleasure and pain, against law and reason, or *logos*.

Dianoia, the thought that binds and traverses, the thought that is a *logos* subject to a law, possesses a paradigm, which is that of mathematics. We can thus claim that what the poem is opposed to, in the realm of thought, is properly speaking the jurisdiction of the mathematical break, or of the power of intelligibility of the matheme, over thought itself.

---

2   Plato, *Republic*, 607b.
3   Ibid., 608b.
4   Ibid., 602d.
5   Ibid., 602e (translation modified).

The founding opposition is ultimately as follows: philosophy cannot begin, philosophy cannot take hold of the real of politics, except if it substitutes the authority of the matheme for that of the poem.

The profound motif of this opposition between matheme and poem is twofold. On the one hand, which is the clearest, the poem remains subservient to the image, to the immediate singularity of experience; whereas the matheme takes as its point of departure the pure Idea, and subsequently has confidence only in the power of deduction. In this way the poem maintains with sensible experience an impure link, which exposes language to the limits of sensation. From this point of view, it is always doubtful whether there really is such a thing as a thought of the poem, or whether the poem thinks.

But what is a doubtful thinking for Plato, a thinking that is indiscernible from non-thought? It is a sophistics. It could well be that the poem is in reality the capital accomplice of sophistics.

This is certainly what is suggested in the dialogue *Protagoras*. For Protagoras finds shelter behind the authority of the poet Simonides, and it is he who declares that 'the greatest part of a man's education is to be skilled in the matter of verses.'[6]

We could thus posit that what poetry is to the sophist, mathematics is to the philosopher. The opposition between matheme and poem would support, within the disciplines that condition philosophy, the incessant labour of philosophy to disjoin itself from its discursive double, from that which resembles it and, due to this resemblance, corrupts its act of thinking: sophistics. The poem, like the sophist, would be a non-thought that presents itself in the linguistic power of a possible thought. Interrupting this power would be the function of the matheme.

But, on the other hand, and more profoundly, even if we were to suppose that there is a thinking of the poem, or

---

6 *Translator's note*: See Plato, *Protagoras*, trans. W. R. M. Lamb (Cambridge, MA: Harvard University Press, 1967), 338e–339a.

that the poem is a form of thought, this thinking is inseparable from the sensible – it is a form of thought that *we
cannot discern or separate as thought*. Let us say that the
poem is an unthinkable thought, whereas mathematics is
a thought that immediately inscribes itself as thought, a
thinking that precisely exists only insofar as it is thinkable.

We could thus also posit that, for philosophy, poetry is
a thinking that is neither thinking nor even thinkable. But
it is precisely philosophy that has no other stakes but to
think thinking, to identify thought as the thinking of thinking. And thus it must exclude from its field any immediate
thinking, and do so by finding support in the discursive
mediations of the matheme.

'Let no one ignorant of geometry enter here': Plato
introduces mathematics through the grand entrance as
an *explicit* procedure of thought, or a form of thinking
that can expose itself only as thinking. As a consequence,
poetry must be escorted out via the back stairs. This poetry,
still omnipresent in Parmenides' declaration as much as
in Heraclitus's pronunciations, obliterates the philosophical function because in it thought allows itself the right of
what is inexplicit, which takes on power in language from
another source than the self-exposure of thinking as such.

But this opposition in language between the transparency of the matheme and the metaphorical obscurity of the
poem poses major problems for us moderns.

Plato himself is already unable to hold on until the end
to this maxim, which promotes the matheme and banishes
the poem. He cannot, because he himself explores the limits
of *dianoia*, or of discursive thought. When it is a matter of
the supreme principle, the One or the Good, Plato must
admit that here we are *epekeine tes ousias*, 'beyond substance', and consequently outside everything that lets itself
be exposed in the delimitation of the Idea. He must confess
that the donation in thought of this supreme principle,
which is the donation in thinking of being beyond beings,
cannot be traversed by any *dianoia*. He himself must have
recourse to images, such as that of the sun, to metaphors,

such as those of 'prestige' and 'power', and to myth, such as the myth of Er the Pamphylian, who returns from the kingdom of the dead. In short: where what is at play is the opening of thought to the principle of the thinkable, when thinking must absorb itself into the seizing of that which institutes it as thinking, that is where Plato himself must submit language to the power of poetic speech.

But we moderns endure the linguistic interval between the poem and the matheme in an entirely different manner. First of all because we have taken the full measure not only of everything the poem owes to number, but also of its properly intelligible vocation.

Here Mallarmé is exemplary: the stake of a poetic dice throw in effect is to give rise, 'product of the stars', to what he calls 'the one and only Number that cannot be any other'.[7] The poem belongs to the ideal regime of necessity; it articulates sensible desire onto the aleatory advent of the Idea. The poem is a *duty* of thought:

> Ideas, glory of long desire,
> All within me rejoiced to see
> The irid family aspire
> To this new responsibility.[8]

But, furthermore, the modern poem identifies itself as thought. It is not only the effectiveness of a form of thinking proffered in the flesh of words; it is also the set of operations by which this thinking thinks itself. The great poetic *figures*, whether the Constellation, the Tomb or the Swan for Mallarmé, and the Christ, the Worker or the infernal Husband for Rimbaud, are not blind metaphors. They organize a consistent machine in which the poem assembles the sensible presentation of a regime of thought: subtraction and isolation for Mallarmé; presence and interruption for Rimbaud.

---

7 *Translator's note*: See Mallarmé, 'A Dice Throw', in *Collected Poems*, pp. 176 and 166–7.

8 *Translator's note*: See Mallarmé, 'Prose (for des Esseintes)', in *Collected Poems*, p. 55.

Symmetrically, we moderns know that mathematics, which directly thinks the configurations of being as multiplicity, is traversed by a principle of errancy and excess on which it cannot put a measure all by itself. The great theorems of Cantor, Gödel and Cohen mark the aporias of the matheme in the twentieth century. The discord between set-theoretical axiomatics and categorial description places mathematical ontology under the constraint of several options of thought between which no purely mathematical prescription can assign the norm of a choice.

At the same time that the poem arrives at the poetic thought of the thinking that it is, the matheme organizes itself around a point of flight in which the real appears in the impasse of all formalization.

Let us say that, apparently, modernity idealizes the poem and sophisticates the matheme. In doing so, it inverts the Platonic judgment more assuredly than Nietzsche wished to do from the point of the 'transvaluation of all values'.

The result is a crucial displacement of the relation of philosophy to the poem. Because it is not the opposition between the sensible and the intelligible, or between the Beautiful and the Good, or between the image and the Idea, that henceforth may support this relation. The modern poem is so much not the sensible form of the Idea that it is rather the sensible that presents itself as the persistent, and impotent, nostalgia for the poetic Idea.

In Mallarmé's 'A Faun in the Afternoon', the 'character' who offers a monologue asks himself if there exists in nature, in the sensible landscape, a possible trace of his sensuous dream. Does water not bear witness to the coldness of one of his desired women? Does the wind not remind him of the voluptuous whispers of the other? If this hypothesis must be discarded, it is because water and wind are nothing; they inexist with regard to the power to give rise through art to the Idea of water or the Idea of the wind:

the cool dawn's struggles, not a sound
of water but my flute's outpourings murmurs round
the thicket steeped in music; and the one stir of air
my dual pipes are swiftly shedding everywhere
and then dispersing in a sonorous arid sleet,
is, over the horizon that no ripples pleat,
the visible, serene and artificial sigh
of inspiration reascending to the sky.[9]

Through the visibility of artifice, which is also the thought of poetic thought, the poem surpasses in power whatever the sensible is capable of. The modern poem is the opposite of a mimesis. By its operation it exhibits an Idea, of which the object and objectivity are but pale copies.

Philosophy thus cannot grasp the pair of the poem and the matheme within the simple opposition between the delightful image and the pure Idea. Where then does it situate the disjunction in language between these two regimes of thinking? I would say that it is at the point where one or the other of these forms of thought find their unnameable.

In a diagonal opposition to the Platonic banishment of the poets, let us pose the following equivalence: poem and matheme, examined from the vantage point of philosophy, are both inscribed in the general form of a procedure of truth.

Mathematics establishes the truth of pure multiplicity as primordial inconsistency of being qua being.

Poetry establishes the truth of the multiple as presence arrived at the limits of language – that is, the song of language as the capacity to make present the pure notion of 'there is', in the very effacement of its empirical objectivity.

When Rimbaud enounces poetically that eternity is 'the sea gone off / with the sun';[10] or when Mallarmé sums up the entire dialectical transposition of the sensible into the Idea in the triad of 'night and despair and precious

---

9　Mallarmé, 'A Faun in the Afternoon', in *Collected Poems*, p. 41.
10　Rimbaud, 'Eternity', in *Complete Works*, p. 187.

stone',[11] or 'solititude, star, or rocky coast',[12] they fuse into the crucible of nomination the referent that sticks to the words, in order to give atemporal existence to the temporal disappearance of the sensible.

In this regard, it is always true that a poem is an 'alchemy of the word'.[13] But this alchemy, as opposed to the other one, is a form of thought, the thinking of what there is, a 'there' henceforth suspended from the powers of evacuation and evocation that belong to language.

Of the unpresented and insensible multiple, which mathematics makes into its truth, the emblem is the void, the empty set.

Of the multiple given or disclosed, retained at the outer limits of its disappearance, which the poem makes into its truth, the emblem is the Earth, this affirmative and universal Earth about which Mallarmé declares:

> Yes, Earth has cast into this night afar
> the startling mystery of sheer dazzlingness.[14]

Now any truth, whether it is linked to the mathematical account or extracted from the song of natural language, is first and foremost a *power*. It has power over its own infinite becoming, from which it can fragmentarily anticipate the unachievable universe. It can *force* the supposition of what the universe would be, if the complete effects of a truth in process were to unfold themselves without limit.

It is thus that, from a new and powerful theorem, one posits the consequences which reorient thought and subordinate it to entirely new exercises.

But it is also thus that, from a foundational poetics, new methods of poetic thinking can be drawn – a new prospectus of the resources of language, and not only the dazzling delight of a radiant presence.

---

11   Mallarmé, 'For the sole task of travelling', in *Collected Poems*, p. 213.

12   Mallarmé, 'Toast', in *Collected Poems*, p. 3.

13   Rimbaud, *A Season in Hell*, in *Complete Works*, p. 285.

14   Mallarmé, 'A Few Sonnets', in *Collected Poems*, p. 67.

It is not for nothing that Rimbaud exclaims: 'We assert you, method!' or or that he declares himself 'impatient to find the place and the formula';[15] or that Mallarmé proposes that he install the poem as a science:

> for by my science I instill
> the hymn of spiritual hearts
> in the work of my patient will
> atlases, herbals, sacred arts.[16]

Just as the poem, as thought of presence against the backdrop of disappearance, is an immediate action, it is also at the same time, like any local figure of a truth, a programme of thought, a powerful anticipation, a forcing of language by the advent of an 'other' language that is both immanent and created.

But, at the same time as it is a power, all truth is a powerlessness. For that over which it has jurisdiction can never be a totality.

That truth and totality are incompatible is no doubt the decisive – or post-Hegelian – lesson of modernity.

Jacques Lacan expresses this with a famous aphorism: truth cannot 'all' be said, it can only be half-said. But already Mallarmé criticized the Parnassians because, he said, they 'take the thing in its entirety and show it'. In this, he added, 'they lack the mystery'.[17]

Of whatever a truth is the truth, one should not pretend that it can invest it 'entirely', or be its integral monstration. The poem's power of revelation encircles an enigma, so that the *pinpointing* of this enigma makes up the real powerlessness of the power of truth. In this sense, the 'mystery in letters' is a veritable imperative. When Mallarmé claims that 'there must always be some enigma in poetry',[18] he

---

15 Rimbaud, 'Morning of Drunkenness', in *Complete Works*, p. 323; and 'Vagabonds', in *Complete Works*, p. 331.

16 Mallarmé, 'Prose (for des Esseintes)', in *Collected Poems*, p. 53.

17 *Translator's note*: See Mallarmé, 'Sur l'évolution littéraire (enquête de Jules Huret)', in *Œuvres complètes*, p. 869.

18 Ibid. See also Mallarmé, 'The Mystery in Letters', in *Divagations*.

founds an ethics of mystery that is the respect, through the power of a truth, for its point of powerlessness.

The mystery is, properly speaking, that any poetic truth leaves at its centre something that it has no power to bring to presence.

More generally, a truth always encounters, at some point in that which it investigates, the limit that proves that it is *this* singular truth, and not the self-consciousness of the Whole.

That any truth, even though it proceeds to infinity, is also always a singular procedure is attested in the real by at least one point of powerlessness, or, as Mallarmé says, 'a false mansion suddenly dispelled in mists which laid a limit on the infinite'.[19]

Any truth stumbles upon the rock of its own singularity, and only there can it be announced, as powerlessness, that *there is* a truth.

Let us call this stumbling block the *unnameable*. The unnameable is that over which a truth cannot force the nomination. It is that of which it cannot anticipate the *putting into truth*.

Any truth regime is founded in the real on the unnameable that is its own.

If we now return to the Platonic opposition between poem and matheme, let us ask ourselves: what differentiates 'in the real', and thus in terms of the unnameable that is proper to them, mathematical truths from poetic truths?

What characterizes mathematical language is deductive fidelity. By this let us understand the capacity to link statements into a chain so that this chain is subject to *constraint*, and the set of statements that is thus obtained successfully withstands the test of *consistency*. The effect of constraint stems from the logical codification that underlies mathematical ontology. The effect of consistency is central. In effect, what is a consistent theory? It is a theory which is such that there exist statements that are impossible within

---

19   Mallarmé, 'A Dice Throw', in *Collected Poems*, p. 175.

it. A theory is consistent if there exists at least one 'correct' statement according to the language of this theory that cannot be inscribed in the theory, or that the theory does not admit as being veridical.

From this point of view, consistency attests to a theory as being a *singular thought*. Because if any statement whatsoever were to be acceptable in the theory in question, this would mean that there was no difference between a 'grammatically correct statement' and a 'theoretically veridical statement'. The theory in question, then, would be merely a grammar, and it would think nothing.

The principle of consistency is what assigns mathematics to a situation of being for thought, so that it is not a simple set of rules.

But we have known since Gödel that consistency *is precisely the point of the unnameable of mathematics*. It is not possible for a mathematical theory to establish as veridical the statement of its own consistency.

If we now turn towards poetry, we see that what characterizes its effect is the monstration of the powers of language itself. Any poem brings into language a power – the power to fix for eternity the disappearance of that which presents itself, or the power to produce presence itself as Idea by the poetic restraint of its disappearance.

But this power of language is precisely that which the poem cannot name. It effectuates this power by delving into the latent song of language, in the infinity of its resources, in the novelty of its assemblage. And precisely because the poem addresses itself to the infinity of language in order to orient its power towards the restraint of a disappearance, it cannot fixate this infinity itself.

Let us say that language as infinite power articulated onto presence is precisely the unnameable of poetry. The linguistic infinity is the powerlessness immanent to the power effect of the poem.

This point of powerlessness, or of the unnameable, is represented by Mallarmé in at least two ways. First, by the fact that the poem's effect supposes a guarantee that it cannot constitute, or validate, poetically. This guarantee is language itself grasped *as order*, or syntax: 'What pivot, in these contrasts, am I assuming for intelligibility? We need a guarantee. – Syntax.'[20] Syntax, in the poem, is the latent power wherein the contrast between presence and disappearance (being as nothingness) can present itself to the intelligible. But syntax cannot be poeticized, no matter how far I push its distortion. It operates without ever presenting itself.

Furthermore, Mallarmé clearly indicates that there cannot be a poem of the poem, or metapoem. This is the meaning of the famous 'ptyx' – that name which nominates nothing, which is 'abolished bauble, sonorous inanity'.[21]. No doubt, the ptyx would be the name of that which the poem is capable of: to give rise in language to a coming into presence that was previously impossible. Except that, precisely, this name is not a name – this name does not name anything. As a result, the poet (the Master of language) carries this false name with him until death:

Master has gone to draw tears from the Styx
with that one thing, the Void's sole source of vanity.[22]

The poem itself, insofar as it locally verifies the infinity of language, remains, for the poem, unnameable. The power of language is all that the poem has the task of manifesting, but it is powerless to name this power veridically.

This is also what Rimbaud wants to say when he labels his poetic project a form of 'madness'. Certainly, the poem 'annotates the inexpressible' or 'fixates the vertiginous frenzies'.[23] But it is madness to believe that it can also recapture and name the profound and general resource of these annotations, or of these fixations. As an active thinking

---

20   Mallarmé, 'The Mystery in Letters', in *Divagations*, pp. 234–5.

21   Mallarmé, 'With her pure nails offering their onyx high', in *Collected Poems*, p. 69.

22   Ibid.

23   Rimbaud, 'Alchemy of the Word', in *Complete Works*, p. 286 (translation modified).

which cannot name its own power, the poem remains forever unfounded. This is what, in the eyes of Mallarmé, makes it similar to a sophism: 'I explained my magic sophisms with the hallucination of words!'[24]

Besides, from the early beginnings of his work, Rimbaud observed that in the poem, conceived subjectively, there lies an irresponsibility. The poem is like a power that involuntarily traverses language: 'It is too bad for the wood which finds itself a violin', or 'if brass wakes up a trumpet, it is not its fault.'[25]

At bottom, for Rimbaud, the unnameable of poetic thought is this thought itself *in its advent*, or its coming into being. This is also the coming into being of the infinity of language as song, or symphony, which enchants with presence: 'I am present at this birth of my thought: I watch it and listen to it: I draw a stroke of the bow: the symphony makes it stir in the depths, or comes on to the stage in a leap.'[26]

Let us say that the unnameable proper to the matheme is the consistency of language, whereas the unnameable proper to the poem is its power.

Therefore, philosophy will place itself under the double condition of the poem and the matheme, both from the side of their power of veridiction and from the side of their powerlessness, or their unnameable.

Philosophy is the general theory of being and of the event, insofar as they are tied together by truth. For a truth is the work *upon* the being of a vanished event, of which only the name remains.

Philosophy will recognize that any naming of an event, which summons the restraint of what disappears, any nomination of the presence of an event, is essentially poetic.

It will also recognize that all fidelity to the event, all the work upon being guided by a prescription that nothing can

---

24   Ibid., p. 289.
25   Rimbaud, 'To Georges Izambard', in *Complete Works*, p. 371; and 'To Paul Demeny', in *Complete Works*, p. 375.
26   Rimbaud, 'To Paul Demeny'.

found, must have the rigor of which mathematics is the paradigm, and subject itself to the discipline of a continuous constraint.

Moreover, from the fact that consistency is the unnameable of the matheme, philosophy will retain the impossibility of an integral reflexive foundation; and the fact that every system contains a breaking point, a subtraction from the powers of truth. A point that is properly impossible to force by the power of a truth, whatever this truth may be.

Finally, from the fact that the infinite power of language is the unnameable of the poem, philosophy will retain the notion that no matter how strong an interpretation may be, the meaning that it obtains will never do justice to the capacity for meaning. Or again, that no truth can ever deliver the meaning of meaning, or the sense of sense.

Plato banned the poem because he suspected that poetic thought could not be the thought of thought. We once again welcome the poem in our midst, because it keeps us from supposing that the singularity of a thought can be replaced by the thought of this thought.

Between the consistency of the matheme and the power of the poem, these two unnameables, philosophy gives up on the pretence to establish the names that close off that which subtracts itself. In this sense, after the poem and after the matheme, but under their thinking condition, philosophy is the most lacunary thinking of the multiplicity of thoughts.

5

ONE MUST DESCEND INTO LOVE: ON THE POETRY OF HENRY BAUCHAU

The poetry of Henry Bauchau is above all loyal. He has often explained how he came into the grip of the poem, subjected to its imperative, and how it was a matter of obeying without ever being able to calculate the result. This is not because he adopts the pose of the inspired. On the contrary, it is because the poetic exercise gives access to a truth dispensed by the course of history, or even the course of prose. Because 'Pilate by washing his hands says that the truth is sad'.[1] The poem both transmits and contests the likelihood of this sadness. Hence the aspect of tenacity, and even of laboriousness, of Bauchau's long poems: in them one returns without joy to the youthful truth, and one accepts the face-to-face confrontation with what is involuntarily delivered to us. For 'at nineteen years, your body is sad and grey and the women are deaf'.[2]

---

1 *Translator's note*: See Henry Bauchau, 'Selon Pilate', in *Heureux les déliants: Poèmes 1950–1995*, preface Alain Badiou (Brussels: Labor, 1995), p. 314. The title of Badiou's text, 'One Must Descend into Love', is borrowed from 'Paroles du corps endormi', a poem from 1995 that Bauchau in turned dedicates 'To Alain Badiou', in *Heureux les déliants*, p. 35.

2 Ibid., 'La sourde oreille ou le rêve de Freud', p. 87.

This somewhat elementary sentence – with Bauchau
we can talk about the elements of the subject in the same
way that the Greeks spoke about air and water and fire
(and is it not a matter of answering, like the Ancients
did regarding the cosmos, the question, 'Who are you
and who are you not, what is this point that you have
not traced, in the chaos before the intensity of the great
open sea?') – contains two major resources of Bauchau's
poetry.

First of all, the word 'deaf' defines the site of the
poem. The language that his poetry delivers demands
that ordinary noise fall silent. As early as 1955, when
he identifies himself with Heraclitus as he dreams of
him (how he has dreamed of all of them, the Greeks:
Oedipus, Diotima, Antigone ...), Bauchau writes: 'And I
depart, street singer, carrying the infant sun in my deaf
man's ear and an armful of stars in my blind beggar's
bowl.'[3]

Twenty years later, the most dense, tight and grandiose
of his poems bears the title 'La sourde oreille' ('The Deaf
Ear'). Without a doubt, this is an allusion to the floating
attention of the psychoanalyst, at the moment when 'the
word has deciphered the frightened bosom', liberating the
poet from an obliterated youth, between the mother who
'did not understand' and the father who 'does not know
love, its tremors, its celestial and harrowing march'.[4] But
it is above all a question of the capacity for hearing that
the poem itself produces and that previously did not exist.
Whether it is about the Gare de Lyon ('the locomotives of
sleep rust without deciphering you') or the moon (when
it 'advances with measured steps on the alexandrines of
the sky'), or the watercress bed ('its collar of herbs and
reeds'), the point is always to hold that 'the poem only
talks in order to listen'[5] – and therein lies the revealing
deafness with which we may receive it.

---

3   Ibid., 'Chemin d'Héraclite', p. 305.
4   Ibid., 'La sourde oreille ou le rêve de Freud', pp. 86–7 and 100.
5   Ibid., 'La sourde oreille', p. 88; and 'La cressonnière', p. 68.

And then there is this singular 'you', which Paul Celan introduces into poetry and Michel Butor unfolds into prose, but which Bauchau uses in an entirely different way. Because it is he himself whom he pins down into the stanzas with this second person, thus indicating that he expects poetry to produce sufficient distance to let the 'I', overburdened with intimate prose, be succeeded by the almost objective serenity of this entity addressed with the familiar 'you' or *tu* in French.

This is because 'you needed many years for the deconstruction of the erroneous edifice of me'.[6]

Let us understand that the possibility of this 'you', against the edifice of me, is already a joint victory of psychoanalysis and poetry – a result of the 1960s in which 'the frightened bosom' of infancy was finally able to find 'its place on the wall without grief of the poem'.[7] Before that, Bauchau could still wonder 'whether I believe in God, I do not know / I no longer know, I must forget.'[8] He can trace the paths of his effort in the footsteps of Saint Paul: 'Neither hope, nor wilfulness, I try hard. / I try hard without trying, to be in the world / without being there.'[9] Under the banner of Genghis Khan, he does not forgo the great subjective impulse of the powerful dreamer, whom one would almost associate with Victor Hugo: 'I float and I contemplate / The river bed of ebbing waters, the great grey mules in the irresistible valleys.'[10]

Let us compare these great impulses, sometimes painful and at other times heroic, but in which the lyric 'I' remains essential, to the strange and captivating fraternity with the self that Bauchau encounters in the familiar second-person address of the most limited movements:

---

6 Ibid., 'La sourde oreille', p. 115.
7 Ibid., p. 100.
8 Ibid., 'La Dogana', p. 196.
9 Ibid., 'Géologie', p. 277.
10 Ibid., 'L'arbre de Gengis Khan', p. 299.

'You take a cheque to the bank and you are afraid of the future.'[11]
'You are going to Vincennes this morning.'[12]
'You were daydreaming at the new doctor's.'[13]

And it is not that these almost imperceptible gestures introduce a kind of prosodic limitation into the poem. On the contrary, they give the poem a close support, an intimate and pressing force, which in a series of steps that are both measured and tenacious, sweet and unpredictable, lead the poem to an agreement with the world, after its inhabitant – the Bauchau addressed in the poem by the familiar second person – has gone to great lengths to describe its difficulty, only to emerge from the effort purified and victorious.

Thus, the poem that begins with the cheque at the bank ('La Sibylle') transforms an opaque meditation, in the cold, on old age and fear into a salvific rage in which 'the body is seized with hope'.[14] The poem which takes us to the university of Vincennes talks of the dialectic, of the fecundity of disorder ('To prefer order to disorder is the negation of the spirit'), and balances the image of Mao, who 'has confidence in the trees, because in the making of the world / China is perhaps the vegetal hope', with that of life's dissemination ('The tiredness of living while waiting for death looks at his dispersed organs and body'[15]). And the great fourth part of 'The Deaf Ear', which begins with the dream of the doctor, goes through a condensed and subjectivized recollection of the war of 1914–18 ('When the peasants and the workers killed one another, bogged down in the mud, when they dug their trenches which continued all the way into you'), only to return with energy to the lovelessness of childhood and the observation, both bitter

---

11 Ibid., 'La Sibylle', p. 177.
12 Ibid., 'La pensée végétale', p. 180.
13 Ibid., 'La sourde oreille', p. 89.
14 Ibid., 'La Sibylle', p. 177.
15 Ibid., 'La pensée végétale', pp. 180–1.

and pacified, of 'the refusal by those who are solid / of the one who has no armour.'[16]

In this way, Bauchau's poetic 'you' anchors the meditation in the modest exactitude of a distance from the self that takes the measure of the fact that the poem, according to one of its oldest intuitions, has no other necessity 'except to be there, at each instant, more and more'.[17]

I admire how this 'being-there' knows to keep the balance between the poem's natural resource and its historic resource.

Certainly, Bauchau does not fail to illuminate the slow path – or the sudden eruption – of an excess of truth with an image trapped in perception. And like all genuine poets, he knows how to do this on the scale of a general or elementary vision ('And I mean to compose in myself according to the rule of the larch / a slow corporeal poem on the matter of snow'),[18] as well as with the precision of a place from memory that drags with it the sensible destiny of subjective truths: 'In the woods, between the hedges, in the citadel of trees, it is a scene from the silent theatre, for the monumental and circumstantial stay of the sun'[19] – or, finally, with the humility of that which conceals its splendour: 'Wild strawberry under the leaf / will be better praise of redness / One cannot stay a snowflake / One must descend into the snow.'[20]

But in these poems we can also hear, with an insistence that is as discreet as it is original, the rumour of History and Bauchau's concern for its twists and turns, its injustice, or its promises. In 1956, after the crushing of the revolt in Hungary by the Soviets, he writes superbly: 'The war chariots of November roll in vain over the knowledge of suffering.'[21] I have already mentioned what he thought of

---

16 Ibid., 'La sourde oreille', pp. 90 and 92.
17 Ibid., 'Géologie', p. 277.
18 Ibid., 'Les mélèzes', p. 189.
19 Ibid., 'La sourde oreille', p. 119.
20 Ibid., 'Regards sur Antigone', p. 29.
21 Ibid., 'Les chars de Budapest', p. 309.

the war of 1914–18, or of his hopes tied to China, to this
Mao – a poet, also – to whom he devoted the most beautiful and subtle study available. But consider also this poetic
capture of the sinister time of the 1930s:

> It was a time of involuntary poverty, the time of closed
> workshops and unemployment.
> In Germany, you saw thousands of unemployed march in
> the streets to the slogan: *Arbeit und Brot*.
> Hitler too called for work and bread, promising – how?
> how? – justice and peace.
> In the nocturnal flights of discourse, in the husky celebra-
> tions of war,
> One could hear his voice, his dark and twisted cross, raise
> the tumours of the crowd. One could hear the deviated
> sacrament of its apocalyptic mass.[22]

I love how Bauchau does not reserve for the sole epipha-
nies of being what in the poem is both the instruction of a
saying and the foundation of a listening. I love that he says:
'One must lean in, with a deaf ear, to listen to the voice of
revolution.'[23]

And yet, I would not say that what dominates his
thought-poem is the passage from the desolations of the
subject to the reflexive distance of the other, from the 'I'
to the 'you' (Celan). Nor would I say that we just reduce
everything to the 'deaf' dialectic of silence and the letter
(Mallarmé); nor, finally, that song emerges from an excessive tension between the suddenness of 'nature light' and
the slowness of human hopefulness (Rimbaud). All this is
summoned up by Bauchau, but as the available means for
an entirely different ambition: to surmount death with love.

Someone will say that we thus come back to the safest
themes of lyric poetry. Yes, except that Bauchau gives them
a form and a scope without any equivalent today. One will
also say that to tie the poem to a concern for the victory of
love brings Bauchau closer to twentieth-century Christian

---

22 Ibid., 'La sourde oreille', p. 104.
23 Ibid., p. 112.

poetry – first and foremost that of his teacher, Pierre Jean Jouve, who likewise combined this inspiration with the experiments and experiences of psychoanalysis. Yes, except that this 'Christianity' is without God ('Don't consume your life anymore / in works of earth or bricks / for God is dead') and without dogma. In a recent poem, after having mentioned that 'Each morning without Church / on the wild cement ... I kneel down before nothing', Bauchau also says that when he is 'in his rightful place', he 'kneels down before everything'.[24] This poetic equivalence in the gesture of adoration between nothing and everything indicates what the 'Christianity' of the poet might be: reduced to that alone which counts, the disentangling of love and death.

Bauchau starts from two observations, to which the poem gives an unsuspected power: we are mixed up with death, and love is a promise without any guarantee.

First, we are never separated from death; it is not summed up in the solidity of the tombstone, nor in ceremonial glorification. It insinuates itself everywhere, taking advantage of the uncertainty of love:

> We are not separated from death by the construction of a
>   tomb,
> nor by a church's song of stones, nor by way of
>   contemplation ...
> On the side of the road where the shadow is rare and love
>   uncertain
> we are not separated from death in the midst of the
>   bushes and the common things.[25]

Furthermore, love – supposing that it confronts death and descends all the way down to death – risks being misrecognized, for no longer being that living beauty that we must incessantly recommence. Eternity no doubt proves fatal to it:

---

24   Bauchau, 'Exercice du matin', in *Heureux les déliants*, p. 34.
25   Bauchau, 'Nous ne sommes pas séparés', in *Heureux les déliants*, p. 257.

> When love will be under the shroud
> Of the dead, when love spread out
> In the sea will have descended
> With the edifice of sails.
>
> Will it still be the beautiful wind
> The beautiful blood, the numerous wave
> And always the vigorous beauty
> To be broken indefinitely.[26]

Hence the cruel question: 'Must we always decipher and translate / Love in the bitter language?'[27] Because if we are never separated from death and if love cannot overcome this inseparation, there subsists in the human being a torn and unreconciled part, and the poem will fail to accomplish its own dictate of accessible serenity.

To this question, the whole progress of the thought-poem, of which 'The Deaf Ear' retraces the harsh steps, ends up by answering in the negative: no, the 'bitter language' is not the obligatory destination of love and we can separate ourselves from death. We have the right to uphold 'the essential liberty that love can or could institute'.[28] We can affirm the 'amorous dependence of the poem' and conclude explicitly that 'one lives fully only in love'.[29] And as a consequence we are, if not relieved, then at least capable of being relieved of the omnipresence of death. This is the singular hallelujah that closes 'The Deaf Ear':

> Is this the reason of love, is this a mad madness? The poem doesn't say. It advances in the midst of the forgotten mine, it advances in the shadow of the woods and you follow it from afar.
>   Walking in the footsteps of the old man who descends toward his farm and the house of eternity that will be his native home.

---

26 Ibid., 'Quand l'amour sera', p. 255.
27 Ibid., 'La grille', p. 197.
28 Ibid., 'La sourde oreille', p. 105.
29 Ibid., 'Dépendance amoureuse du poème', p. 21.

Poetry tells you not to die and you, in this very instant
in which you lose sight of it, you see – how, how by
following Freud and his poem? –
You see that the interior writing is right.[30]

In the end, the dictatorship of the poem that Bauchau talks
to us about, if he endures it and transmits to us its result in
language, has no other stakes than to persuade us, against
all reason, against the laughter of reason, that if we manage
to entrust ourselves to love, we will be immortal.

And this explains why Bauchau has always written two
kinds of poem. There are the 'short forms' in which the
shock is instantaneous, in which it is a question only of a
flash of confidence, a sudden clearing of love in the ordinary interlacing of things and death. For example:

> In father's garden
> On the shores of the Meuse
> There were
> Days of festivity
> There was
> A cherry tree
> Which was all
> Covered with love.[31]

This is a text that instantaneously declares (and we
must obey this declaration) that it is poetically possible
to associate love with a father about whom other poems
nonetheless tell us that he knew nothing of love. Thus the
poem surpasses ignorance and restores love, against death,
to he who turned his back to it.

And then there are the 'long forms', in which the poem
justifies its powers, retracing their genealogy, and constructs its victory only via the experience of obstacles,
reaching transparency only in an obstinate poeticization
of thick substance. Here, death is described and absorbed,
and love is a result that is simultaneously radiant and

---

30 Ibid., 'La sourde oreille', pp. 122–3.
31 Ibid., 'Le cerisier', p. 76.

difficult. Its comprehension is so mixed up with that of death that the whole poem is needed, as well as its reading by a captivated reader, for it to be effective. As early as 1956, Bauchau notes:

> I enter the current, I submerge myself, I swim. It happens that, no longer understanding, I am understood.[32]

This is also the meaning of the mysterious and magnificent conclusion in 'The Great Troménie':

> You will be, awakened to your own light, the last to
> appear among those who set sail
> and who returned from the great metaphors
> to enter, without plan, into the metamorphosis.[33]

However, whether as visible radiance of the imperative or as slow moving of the peat bogs of childhood and dream, Bauchau's poem remains faithful to its loyalty. The conviction that it nourishes is never rhetorical – no more when it strikes us with the unpredictable precision of its notation than when it summons us fraternally to share a long and painful experience, by following, verse after verse, its meandering path (and Bauchau confesses to us, as he whispers to himself: 'for the straight line, you were not cut out'[34]). Whoever reads him, whoever turns a deaf ear to the world's commercial language so as to read him, will find poetry of two kinds: 'with its sudden illuminations, with his day between two nights'.[35] This reader will be able to hear both 'the patience and the parables of the sun'.[36] This reader, then, is immortally recompensed.

---

32   Ibid., 'Géologie', p. 284.
33   Ibid., 'La grande Troménie', p. 131.
34   Ibid., 'La sourde oreille', p. 114.
35   Ibid., p. 109.
36   Ibid., 'De la ténacité des rivières', p. 40.

6

THE UNFOLDING OF THE DESERT

It would no doubt be easier to restore these poems for the West, comparable to the *Iliad* or the *Odyssey*, if first they did not have to be restored, as Salam Al-Kindy proposes, to their precise East, or even to themselves.[1]

I still remember the amazement I felt when, already through the mediation of Salam, I finally received – no doubt dimmed by the confusing mirages of translation, but still intact – these declarations in which the old Mallarméan that I was promptly recognized that, long before the French language freed itself from a rotting Latin, they seized hold of the void as of that point from where being prescribes its task to language and, in a desert in which every trace is but sand dust on writing, anticipated not only the 'elocutionary disappearance of the poem' but also that 'nothing has taken place but the place'.[2]

What a shame, at the same time! It is in such moments

---

1 *Translator's note*: Badiou is referring to the 'pre-Islamic' poetry anthologized and discussed in Salam Al-Kindy's study, *Le Voyageur sans Orient: Poésie et philosophie des Arabes de l'ère préislamique*, preface Alain Badiou (Arles: Actes Sud, 1998).

2 *Translator's note*: Badiou is referring to Stéphane Mallarmé, 'Crisis of Verse', in *Divagations*; and 'A Dice Throw', in *Complete Poems*.

that one takes the measure of the endless arrogance and the thick ignorance in which the dominant Westerners, perched much more than they think on centuries of imperialism and cruelty, have prospered in the denial of that which ought to have been a lesson to them. Even today, the phantasmagoria of a terrifying Islam separates us from the profundity of the gardens of Granada, from the inventors of algebra, from the subtle discoverers of Aristotle and Plato, from the poets of great love (which does not distinguish between flesh and thought), from the meditating warriors who held still at the foot of the dunes; in short, from these interior Arabs who constituted us, who relieved and surpassed us, and to whom we owe the Greek baptism of our vulgar Latinhood.

How could I for so long have ignored these great poems about which it is an understatement to say that they are essential? This bitter feeling of being, without knowing it, spiritually mutilated, was comparable only to the effect it had on me to discover, while reading *The Tale of Genji*, that in the eleventh century, when we were barely able to produce some rugged epics, in Japan Lady Murasaki was easily nine centuries ahead of Marcel Proust, not only in terms of analytical subtlety about the nadirs and zeniths of love but also in meditating on what a fan, a strumming of the zither or the blue waist-band of a dress has the potential to reveal about the powers of a subject over the timeless essence of time.

It is true that Salam Al-Kindy generously proposes an excuse for us: in Arab lands, too, and perhaps above all, the odes that he finally proposes to *think* have undergone a major phase of concealment because they had to present themselves as 'pre-Islamic', in a universe in which the Prophet is supposed to found in a single gesture, as clerk of the divine Saying, the language, the poetics and finally the law of the world. Thus, forever the captives of a religious retroaction and sometimes contested in terms of their very emergence (much later! apocryphal! post-Islamic fabrication!), the odes have been subtracted from the loyal examination of those who would expose themselves, oblivious to everything that followed them, to the poetic nudity of their power.

This is how I interpret the decentring to which Salam, in a gesture that can only be called iconoclastic, subjects the approach to these unprecedented texts. In order to abolish the retroaction that the qualification as 'pre-Islamic' already imposes, he connects – in a short circuit that frees up an almost unbearable energy – the textual nudity of the odes directly to the heart of the poetico-speculative machinery of the dying West. Mallarmé and Heidegger are required so that, obliterating a convenient 'Arabness' (whose resources he otherwise knows inside out), Salam Al-Kindy reconnects this poetics of the desert with its auroral universality.

From this point of view, Salam Al-Kindy takes a major risk, which is that of firmly *separating* the signifier 'Arab' from its reference, which has everywhere become obligatory, to Islam. Because if there exist poets in Arabic whose contribution to generic thinking can do without the detour through Revelation, or through the Book, must we not suppose that even in the element of this Revelation, the Arabic language persists in telling us in secret, universally, some truths that are subtracted from whatever religion demands from this language?

In this endeavour I can say that Salam is a brother. Have I not tried to show that, in the texts of Saint Paul, in this commercial Greek of the Roman East, a thinking is at work that one can *delink* from any consent to the Christian fable?

In this sense, Salam Al-Kindy finds support in the odes independently of their qualification ('pre-Islamic'); he de-situates them with regard to the becoming, which he suspends (in a kind of historical *epokhè*), of the fatal equation Arab = Muslim. The odes are no longer odes; the Arabic language is no longer a language – which can also be said as follows: the odes are accountable only for themselves; they need not be judged in terms of their results within Islam. Or again: this language is that of these poems, identified by them alone, and subtracted from any sacralized foundation.

All this means in the end that, for Salam Al-Kindy, the poetics of the desert is sovereign; the gods will pass faster than the question asked of language by the infinite duration and mobile dissemination of the sand.

The poet in these odes is a man of wandering and beatitude. He returns to the encampment, after who knows what solitary pilgrimage, and observes that there is nothing left, only the buried traces of departure or destruction. At the heart of this disappearance that the fugitive permanence of the desert in turn makes disappear, the memorable essence of the beloved introduces us to suffering. Not, however, the pathetic suffering of the romantic faced with the impassivity of nature, or with its indifference to earthly sentiments. But rather a thinking-suffering, which finds in nothingness the resource with which to nourish the courage of great declarations. The romantic, at bottom, mentions the immobility of nature only to vaunt the temporal intensity of his passion. The poet of the desert has no concern for time. He addresses himself to the open space, and his dereliction populates this deserted opening with all the symbols of community, without this population becoming a restitution.

Salam Al-Kindy, I believe, is particularly sensible to a kind of *arrested* courage, which looks upon the lamentation only as the pure poetic form of a thought. For him, the desert void of the odes is more radical than Mallarmé's absence. Because for the latter, as a continuator of dialectical philosophy, the negative is transitory. It is an experience that will finally be sublated by the upsurge of the pure Notion, when the Constellation, the Rose, the Swan or the Tomb will come and close the poem on a fragment of the Absolute. What Salam Al-Kindy seeks to transmit to us is a poetry that frontally takes on the fact that loss may be without remedy, the erasure of traces without future, the desert without oasis, and the dereliction of the solitary witness without consolation, neither collective nor private.

But the whole point is that we are not for this reason dealing with a form of nihilism. For all nihilism argues from nothingness against the nostalgia for meaning. Now, the odes, in the precise demonstration of Salam Al-Kindy, may well articulate disappearance with erasure, but they do not pretend to fixate, not even negatively, a possible horizon of meaning. Their poetic courage does not contain as their obverse a nostalgia for donation and plenitude. It is on the contrary in the direct exercise of a pure void that the poet institutes his visible thinking, and adapts to being qua non-being. Therein resides no doubt the singular collusion between the odes and Heidegger, which Salam Al-Kindy reveals in all its depth. In the desert, non-being is by no means the mediation of being; it is its essence. And consequently, the poem need not bear witness to the becoming of meaning, but rather to the fact that thinking, without any guarantee other than the assertive force of language, *stumbles* upon the nondialectical identity of being and non-being. In this way the poem borrows, almost by force, the path of a linguistic elaboration of this stumbling, in which the symbol – which is, as Lacan said, the murder of the thing – is neither a salvation nor an expectation, but an austere assent to the indifference of what happens.

Today there is a relation of what we might call complicity amid allergy between a satisfied but crepuscular West and an Arab world that is partially hystericized by a clinging to signs. In a time like this, Salam Al-Kindy's endeavour is admirably heteronomous. Because against the backdrop of the knotting together of the poem and being, it puts together an Arabness without Islam and a West without Empire. It is fitting in this regard that Salam Al-Kindy does not nourish any particular resentment with regard to the West, nor any identitarian allegiance that would be a captive of dead signs with regard to the Arab world. This young man to whom great universal poems have been confided presents himself to us as a free traveller, the truly modern heir to those Andalusian sovereigns who summoned in their gardens both grandiose and subtle conferences of speculative theology, where the experts in all monotheisms confronted their respective interpretations of Aristotle or Plato. In the interior garden of Salam Al-Kindy, of which *Le Voyageur sans Orient* offers the first map, Mallarmé, Labîd, Heidegger and many others converse about the vocation of the poem, while all territorial disputes have been suspended.

For me to be invited to accompany them on these grounds, where the rustle of the water is like the signature of the great nomadic desert, is a nurturing honour.

7

DRAWING: ON WALLACE STEVENS

I intend simply to propose a very general definition of the arts, more precisely of contemporary arts; and, after that, a short definition of drawing. These definitions take their inspiration from a very beautiful and in fact fundamental poem of the American poet Wallace Stevens. The title of the poem is: 'Description without Place.'[1]

In a very simple and very short talk, it would be possible for me to say that this is my definition of art: every work of art, especially every work in contemporary arts, is a description without place. An installation, for example, is the description of a set of things outside their normal place and the normal relationship between them. So it is the creation of a place which (dis)places all things in it. A performance, or a happening, is a sort of vanishing succession of gestures, pictures, voices, so that the action of bodies describes a space that is strictly speaking outside itself. But what is a drawing? A drawing is a complex of marks. These marks have no place. Why? Because in a true drawing, a creative one, the marks, the traces, the

---

1 Wallace Stevens, 'Description without Place', in *The Collected Poems of Wallace Stevens* (New York: Alfred A. Knopf, 1965), pp. 339–46.

lines, are not included or closeted in the background. On the contrary, the marks, the lines – the forms, if you will – create the background as an open space. They create what Mallarmé names 'the blank paper guarded by its white'.[2]

In the first case – the installation – the new place displaces all things in it; in the second case – the happening – the new things, the new bodies, displace the place; in the third – the drawing – some marks create a nonexistent place. As a result, we shall see, we have a description without place. So my general definition of arts is good, and I have apparently no reason for continuing my lecture, for I can propose a short definition of drawing. There is a drawing when some trace without place creates as its place an empty surface.

Fortunately, one point in the poem of Wallace Stevens surprises me; and I cannot stop my lecture without making myself clear about it. The best thing probably is to read and to comment on some passages of the poem. First, the beginning:

> It is possible that to seem – it is to be,
> As the sun is something seeming and it is.
> The sun is an example. What it seems
> It is and in such seeming all things are.[3]

So the artistic idea of a description without place is in a close relationship with the old philosophical question of being and seeming. Or of being qua being and appearing – to be and to appear – appearing precisely in a place, in a tangible world. The sun is, and it is something seeming, and in poetry, we must name 'sun' neither the fact that the sun is, nor the fact that the sun seems, or appears, but we must name 'sun' the equivalence of seeming and being, the inseparability of being and appearing. And finally, the equivalence of existing and not existing.

---

2   Mallarmé, 'Sea Breeze', in *Collected Poems*, p. 25.
3   Stevens, 'Description without Place', p. 339.

That is exactly the problem of drawing. In one sense, the paper exists, as a material support, as a closed totality; and the marks, or the lines, do not exist by themselves: they have to compose something upon the paper. But in another and more crucial sense, the paper as a background does not exist, because it is created as such, as an open surface, by the marks. It is that sort of movable reciprocity between existence and nonexistence that constitutes the very essence of drawing. The question of drawing is very different from the question in Hamlet. It is not 'to be or not to be', it is 'to be and not to be'. And that is the reason for the fundamental fragility of drawing: not a clear alternative, to be or not to be, but an obscure and paradoxical conjunction, to be and not to be. Or, as Gilles Deleuze would say: a disjunctive synthesis.

This fragility of drawing is its essential feature. And if we remember another famous sentence of Hamlet: 'Frailty, thy name is woman', we can perceive a secret relationship between drawing and femininity.

I shall return in a moment to these points.

We have found here, in Wallace Stevens, a critic of two historical definitions of beauty and art. The first definition holds that real beauty is always beyond appearances. So a work of art, as a creation with material means, is only a sign or a symbol of something infinite that is beyond its proper appearance. Appearing is only a passage to real being. Wallace Stevens summarizes this classical theory of beauty when he writes: 'Description is composed of a sight indifferent to the eye.'[4] The eye, the concrete vision, is not in art the true sight, the real vision of beauty. The real vision of beauty is indifferent to the eye. It is an act of thinking. But Stevens does not agree, and I do not agree either. In the work of art, there is not the absolute dependence of appearing on a transcendent being. On the contrary, we have to fix a point where appearing and being are indiscernible. In drawing this point is precisely the point, the

---

4   Ibid., p. 343.

mark, the trace, when it is hardly discernible from the white background.

Another conception of the beauty of art, more romantic than classical, is that beauty is the sensitive form of the Idea. The work of art as a composition, in appearing, realizes an effective presence of the infinite, of the absolute Idea. It is not a question of going beyond seeming. The movement goes in the opposite direction: the Idea, the real being, comes down in a material form and appears as beauty.

But Wallace Stevens does not agree with this romantic vision, and I do not agree either. Stevens may seem to agree, when he writes: 'description is revelation'.[5] Is not 'revelation' a name for the coming down of the absolute Idea in the appearance of a beautiful form? But here, in the poem, this is not the case. Because the work of art, as description without place, 'is not the thing described'.[6] So Beauty is not the sensitive form of the Idea. The work of art is a description that has no immediate relationship with a real that would be outside the description; as in the romantic conception, the absolute Idea is outside its sensible glory.

For example, a contemporary drawing is not the realization of an external motif. It is much more completely immanent to its proper act. A drawing is the fragmentary trace of a gesture, much more than a static result of this gesture. In fact, a romantic drawing cannot be simply a drawing. There is always something else: heavy darkness, black ink, violent contrasts. A contemporary drawing is without those sorts of effects. It is more sober, more invisible. The pure drawing is the material visibility of invisibility.

We can sum up briefly:

1. The best definition of a work of art is: description without place.

---

5   Ibid., p. 344.
6   Ibid.

2. This description is always a link between real being and seeming, or appearing.
3. This link is not purely symbolic. We do not need to go beyond appearances to find the Real. The description is not a sign for something that lies outside its form.
4. This link is not a pure revelation. It is not the coming down of the absolute Idea, or of the infinite, in a beautiful form. Appearing is not like a formal body of being. It is therefore necessary to consider a new link between appearing and being. Wallace Stevens writes:

> It is an artificial thing that exists,
> In its own seeming, plainly visible,
> Yet not too closely the double of our lives,
> Intenser than any actual life could be.[7]

Our new task is to explain four features of the work of art as a description without place:

1. The description is an 'artificial thing that exists'. Artificiality. Drawing is something that is composed. It is the question of technology. Today the background can be a screen, and not a piece of paper, and the marks can be the visible projection of immaterial numbers.
2. The description is 'in its own seeming'. There is an independent existence in appearances. Drawing must exist without any external explanation, and without external references.
3. But the description is not 'too closely the double of our lives'. A true drawing is not a copy of something. It is a constructive deconstruction of something, and much more real than the initial thing.
4. The description is 'intenser than any actual life'. A drawing is fragile. But it creates a very intense fragility.

---

7 Ibid.

In other words: first, being is purely a mathematical abstraction. It is, in any thing, the multiple without any quality or determination. Drawing seizes this definition by reducing any thing to a system of marks. Second, when a thing appears as a degree of intensity, we have nothing else than the existence of the thing in a world. A thing exists more or less, and the intensity has no relation with being, but only with the concrete world in which the thing appears. In drawing, the world is symbolized by the background, pages, screen, or wall. Third, there is no question of imitation or of representation. The existence of a multiplicity is directly its appearing in a world, with a new measure of the intensity of this appearing.

Within this framework, we can reconstruct our theory of a work of art as a point where appearing and being are indiscernible.

I shall begin with two examples, a poetic one and one of drawing, about the same type of thing: a musical instrument, a guitar. Wallace Stevens wrote a book under the title *The Man with the Blue Guitar*. What is a 'blue guitar'? It is the poetical intensity of the thing 'guitar' in the work of Stevens, in the artificial world created in language by Stevens. At the point of 'blue guitar' there is no possible distinction between 'guitar' as a word, 'guitar' as a real thing, guitar as being, and guitar as appearing. Because this guitar, which appears in Stevens's poems, is the blue guitar. So we can say that, with the blue guitar, we have a poetical intensity in which being and existence are identical. That is probably the best definition of a work of art: in the description without place you have a sort of fusion of being and existence. That is why Stevens writes:

> Thus the theory of description matters most
> It is the theory of the word, for those
> For whom the word is the making of the world.[8]

---

8   Ibid., p. 345.

Here the description is thought as the point inside the poetic language where we have a creation of the world. But if a world is created before us, we have no distinction between the appearing of the thing, its existence and its being. All that is included in the same intensity, the intensity of the blue guitar.

We can immediately transfer all that to the experience of drawing. As you know, the guitar is something like a fetish in cubist painting at its beginning. It is a thing that appears like a new centre of the composition in Pablo Picasso, Georges Braque or Juan Gris. And, as a thing-of-drawing, it is a new way of existing for the true being of the thing. It is the creation of a guitar without separation between its being and its existence. Because in drawing, a guitar is nothing other than its pure form. A guitar is a line, a curve.

You see that to say that a drawing is a work of art has a precise meaning. It is a description without place that creates a sort of artificial world. This world does not obey the common law of separation between real being and appearances. In this world, or at least in some points of this world, there is no difference between 'to be' and 'to exist', or between 'to be' and 'to seem', to 'appear'.

All this allows us to proceed in the direction of a relationship between drawing and politics. Classically, politics, revolutionary politics, is a description with places. You have social places, classes, racial and national places, minorities, foreigners, and so on; you have dominant places, wealth, power ... And a political process is a sort of totalization of different objective places. For example, you organize a political party as the expression of some social places, with the aim of seizing state power.

But today, maybe, we have to create a new trend of politics, beyond the domination of places, beyond social, national, racial places, beyond gender and religion. A purely displaced politics, with absolute equality as its fundamental concept.

This sort of politics will be an action without place. An international and nomadic creation with – as in a work of art – a mixture of violence, abstraction and final peace.

We have to organize a new trend in politics beyond the law of places and of the centralization of power. And, in fact, we have to find a form of action where the political existence of everybody is not separated from their being – a point where we exist in so intense a fashion that we forget our internal division. Doing so, we become a new subject.

Not an individual, but a part of a new subject.

Wallace Stevens writes about something like that at the end of a very beautiful poem with a strange title, 'Final Soliloquy of the Interior Paramour':

> Out of this same light, out of the central mind
> We make a dwelling in the evening air
> In which being together is enough.[9]

Yes, we have to build a new dwelling, a new house, where 'being together is enough'. But for that, we must change our mind ('out of the central mind') and change the light. And for that, with the help of new forms of art, we must go into an action without places.

This is precisely the goal of the pure drawing: to institute a new world, not by the strength of means, like images, painting, colours, and so on, but by the minimalism of some marks and lines, very close to the inexistence of any place. Drawing is the perfect example of an intensity of weakness.

Victory of fragility. Victory of femininity, maybe. In a drawing, the 'together' is only the together of some vanishing marks. 'Together is enough.'

For these reasons, we may perhaps speak of a politics of drawing.

---

9 Stevens, 'Final Soliloquy of the Interior Paramour', in *Collected Poems*, p. 524.

8

DESTRUCTION, NEGATION, SUBTRACTION: ON PIER PAOLO PASOLINI

The abstract content of my lecture is very simple. I can summarize it in five points:

1. All creations, all novelties, are in some sense the affirmative part of a negation. 'Negation', because if something happens as new, it cannot be reduced to the objectivity of the situation where it happens. So, it is certainly like a negative exception to the regular laws of this objectivity. But 'affirmation', affirmative part of the negation, because if a creation is reducible to a negation of the common laws of objectivity, it completely depends on them for its identity. So the very essence of a novelty implies negation, but must affirm its identity apart from the negativity of negation. That is why I say that a creation or a novelty must be defined paradoxically as an affirmative part of negation.

2. I name 'destruction' the negative part of negation. For example, if we consider the creation by Arnold Schönberg, at the beginning of the last century, of the dodecaphonic musical system, we can say that this

creation achieves the destruction of the tonal system, which in the Western world has dominated musical creation for three centuries. In the same way, the Marxist idea of revolution is to achieve the process of immanent negation of capitalism by the complete destruction of the machinery of the bourgeois state. In both cases, negation is the evental concentration of a process through which is achieved the complete disintegration of an old world. It is this evental concentration that realizes the negative power of negation, the negativity of negation, which I name destruction.

3. I name the affirmative part of negation 'subtraction'. For example, the new musical axioms that, for Schönberg, structure the admissible succession of notes in a musical work, outside the tonal system, are in no way deducible from the destruction of this system. They are the affirmative laws of a new framework for musical activity. They show the possibility of a new coherence for musical discourse. The point that we must understand is that this new coherence is not new because it achieves the process of disintegration of the system. The new coherence is new to the extent that, in the framework that Schönberg's axioms impose, the musical discourse avoids the laws of tonality, or, more precisely, becomes indifferent to these laws. That is why we can say that the musical discourse is subtracted from its tonal legislation. Clearly, this subtraction is on the horizon of negation; but it exists apart from the purely negative part of negation. It exists apart from destruction.

It is the same thing for Marx in the political context. Marx insists on saying that the destruction of the bourgeois state is not in itself an achievement. The goal is communism – that is, the end of the state as such, and the end of social classes, in favour of a purely egalitarian organization of civil society. But to come to this, we must first substitute for the bourgeois state a new state, which is not the immediate result of the destruction of the first. In fact, it is a state as different from the bourgeois state as the experimental music of today can be from an academic tonal piece of the nineteenth century, or a contemporary performance can be from an academic representation of Olympic Gods. For the new state – which Marx names 'dictatorship of the proletariat' – is a state that organizes its own vanishing, a state that is in its very essence the process of the non-state. Perhaps, as for Theodor W. Adorno, 'informal music' is the process, in a work, of the disintegration of all forms, so we can say that, in the original thought of Marx, 'dictatorship of the proletariat' was a name for a state that is subtracted from all classical laws of a 'normal' state. For a classical state is a form of power; but the state named 'dictatorship of proletariat' is the power of un-power, the power of the disappearance of the question of power. In any case, we name subtraction this part of negation that is oriented by the possibility of something that exists absolutely apart from what exists under the laws of what negation negates.

4. So negation is always, in its concrete action – political or artistic – suspended between destruction and subtraction. That the very essence of negation is destruction has been the fundamental idea of the last century. The fundamental idea of the beginning century must be that the very essence of negation is subtraction.

5. But subtraction is not the negation of destruction, no more than destruction has been the negation of subtraction, as we have seen with Schönberg or Marx. The most difficult question is precisely to maintain the complete concept of negation from the point of view of subtraction, as Lenin, Schönberg, Marcel Duchamp, John Cage, Mao Zedong or Jackson Pollock have maintained the complete concept of negation from the point of view of destruction.

To clarify the very complex interplay between destruction, negation and subtraction, I propose to read a fragment of a magnificent poem of Pier Paolo Pasolini.

Pasolini is well known as a filmmaker; in particular, he created during the sixties and seventies profound contemporary visual readings of the two great Western intellectual traditions: that of ancient Greece, with movies like *Medea* and *Oedipus Rex*, and Judaeo-Christianity, with *The Gospel According to Saint Matthew*, and a very complex script about the life of Saint Paul. All of that constitutes a difficult thinking of the relationship between History, myths and religion. Pasolini was simultaneously a revolutionary Marxist and a man forever influenced by his religious childhood. His question was: is the revolutionary becoming of History, the political negativity, a destruction of the tragic beauty of the Greek myths and of the peaceful promise of Christianity? Or do we have to speak of a subtraction, whereby an affirmative reconciliation of beauty and peace becomes possible in a new egalitarian world?

Pasolini is also well known for the relationship between his private life and public convictions. Not only was he gay, but this was a part of his political vision, many years before the beginning of the gay and lesbian movement. He knew perfectly well that desire – and in his own case the desire for young poor workers of the suburbs of Rome – is not independent of our ideological choices. Once more, the task is to inscribe sexual desire in the political negativity not as a purely subversive and destructive feature, but as a creative displacement of the line that separates the individual subjectivity from the collective one.

Pasolini was murdered in November 1975. He was fifty-three years old. The circumstances of this horrible murder are still obscure today. But certainly they are exactly at the point where political determinations are linked with sexual situations. It is this point that has been, for Pasolini, a constant source of new truths, but also an existential tragedy.

Marvellous movies, political commitments, critical essays, great novels, new existential style ... Beyond all that, Pasolini is the greatest poet of his generation. We can distinguish three major poetical collections:

1. The poems written when Pasolini was twenty years old, in a specific Italian dialect, the Friulan one. Here we have the attempt to subtract poetry from the authority of the official Italian language, and to use a popular language against the state language. It is a characteristic example of what Deleuze names 'minoritarian politics' in poetry.
2. The great collection published in 1957, the heart of which is the magnificent poem *The Ashes of Gramsci*, a complex meditation concerning history, Marxist ideology, Italian landscape and personal feelings. The title is itself a metaphor of melancholic negation. It is as if Gramsci, the Master, the Father of Italian Marxism, is here dissipated in the dust of History.
3. The two collections of the beginning of the sixties: *The Religion of My Time* (1961) and *Poetry in the Form of a Rose* (1964). Here we have the context of the fragment I shall explain today. Fundamentally, it is the bitter disappointment of Pasolini concerning the practices of the Italian left – and more precisely, two very serious failures of the Communist Party: first, an infidelity to the armed struggle of thousands of young men against fascism and Nazism during the war; second, the inability of the Communist Party to organize the revolt of thousands of young workers in the suburbs of Italian towns.

So we have here a double negation of popular young people: in the past, where their fighting is forgotten; and in the present, where their revolt is despised. But Pasolini has two very important reasons for being passionately interested in the existence and the struggles of young people. First, his younger brother, Guido, has been killed in battle during the war as a partisan, a resistance fighter. And the terrible problem is that he has been killed not by fascists, but by communists

of another country, Yugoslav communists, because of
the rivalry between Italians and Yugoslavs concerning the control of some border regions. Second, as a
gay man, Pasolini has always had real and constant
relationships with very poor young workers, or with
the unemployed of the suburbs. That is why many of
Pasolini's poems speak of the contradiction between
history, politics and the concrete existence of proletarian youth.

We shall first listen to one of these poems. It is a fragment
of a very long poem, 'Victory' ('Vittoria'):

'All politics is Realpolitik', warring

soul, with your delicate anger!
You don't recognize a soul other than this one
which has all the prose of the clever man,

of the revolutionary devoted to the honest
common man (even the complicity
with the assassins of the Bitter Years grafted

onto protector classicism, which makes
the communist respectable): you don't recognize the heart
that becomes slave to its enemy, and goes

where the enemy goes, led by a history
that is the history of both, and makes them, deep down,
perversely, brothers; you do not recognize the fears

of a consciousness that, by struggling with the world,
shares the rules of the struggle over the centuries,
as through a pessimism into which hopes

drown to become more virile. Joyous
with a joy that knows no hidden agenda,
this army – blind in the blind

sunlight – of dead young men comes
and waits. If their father, their leader, absorbed
in a mysterious debate with Power and bound

by its dialectics, which history renews ceaselessly –
if he abandons them,
in the white mountains, on the serene plains,

little by little in the barbaric breasts
of the sons, hate becomes love of hate,
burning only in them, the few, the chosen.

Ah, Desperation that knows no laws!
Ah, Anarchy, free love
of Holiness, with your valiant songs![1]

To achieve an overview of this fragment, we can say something like this: everybody is saying that politics must be realistic, that all ideological illusions have been proved dangerous and bloody.

But what is the real for politics? The real is History. The real is the concrete becoming of struggle and negation. But how is it possible to understand or know History? We can do so if we know the rules of History, the great laws of becoming. This is the lesson of Marxism.

But are not the laws of History the same for us and for our enemies? And if such is the case, how can negation be distinguished from approval?

We are in the situation where destruction being suppressed – the subtraction itself, the opposition, if you want – becomes complicity. As Pasolini writes: we recognize that we are going exactly where the enemy goes, 'led by a History that is the history of both'. And political hope is impossible.

So, if the young dead of the last war could see the present political situation, they would not agree with this complicity. Finally, they cannot accept their political fathers, the leaders of the Communist Party. And they become by necessity barbarian and nihilistic people, exactly like the young unemployed of the suburbs.

---

1 Pier Paolo Pasolini, 'Victory', in *In Danger: A Pasolini Anthology*, ed. and trans. Jack Hirschman (San Francisco: City Lights Books, 2010), pp. 212–13.

The poem is a manifesto for true negation.

If subtraction is separated from destruction, we have as a result hate and despair. The symbol of this result is the fusion of the dead heroes of the last war with the despised workers of our suburbs in a sort of terrorist figure. But if destruction is separated from subtraction, we have as a result the impossibility of politics, because young people are absorbed in a sort of nihilistic collective suicide, which is without thinking or destination. In the first case, fathers, who are responsible for the emancipatory political orientation, abandon their sons on behalf of the real. In the second case, sons, who are the collective strength of a possible revolt, abandon their fathers on behalf of despair.

But emancipatory politics is possible only when some fathers and mothers and some sons and daughters are allied in an effective negation of the world as it is.

Some remarks:

1. The whole beginning: under the idea of 'Realpolitik' we have something like a negation without destruction. I define this as 'opposition', in the common democratic sense. Like democrats against Bush. We find two excellent definitions of this sort of negation: 'the prose of the clever man' and 'protector classicism'. You will note that, in both cases, the comparison is with artistic conservative style.

2. The 'bitter years' are the years of the war, which, in Italy, has largely been also a civil war.

3. The heart of 'opposition' is to substitute some rules for the violence of the real. In my jargon, I can say: to substitute rules of history, or rules of economy, for the rupture of the event. And when you do that, you 'share the rules of the struggle' with your enemy. And finally you become 'slave of your enemy', a 'brother' of your enemy.

4. In this context, Pasolini has a sort of magnificent and melancholic vision. The army of dead young men of the last war, among them certainly his younger brother

Guido, is coming to see their father, their leader. That is, in fact, the revolutionary leaders of today. This army, 'blind in the blind sunlight', comes and waits 'in the white mountains, on the serene plains'. And they see their father, their leader, absorbed in the very weak form of negation, the dialectical negation. This negation is not separate from the power. This negation is only an obscure relationship to the power itself. It is 'a mysterious debate with Power'. So the father is in fact without freedom – he is 'bounded' by the dialectics of power.

5. The conclusion is that this father 'abandons them'. You see the problem, which is clearly a problem of today. The army of dead young men was on the side of destruction, of hate. They existed on the hard side of negation. But they wait for an orientation, for a negation which, under some paternal law, reconciles destruction and subtraction.

    But contemporary leaders abandon them. So they have only the destructive part of negation. They have only 'Desperation that knows no laws!'.

6. And the description of their subjectivity is quite an expressive one. Yes, they were on the side of hate, of destruction. They were 'angry young men'. But now, in a very striking formula, 'hate becomes love of hate'. This love of hate is negation as purely destructive. Without any access to subtraction, without fathers, or leaders, we have to face the nudity of 'the barbaric breasts of the sons'.

7. Great poetry is always an anticipation, a vision, of the collective future. We can see here that Pasolini describes the terrorist subjectivity. He indicates with astonishing precision that the possibility of this subjectivity among young men or women is the lack of any rational hope of changing the world. That is why he creates a poetic equivalence between desperation (the nihilistic consequence of false negation), anarchy (the purely destructive political version) and 'free love

of Holiness', which is the religious context of terror-
ism, with the figure of the martyr. This equivalence
is certainly clearer today than it was forty years ago,
when Pasolini wrote 'Victory'.

We can now conclude: the political problems of the contemporary world cannot be solved, neither in the weak context
of democratic opposition, which in fact abandons millions
of people to a nihilistic destiny, nor in the mystical context
of destructive negation, which is another form of power,
the power of death. Neither subtraction without destruction, nor destruction without subtraction. It is in fact the
problem of violence today. Violence is not, as has been
said during the last century, the creative and revolutionary part of negation. The way of freedom is a subtractive
one. But to protect the subtraction itself, to defend the new
kingdom of emancipatory politics, we cannot radically
exclude all forms of violence. The future is not on the side
of the savage young men and women of popular suburbs –
we cannot abandon them to themselves. But neither is the
future on the side of the democratic wisdom of mothers
and fathers with their law. We have to learn something of
nihilistic subjectivity.

The world is made not of law and order, but of law and
desire. Let us learn from Pasolini not to be 'absorbed in a
mysterious debate with power', not to abandon millions of
young men and women either 'in the white mountains' or
'on the serene plains'.

9

POETRY AND COMMUNISM

In the last century, some truly great poets, in almost all languages on earth, have been communists. In an explicit or formal way, for example, the following poets were committed to communism: in Turkey, Nâzim Hikmet; in Chile, Pablo Neruda; in Spain, Rafael Alberti; in Italy, Edoardo Sanguineti; in Greece, Yannis Ritsos; in China, Ai Qing; in Palestine, Mahmoud Darwish; in Peru, César Vallejo; and in Germany, the shining example is above all Bertolt Brecht. But we could cite a very large number of other names in other languages, throughout the world.

Can we understand this link between poetic commitment and communist commitment as a simple illusion? An error, or an errancy? An ignorance of the ferocity of states ruled by communist parties? I do not believe so. I wish to argue, on the contrary, that there exists an essential link between poetry and communism, if we understand 'communism' closely in its primary sense: the concern for what is common to all. A tense, paradoxical, violent love of life in common; the desire that what ought to be common and accessible to all should not be appropriated by the servants of Capital. The poetic desire that the things of life would be like the sky and the earth, like the water of the oceans and the brush fires on a summer night – that is to say, would belong by right to the whole world.

Poets are communist for a primary reason, which is absolutely essential: their domain is language, most often their native tongue. Now, language is what is given to all from birth as an absolutely common good. Poets are those who try to make a language say what it seems incapable of saying. Poets are those who seek to create in language new names to name that which, before the poem, has no name. And it is essential for poetry that these inventions, these creations, which are internal to language, have the same destiny as the mother tongue itself: for them to be given to all without exception. The poem is a gift of the poet to language. But this gift, like language itself, is destined to the common – that is, to this anonymous point where what matters is not one person in particular but all, in the singular.

Thus, the great poets of the twentieth century recognized in the grandiose revolutionary project of communism something that was familiar to them – namely that, as the poem gives its inventions to language and as language is given to all, the material world and the world of thought must be given integrally to all, becoming no longer the property of a few but the common good of humanity as a whole.

This is why the poets have seen in communism above all a new figure of the destiny of the people. And 'people', here, means first and foremost the poor people, the workers, the abandoned women, the landless peasants. Why? Because it is first and foremost to those who have nothing that everything must be given. It is to the mute, to the stutterer, to the stranger, that the poem must be offered, and not to the chatterbox, to the grammarian, or to the nationalist. It is to the proletarians – whom Marx defined as those who have nothing except their own body capable of work – that we must give the entire earth, as well as all the books, and all the music, and all the paintings, and all the sciences. What is more, it is to them, to the proletarians in all their forms, that the poem of communism must be offered.

What is striking is that this should lead all those poets to rediscover a very old poetic form: the epic. The communists' poem is first the epic of the heroism of the proletarians. The Turkish poet Nâzim Hikmet thus distinguishes lyric poems, dedicated to love, from epic poems, dedicated to the action of the popular masses. But even a poet as wise and as hermetic as César Vallejo does not hesitate to write a poem with the title, 'Hymn to the Volunteers of the Republic'.[1] Such a title evidently belongs to the order of the commemoration of war, to epic commitment.

These communist poets rediscover what in France Victor Hugo had already discovered: the duty of the poet is to look in language for the new resources of an epic that would no longer be that of the aristocracy of knights but the epic of the people in the process of creating another world. The fundamental link organized into song by the poet is the one that the new politics is capable of founding between, on the one hand, the misery and extreme hardship of life, the horror of oppression, everything that calls for our pity, and, on the other hand, the levying, the combat, the collective thought, the new world – and, thus, everything that calls for our admiration. It is of this dialectic of compassion and admiration, of this violently poetic opposition between debasement and rising up, of this reversal of resignation into heroism, that the communist poets seek the living metaphor, the nonrealist representation, the symbolic power. They search for the words to express the moment in which the eternal patience of the oppressed of all times changes into a collective force which is indivisibly that of raised bodies and shared thoughts.

That is why one moment – a singular historic moment – has been sung by all the communist poets who wrote

---

1   César Vallejo, 'Hymn to the Volunteers of the Republic', in *Spain, Take This Cup from Me*, trans. Clayton Eshleman and José Rubia Barcia (New York: Grove Press, 1974), pp. 3–13.

between the 1920s and 1940s: the moment of the civil war in Spain, which as you know ran from 1936 to 1939.

Let us observe that the Spanish civil war is certainly the historic event that has most intensely mobilized all the artists and intellectuals of the world. On one hand, the personal commitment of writers from all ideological tendencies on the side of the republicans, including therefore the communists, is remarkable: whether we are dealing with organized communists, social democrats, mere liberals, or even fervent Catholics, such as the French writer Georges Bernanos, the list is extraordinary if we gather all those who publicly spoke out, who went to Spain in the midst of the war, or even entered into combat on the side of the republican forces. On the other hand, the number of masterpieces produced on this occasion is no less astonishing. I have already noted as much for poetry. But let us also think of the splendid painting by Pablo Picasso that is titled *Guernica*; let us think of two of the greatest novels in their genre: *Man's Hope* by André Malraux and *For Whom the Bell Tolls* by the American Ernest Hemingway. The frightening and bloody civil war in Spain has illuminated the art of the world for several years.

I see at least four reasons for this massive and international commitment of intellectuals on the occasion of the war in Spain.

First, in the 1930s the world found itself in a vast ideological and political crisis. Public opinion sensed more and more that this crisis could not have a peaceful ending, no legal or consensual solution. The horizon was a fearsome one of internal and external warfare. Among intellectuals, the tendency was to choose between two absolutely contrary orientations: the fascist and the communist orientations. During the war in Spain, this conflict took the form of civil war pure and simple. Spain had become the violent emblem of the central ideological conflict of the time. This is what we might call the symbolic and therefore universal value of this war.

Second, during the Spanish war, the occasion arose for

artists and intellectuals all over the world not only to show their support for the popular camp, but also to participate directly in combat. Thus what had been an opinion changed into action; what had been a form of solidarity became a form of fraternity.

Third, the war in Spain took on a fierceness that hit people over the head. Misery and destruction were present everywhere. The systematic massacre of prisoners, the indiscriminate bombing of villages, the relentlessness of both camps: all this gave people an idea of what could be and what in fact was to be the worldwide conflict to which the war in Spain was the prologue.

Fourth, the Spanish war was the strongest moment, perhaps unique in the history of the world, of the realization of the great Marxist project: that of a truly internationalist revolutionary politics. We should remember what the intervention of the International Brigades meant: they showed that the vast international mobilization of minds was also, and before anything, an international mobilization of peoples. I am thinking of the example of France: thousands of workers, often communists, had gone as volunteers to do battle in Spain. But there were also Americans, Germans, Italians, Russians, people from all countries. This exemplary international dedication, this vital internationalist subjectivity, is perhaps the most striking accomplishment of what Marx had thought, which can be summarized in two phrases: negatively, the proletarians have no fatherland, their political homeland is the whole world of living men and women; positively, international organization is what allows for the confrontation and in the end the real victory over the enemy of all, the capitalist camp, including in its extreme form, which is fascism.

Thus, the communist poets found major subjective reasons in the Spanish war for renewing epic poetry in the direction of a popular epic – one that was both that of the suffering of peoples and that of their internationalist heroism, organized and combative.

Already the titles of the poems or collections of poems are significant. They indicate almost always a kind of sensible reaction of the poet, a kind of shared suffering with the horrible fate and hardship reserved for the Spanish people. Thus, Pablo Neruda's collection bears the title *Spain in Our Hearts*. This goes to show that the first commitment of the poet is an affective, subjective, immediate solidarity with the Spanish people at war. Similarly, the very beautiful title of César Vallejo's collection is *Spain, Take This Cup from Me*. This title indicates that, for the poet, the sense of shared suffering becomes its own poetic ordeal, which is almost impossible to bear.

However, both poets will develop this first personal and affective impulse almost in the opposite direction – that of a creative use of suffering itself, that of an unknown liberty. This unknown liberty is precisely that of the reversal of misery into heroism, the reversal of a particular anxiety-ridden situation into a universal promise of emancipation. Here is how César Vallejo puts it, with his mysterious metaphors:

> Proletarian who dies of the universe, in what frantic
> harmony
> your grandeur will end, your extreme poverty, your
> impelling whirlpool,
> your methodical violence, your theoretical & practical
> chaos, your Dantesque
> wish, so very Spanish, to love, even treacherously, your
> enemy!

> Liberator wrapped in shackles,
> without whose labour extension would still be without
> handles,
> the nails would wander headless,
> the day, ancient, slow, reddish,
> our beloved helmets, unburied!
> peasant fallen with your green foliage for man,
> with the social inflection of your little finger,
> with your ox that stays, with your physics,
> also with your word tied to a stick

& your rented sky
& with the clay inserted in your tiredness
& with that in your fingernail, walking!
Agricultural
builders, civilian & military,
of the active, ant-swarming eternity: it was written
that you will create the light, half-closing
your eyes in death;
that, at the cruel fall of your mouths,
abundance will come on seven platters, everything
in the world will be of sudden gold
& the gold,
fabulous beggars for your own secretion of blood,
& the gold itself will then be made of gold![2]

You see how death itself – the death in combat of the volunteers of the Spanish people – becomes a construction; better yet, a kind of nonreligious eternity, an earthly eternity. The communist poet can say this: 'Agricultural builders, civilian & military, of the active, ant-swarming eternity'. This eternity is that of the real truth, the real life, wrested away from the cruel powers that be. It changes everything into the gold of true life. Even the accursed gold of the rich and the oppressors will simply become once more what it is: 'the gold itself will then be made of gold'.

We might say that, in the ordeal of the Spanish war, communist poetry sings of the world that has returned to what it really is – the world-truth, which can be born forever, when hardship and death change into paradoxical heroism. This is what César Vallejo will say later on by invoking the 'victim in a column of victors', and when he exclaims that 'in Spain, in Madrid, the command is to kill, volunteers who fight for life!'[3]

Pablo Neruda, as I have mentioned, likewise starts out from pain, misery and compassion. Thus, in the great epic poem titled 'Arrival in Madrid of the International Brigade', he begins by saying that 'Spanish death, more

---

2   Ibid., pp. 7–9.
3   Ibid., p. 11 (translation modified).

acrid and sharper than other deaths, filled fields up to then
honoured by wheat.'[4] But the poet is most sensitive to the
internationalism of the arrival in Spain from all over the
world of those whom he directly calls 'comrades'. Let us
listen to the poem of this arrival:

Comrades,
then
I saw you,
and my eyes are even now filled with pride
because through the misty morning I saw you reach
          the pure brow of Castile
silent and firm
like bells before dawn,
filled with solemnity and blue-eyed, come from far,
          far away,
come from your corners, from your lost fatherlands,
          from your dreams,
covered with burning gentleness and guns
to defend the Spanish city in which besieged liberty
could fall and die bitten by the beasts.

Brothers,
from now on
let your pureness and your strength, your solemn story
be known by children and by men, by women and by old
     men,
let it reach all men without hope, let it go down to the
mines
          corroded by sulphuric air
let it mount the inhuman stairways of the slave,
let all the stars, let all the flowers of Castile
          and of the world
write your name and your bitter struggle
and your victory strong and earthen as a red oak.
Because you have revived with your sacrifice
lost faith, absent heart, trust in the earth,
and through your abundance, through your nobility,
through your dead,

---

4 Pablo Neruda, 'Arrival in Madrid of the International Brigade',
Spain in Our Hearts: Hymn to the Glories of the People at War, trans.
Donald D. Walsh (New York: New Directions, 2005), p. 27.

as if through a valley of harsh bloody rocks,
flows an immense river with doves of steel and of hope.[5]

What we see this time is first the evidence of fraternity. The word 'comrades' is followed later on by the word 'brothers'. This fraternity puts forward not so much the changing of the real world as the changing of subjectivity. Certainly, at first, all these international communist militants have come 'from far', 'from your corners', 'from your lost fatherlands'. But above all they have come from their 'dreams covered with burning gentleness and guns'. You will note the typical proximity of gentleness and violence. This will be repeated with the image of a 'dove of steel': combat is the building not of naked violence, not of power, but of a subjectivity capable of confronting the long run because it has confidence in itself. The workers and intellectuals of the international brigades, mixed together, have given new birth to 'lost faith, absent heart, trust in the earth'. Because we are at war, the dove of peace must be a dove of steel, but it is also and above all, says the poem, a dove of hope. In the end, the epic of war that Neruda celebrates, what he calls 'your victory strong and earthen as a red oak', is above all the creation of a new confidence or trust. The point is to escape from nihilistic resignation. And this constructive value of communist confidence, I believe, is also needed today.

The French poet Paul Éluard picks up on two of the motifs that we have seen so far, and mixes them together. On one hand, as César Vallejo says, the international volunteers of the Spanish war represent a new humanity, simply because they are true human beings, and not the false humanity of the capitalist world, competitive and obsessed with money and commodities. On the other hand, as Pablo Neruda says, these volunteers transform the surrounding nihilism into a new confidence. A stanza of the poem 'The Victory of Guernica' says this with precision:

---

5 Ibid., pp. 27–9.

> True men for whom despair
> Feeds the devouring fire of hope
> Let us open together the last bud of the future.[6]

However, in the Spanish war Éluard is sensitive to another factor with universal value. For him, as for Rousseau, humanity is fundamentally good-natured, with a good nature that is being destroyed by oppression through competition, forced labour, money. This fundamental goodness of the world resides in the people, in their obstinate life, in the courage to live that is theirs. The poem begins as follows:

> Fair world of hovel
> Of the mine and fields.[7]

Éluard thinks that women and children especially incarnate this universal good nature, this subjective treasure that finally is what men are trying to defend in the war in Spain:

> VIII
> Women and children have the same riches
> Of green leaves of spring and pure milk
> And endurance
> In their pure eyes.

> IX
> Women and children have the same riches
> In their eyes
> Men defend them as they can.

> X
> Women and children have the same red roses
> In their eyes
> They show each their blood.

---

6 Paul Éluard, 'The Victory of Guernica', *Selected Poems*, trans. Gilbert Bowen (New York: Riverrun Press, 1987), p. 55.

7 Ibid., p. 53 (translation modified; Badiou's version has *De la nuit et des champs*, 'Of the night and fields' instead of *De la mine et des champs*, 'Of the mine and fields').

XI
The fear and the courage to live and to die
Death so difficult and so easy.[8]

The Spanish war, for Éluard, reveals what simple riches are at the disposal of human life. This is why extreme oppression and war are also the revelation of the fact that men must guard the riches of life. And to do so you must keep the trust, even when the enemy is crushing you, imposing on you the easiness of death. We clearly sense that this trust is communism itself. This is why the poem is titled 'The Victory of Guernica'. The destruction of this town by German bombers, the 2,000 dead of this first savage experience that announces the world war: all this will also be a victory, if people continue to be confident that the riches of simple life are indestructible. This is why the poem concludes as follows:

> Outcasts the death the ground the hideous sight
> Of our enemies have the dull
> Colour of our night
> Despite them we shall overcome.[9]

This is what we can call poetic communism: to sing the certainty that humanity is right to create a world in which the treasure of simple life will be preserved peacefully, and that, because it has reason on its side, humanity will impose this reason, and its reason will overcome its enemies. This link between popular life, political reason and confidence in victory: that is what Éluard seeks to confer, in language, upon the suffering and heroism of the Spanish war.

Nâzim Hikmet, in the truly beautiful poem titled 'It Is Snowing in the Night', will in turn traverse all these themes of communist poetics, starting out from a subjective identification. He imagines a sentry from the popular camp at the gates of Madrid. This sentinel, this lonely man – just as the poet is always alone in the work of language – carries

---

8   Ibid., pp. 53–5.
9   Ibid., p. 55.

inside him, fragile and threatened, everything the poet
desires, everything that according to him gives meaning to
existence. Thus, a lonely man at the gates of Madrid is in
charge of the dreams of all of humanity:

> It is snowing in the night,
> You are at the door of Madrid.
> In front of you an army
> Killing the most beautiful things we own,
>> Hope, yearning, freedom and children,
>>> The City ...[10]

You see how all the Spanish themes of communist poetics
return: the volunteer of the Spanish war is the guardian of
universal revolutionary hope. He finds himself at night, in
the snow, trying to prohibit the killing of hope.

Nâzim Hikmet's singular achievement no doubt consists
in finding the profound universality of nostalgic yearn-
ing in this war. Communist poetics cannot be reduced to
a vigorous and solid certainty of victory. It is also what
we might call the nostalgia of the future. The hymn to the
sentry of Madrid is related to this truly peculiar sentiment:
the nostalgia for a grandeur and a beauty that nevertheless
have not yet been created. Communism here works in the
future anterior: we experience a kind of poetic regret for
what we imagine the world will have been when communism has come. Therein lies the force of the conclusion of
Hikmet's poem:

> I know,
> everything great and beautiful there is,
> everything great and beautiful man has still to create
> that is, everything my nostalgic soul hopes for
> smiles in the eyes
> of the sentry at the door of Madrid.
> And tomorrow, like yesterday, like tonight
> I can do nothing else but love him.[11]

---

10   Nâzim Hikmet, 'It Is Snowing in the Night', in *Selected Poems*
(Calcutta: Parichaya Prakashani, 1952).
11   Ibid.

You can hear that strange mixture of the present, of the past and future that the poem crystallizes in the imagined character of the solitary sentry, confronted with the fascist army, in the night and snow of Madrid. There is already nostalgia for what true humanity, the combatant people of Madrid, is capable of creating in terms of beauty and grandeur. If the people are capable of creating this, then humanity will certainly create it. And, then, we can have the nostalgia for that which the world would be if this possible creation had already taken place. Thus, communist poetry is not only epic poetry of combat, historic poetry of the future, affirmative poetry of confidence. It is also lyric poetry of what communism, as the figure of humanity reconciled with its own grandeur, *will have been* after victory, which for the poet is already regret and melancholy as well as 'nostalgic hope' of his soul, past as well as future, nostalgia as well as hope.

With regard to the Spanish civil war properly speaking, Bertolt Brecht also committed himself by writing a didactic play, *Señora Carrar's Rifles*, which is devoted to the interior debate over the need to participate in the right battle, whatever the excellent reasons may be to stay at a safe remove.

But perhaps the most important aspect is the following: as the independent communist that he has always been, Brecht is the contemporary of very serious and bloody defeats of the communist cause. He has been directly present and active in the moment of the defeat of German communism in the face of the Nazis. And of course he has also been the contemporary of the terrible defeat of Spanish communism in the face of Franco's military fascism. But one of the tasks that Brecht has always assigned to himself as a poet is to give poetic support to confidence, to political confidence, even in the worst of all conditions, when the defeat is at its most terrifying. Here we rediscover the motif of confidence, as that which the poem must stir up based on the reversal of compassion into admiration, and of resignation into heroism. To this subjective task Brecht devoted some of his most beautiful poems, in which the almost abstract focus of the topic aims to produce an enthusiasm of sorts. I am thinking of the end of the poem 'In Praise of Dialectics', in which we again find the temporal metamorphoses that I have already talked about – the future that becomes the past, the present that is reduced to the power of the future – all of which makes a poem out of the way in which political subjectivity supports a highly complex connection to historical becoming. Brecht, for his part, poeticizes the refusal of powerlessness in the name of the future's presence in the present itself:

> Who dares say: never?
> On who does it depend if oppression remains? On us.
> On who does it depend if its thrall is broken? Also on us.
> Whoever has been beaten down must rise up!
> Whoever is lost must fight back!
> Whoever has recognized his condition – how can anyone
>   stop him?
> Because the vanquished of today are tomorrow's victors
> And never will become: already today![12]

Must we, too, not desire that 'never' become 'already today'? They pretend to chain us to the financial necessities of Capital. They pretend that we ought to obey today so that tomorrow may exist. They pretend that the communist Idea is dead forever, after the disaster of Stalinism. But must we not in turn 'recognize [our] condition'? Why do we accept a world in which one per cent of the global population possesses 47 per cent of the world's wealth, and in which 10 per cent possesses 86 per cent of the world's wealth? Must we accept that the world is organized by such terrible inequalities? Must we think that nothing will ever change this? Must we think that the world will forever be organized by private property and the ferocity of monetary competition?

Poetry always says what is essential. Communist poetry

---

12 Bertolt Brecht, 'Lob der Dialektik', in *Die Gedichte* (Frankfurt am Main: Suhrkamp, 2000), p. 182.

from the 1930s and 1940s recalls for us that the essential aspect of communism, or of the communist Idea, is not and never has been the ferocity of a state, the bureaucracy of a party, or the stupidity of blind obedience. These poems tell us that the communist Idea is the compassion for the simple life of the people afflicted by inequality and injustice – that it is the broad vision of a raising up, both in thought and in practice, which is opposed to resignation and changes it into a patient heroism. It tells us that this patient heroism is aimed at the collective construction of a new world, with the means of a new thinking about what politics might be. And it recalls for us, with the riches of its images and metaphors, with the rhythm and musicality of its words, that communism in its essence is the political projection of the riches of the life of all.

Brecht sees all this very clearly, too. He is opposed to the tragic and monumental vision of communism. Yes, there is an epic poetry of communism, but it is the patient epic, which is heroic for its very patience, of all those who gather and organize themselves to heal the world of its deadly diseases that are injustice and inequality; and to do so requires going to the root of things: limit private property, end the violent separation of the power of the state, overcome the division of labour. This, Brecht tells us, is not an apocalyptic vision. On the contrary, it is what is normal and sensible, reflecting the average desire of all. This is why the communist poem recalls for us that sickness and violence are on the side of the capitalist and imperialist world as we know it, and not on the side of the calm, normal and average grandeur of the communist Idea. This is what Brecht is going to tell us in a poem that carries the absolutely surprising title, 'Communism is the Middle Term':

> To call for the overthrow of the existing order
> May seem a terrible thing
> But what exists is no order.
> To seek refuge in violence
> May seem evil.
> But what is constantly at work is violence

And there is nothing special about it.
Communism is not the extreme outlier
That only in a small part can be realized,
And until it is not completely realized,
The situation is unbearable
Even for someone who is insensitive.
Communism is really the most minimal demand
What is nearest, reasonable, the middle term.
Whoever is opposed to it is not someone who thinks
      otherwise
It is someone who does not think or who thinks only
      about himself
It is an enemy of the human species who,
Terrible
Evil
Insensitive
And, in particular,
Wanting the most extreme, realized even in the tiniest
      part,
Plunges all humankind into destruction.[13]

Thus, communist poetry presents us with a peculiar epic: the epic of the minimal demand, the epic of what is never extreme nor monstrous. Communist poetry, with its resource of gentleness combined with that of enthusiasm, tells us: rise up with the will to think and act so that the world may be offered to all as the world that belongs to all, just as the poem in language offers to all the common world that is always contained therein, even if in secret. There have been and continue to be all kinds of discussions about the communist hypothesis: in philosophy, sociology, economics, history, political science ... But I have wanted to tell you that there exists a proof of communism by way of the poem.

---

13 Bertolt Brecht, 'Der Kommunismus ist das Mittlere', in ibid., pp. 700–1.

II. On Prose

10

THE AUTONOMY OF THE AESTHETIC PROCESS

The following developments are meant to clarify the implications of two dogmatic statements:

STATEMENT I

Art is not ideology. It is completely impossible to explain art on the basis of the homological relation that it is supposed to maintain with the real of history. The aesthetic process decentres the specular relation with which ideology perpetuates its closed infinity. The aesthetic effect is certainly imaginary; but this imaginary is not the reflection of the real, since it is the real of this reflection.

STATEMENT 2

Art is not science. The aesthetic effect is not an effect of knowledge. However, as differentiating realization and denunciation of ideology, art is closer to science than to ideology. It produces the imaginary reality of that which science appropriates in its real reality.

In the Marxist tradition, art is classified among the 'ideological forms'.[1] And yet, in the same tradition, the evaluation of
certain artworks involves criteria derived from the concept
of *truth* (the work is a 'real reflection of life'), the use of
which implicitly assimilates certain levels of the work to
the functioning of a theoretical knowledge. Everything
appears as if the *general theory* of art were a region of
the theory of ideologies – and as if, at the same time, the
critical practice tended to differentiate art from ideology
by conferring upon it a complex function, simultaneously
descriptive and critical, through which ideology ends up
being denounced and the 'real' is exhibited. In short, we
are in the presence of a chiasmic discord: theory assigns art
an ideological function, but the good (ideological) use of
this function – the determination of the *useful* work – presupposes a clandestine relation of some sort between the
work and truth, and thus between the work and theoretical practice. It is the form of this relation that supports the
evaluations. Leo Tolstoy, Lenin explains, must be valued
as the real reflection of the contradictions of the Russian
peasantry. By contrast, Fyodor Dostoevsky is 'supremely
bad',[2] for the same reasons: as real reflection as well, but
this time of a counter-revolutionary class. The great work
is thus represented as a theoretical essence (the truth that
it envelops) veiled by an ideological existence (the imaginary of the forms). Whence the ambiguity of the critical
task of socialist realism. This critical task indeed consists in
determining the ideological existence of the artworks, by
producing the concepts of their historical belonging. But it
also consists in unveiling the theoretical essence that marks
the singularity of the 'great works' – those that gain right
of access to the socialist pantheon. It is in these general

---

1   This tradition is strong enough to have brought Louis Althusser
in 1963 to write 'ideology, whether religious, political, moral, juridical or
artistic', in *For Marx*, trans. Ben Brewster (London: Verso, 1990), p. 167.

2   V. I. Lenin, 'Letter to Inessa Armand', *Collected Works*, vol. 35
(Moscow: Progress, 1976), pp. 144–5. Also available in *Lenin on Literature
and Art* (Rockville, MD: Wildside Press, 2008), p. 178.

terms that Mao Zedong defines the relation of criticism to the old aesthetic tradition: 'To study the development of this old culture, to reject its feudal dross and assimilate its democratic essence is a necessary condition for developing our new national culture.'[3] The democratic interiority of the work is thus the unchangeable residue of a critical reduction. This means that the theory of feudal literature, *insofar as it is feudal*, brings out that which this theory could not foresee – namely, its essential anti-feudalism. Or again: the theory of literature as historical process contains a truth, which is not what it signifies, the work's historicity, but what it is incapable of signifying: its trans-historical and prophetic value.

We can see that such an approach can be sustained only by reflecting upon aesthetic products according to what are essentially hybrid operators: neither theory nor ideology, the artwork is the ideological appearance of the theoretical, the non-true as the glorious envelope of the true. In reality, this approach has exactly the same status as the one that Plato attributes to the right opinion: truth by chance, or truth produced as pure fact, the work of art stands between being and non-being. And this hybridity is so fundamental that Lenin ends up recognizing theoretical falsity as an almost inevitable condition of the practical effectiveness of works of art. In art, eclecticism is almost compulsory. This enables Lenin to write to Maxim Gorky:

> I believe that an artist can glean much that is useful to him from philosophy of all kinds ... [I]n matters that concern the art of writing you are the best judge, and in deriving *this* kind of view both from your artistic experience *and from philosophy, even in idealistic philosophy*, you can arrive at conclusions that will be of tremendous benefit to the workers' party.[4]

---

3   Mao Zedong, 'On New Democracy (January 1940)', *Selected Works*, vol. 2 (Beijing: Foreign Languages Press, 1965), p. 381.

4   V. I. Lenin, 'A Letter to M. Gorky (1942)', *Collected Works*, vol. 13 (Moscow: Progress, 1972), pp. 453–4 (italics in the original).

As in the case of the right opinion, art's concluding validity can accommodate false premises.

Now, all these remarks do indicate the true problem: that of the ambiguity of art in regard to the binary opposition science/ideology. We cannot declare at the same time that there is a democratic essence to feudal art and that this art is a purely ideological reflection, with a universal vocation, of the 'lived experience' of the dominant class. We cannot observe that art produces the true on the basis of the false and declare, as in a certain socialist realism, that in the final instance theoretical truth conditions aesthetic validity.

Mao Zedong was so sensitive to this problem that in order to elucidate the relation of aesthetic production to the theoretically constructed reality of classes, he needed no fewer than *four* concepts, whereas lazy Marxist criticism establishes a simple binary between the meaning of the work and the ideology of a class. Mao in effect distinguishes the following:

- *The class-being*. The class to which the writer belongs by birth.
- *The class-stand* or *class-position*. The general space of the problematic on the basis of which every theoretical practice is defined: the progressive writer must stand 'on the positions' of the working class – in other words, formulate problems according to the 'outlook' of the working class. The stand is *the space of the questions*. But in the sense in which Georges Canguilhem says that one can *be in* the true without *saying* the true, one can *stand on* a certain class position without the *particular* theoretical practice for this reason corresponding to that of the same class.
- *The class-attitude*. The investment of one's class-stand in a particular practical problem. The attitude thus structures not the problematic, but the articulation of problems onto the problematic. The attitude is the *space of the answers*.

- *The class-study* or *class-culture*. The structure and instruments of the theoretical realm, insofar as they are charged with producing the legitimacy of the class-stand.[5]

It is clear that these terms are not necessarily linked. If we take, for example, the case of Tolstoy, to which I will return, we can say that

- his *class-being* defines him as a member of the land-owning aristocracy and anchors him in feudalism;
- his *class-stand* is that of the peasantry;
- his *class-attitude* is complex, depending on the negative or positive structure of the problem: an attitude *coherent with the stand* of the critique of the landowning regime, but also on the other hand *coherent with his class-being* in its vehement anti-socialism, and even in its hostility towards bourgeois liberalism;
- his *class-culture* is essentially bourgeois.

We see that the concepts Mao put in place solely for the sake of salvaging the validity of ancient artworks break up the simple relation of the writer to his class, disarticulating and recomposing it in such a way that it appears as a series of decentrings between the historical reality, ideology, and the aesthetic process. This distortion is what Lenin highlights in a famous witticism referring to Tolstoy: 'Before this Count there was no authentic *muzhik* in literature.'[6]

Unfortunately, Lenin, like Mao, takes these decentrings to be discrepancies that are certainly understandable, but in the final instance regrettable. No sooner are they theoretically pinpointed than they are practically designated as that which revolutionary art must reduce. Thus what

---

5   Mao Zedong, 'Talks at the Yenan Forum on Literature and Art (May 1942)', *Selected Works*, vol. 3 (Beijing: Foreign Languages Press, 1965), pp. 69–98.

6   See Maxim Gorky's recollection in *Lenin on Literature and Art*, p. 226.

reappears is the chiasmic discord of theory (art is ideological) and criticism (art tells the true), but in its inverted form:
in the evaluation of past works, what matters is to discover
by way of reduction a theoretical essence steeped in an ideological appearance. In the production of future works, the
ideological appearance should be reduced in such a way
that it manifests directly the theoretical truth. The regres-
sive reduction, which involved the concepts of decentring,
is here inverted in a progressive reduction, which dissolves
the specificity of this decentring. This is what enables the
dogmatic aberrations of socialist realism. If we want to
submit these descriptions to a fair judgment, I think we
can say the following: they have staked out what is essential (the decentring), but they have also inverted it into the
inessential. The desired art no longer fitted the concepts of
real art. The programmatic aspect of Marxist criticism hid
the true theoretical bearing of the descriptions and evaluations on the basis of which this programme pretended to
establish its truth: a remarkable example of a theoretical
project that is literally foreclosed by the normative productions it enables.

To my knowledge, we owe it to Pierre Macherey to
have problematized what was practised in the chiasmic
discordance between description and evaluation. In an
article in *La Pensée*, Macherey indeed posits the principle
of the irreducibility of the aesthetic process. We should not
confuse this process, he declares, either with the theoretical
grasping of reality or with the ideological process – even
if evidently, in Macherey's own words, the writer 'confronts' ideology: 'The analysis of a literary work will use
neither the scientific concepts used to describe the historical process, nor ideological concepts. It will require new
concepts which can register the literariness of the text.'[7]
Going one step further, Macherey explicitly introduces
the concept of reversal [*retournement*] to characterize

---

7   Pierre Macherey, 'Lénine critique de Tolstoï', *La Pensée* 121 (June
1965); 'Lenin, Critic of Tolstoy', *A Theory of Literary Production*, trans.
Geoffrey Wall (London: Routledge & Kegan Paul, 1978), p. 119.

the operation to which the work submits the ideological concepts: 'The spontaneous ideology ... is not simply reflected by the mirror of the book; ideology is broken, reversed [*retournée*], or turned inside out by it insofar as the elaboration of a specific form gives it a different status from being a state of consciousness.'[8] For Macherey, the artwork is not what translates ideology, nor what effaces it: it is what renders it visible, decipherable, insofar as it confers upon it the discordant unity of a form; exposed as content, ideology speaks of that whereof *it cannot speak* as ideology: its contours, its limits. The *mise en œuvre*, as elaboration of a specific form – that is, the assemblage of significations in a network of signs – affects ideology so to speak with an outside which is its inevitable reversal, since the law of ideology's functioning is the *closed infinity* of the specular relation, a closed infinity that cannot show its closure without breaking the mirror in which it is reduplicated.

In the metaphor of the visible, of ideology not known but shown, Macherey found the means to indicate, if not operate, the determination of the structural autonomy of the aesthetic process, at the same time as he announced the 'polemical' proximity of art and science.

But I am convinced that Pierre Macherey did not go all the way to the end with his idea. I would like to indicate the reason for this by commenting upon the following dogmatic statement, in which the concept of reversal figures.

STATEMENT 3

We must conceive of the aesthetic process not as a redoubling but as a reversal [*retournement*]. If ideology produces an imaginary reflection of reality, then the aesthetic effect produces in return [*en retour*] ideology as imaginary reality.

---

8 Macherey, 'Lenin, Critic of Tolstoy', pp. 132–3 (translation modified, as the English version skips precisely the term for *retournement*).

We might say that art repeats in the real the ideological repetition of this real. Nevertheless this reversal does not produce the real; it *realizes* its reflection.

Refusing to identify it with knowledge, Macherey nevertheless problematizes the decentring of literary production in relation to ideology. How does he schematize this decentring, and what are for him the successive operations of aesthetic theory? If I understand him correctly, we must take into consideration not two terms (the work and the real), but four: to think the relation of the work to the historical real implies the representation of a double unhinging of this relation – the ideological unhinging and the 'topological' unhinging, which concerns the 'place' or point of view of the author. In short, we would obtain a schema that looks like Figure 1.

Let us clearly fix the meaning of the words:

- By *real*, we must understand the global historical structure as it is scientifically determined. For example, in the case of Tolstoy, the real is the product of the combination of four terms in a displaceable structure-in-dominance: landowning aristocracy, bourgeoisie, peasant masses, working class.[9]
- *Ideologies* are organized in *series*. The theory of ideologies describes them as fragmentary meaningful reflections. They are defined 'by the ensemble of pressures upon the class they represent'.[10] In this way, for example, the peasant ideology reflects the structural position of the peasantry with regard to the economic and cultural domination of the bourgeoisie, the political domination of the landowning aristocracy, and the organizational and theoretical domination of the working class. Thus, it juxtaposes a revolutionary representation of the ends (critique of large landownership)

9   For the concept of structure-in-dominance, see Althusser, *For Marx*, pp. 200–18.

10   Macherey, 'Lenin, Critic of Tolstoy', p. 115 (translation modified).

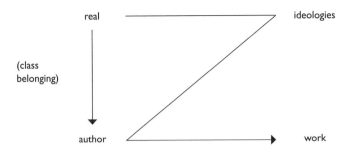

Figure 1 Schema in Z

with an archaic representation of the means (evangelical non-violence).

- By *author* we obviously should not understand a creative subjectivity, a projective interiority, and so on. The author is the concept of a place, defined as point of view – that is, situated theoretically in the ideological series. Thus, Tolstoy is assigned a mobile place, a displaced place: spontaneous representative of the landowning aristocracy, he is a peasant ideologue. Without a doubt this is where Mao's concepts must be invested: being, stand, attitude and culture. In other words, the concept of the author is not a psychological concept, but exclusively a topological one.

- The *work*, finally, maintains with its production the specific relation of decentring that is not a translation of point of view, but the donation of form and, thus, the exhibition of limits. In this sense, Tolstoy's novels are not treatises on peasant ideology but, in Lenin's expression, the 'mirror' of a Russian revolution that Tolstoy nevertheless could not understand at all.

This is the complex meaning of the schema in Z from Figure 1. And such as it is, this schema answers rather well the question that Macherey poses with regard to the structure of the problem: 'To study Tolstoy's work consists in showing which relations it maintains with the determinate historical structure.'[11] The schema in Z shows that this relation is not diagonal, direct, or even simply mediated by the author. In fact, it is a relation that is doubly decentred:

- first, by what we might call the ideological 'defile' in which the global historical structure announces itself in the metonymical reflection produced by one of its elements under the 'pressure' of the others;
- second, by the singular topology in which Tolstoy appears as a displaced element.

If, however, this description does not seem fully satisfying to us, it is because the very question that it poses is not entirely disengaged from an ideological perception of the literary work. Literary theory remains for Macherey the description of a relation – that is, the relating of the work's being, or its assemblage of signs, with its (ideological or historical) outside. To be sure, Macherey no doubt *deforms* the ordinary schema of ideological critique on two crucial points:

- The work for him is not a totality, but an effective multiplicity of levels.
- The relation of the work to its outside is not causal or analogical, but decentred.

However, more so than a rupture, this is in fact a deformation. And I see a sign of this pre-theoretical character in the fact that Macherey maintains the work as the *pertinent unity* of the object of critical study. For Macherey, whereof we must represent the discrepancy remains, at bottom, the relation real–work, conceived of as the ultimate problematic given.

But in reality it is within his conception of the aesthetic process that we must look for the last obstacle that

---

11   Ibid., p. 112 (translation modified).

separates Macherey from the conceptual construction of this very process, as well as for the possibility of this construction. Macherey manifestly thinks that art belabours certain ideological contents. Or again, he places the autonomy of the aesthetic process within the *operators* of transformation, but not in the transformed contents. The discrepancy that can be grasped from within the work itself lies precisely in the fact that there are heterogeneous elements or ideological generalities that figure in it: 'The work can only exist if it introduces into itself this alien term which precipitates an internal contradiction.'[12] Within the work there is the *other* as such, shown in its difference. The result is that the mapping of ideological and heterogeneous elements is presupposed in the explanation of the work as the production of a difference. From this point of view, the work remains internally related to that from which it differs. We should not be surprised to see that Macherey at this point is capable of retrieving and salvaging the vocabulary of expressive causality: as internal relation to its alterity, as immanent contradiction, the work is the phenomenon of internal difference; and whatever in the work belongs to presence takes its manifest value from that which is not manifested, from that which is kept in absence: 'The absence of certain reflections, or expression – that is the true object of criticism. The mirror, from certain sides, is a blind mirror: but it is still a mirror for all its blindness.'[13] In my language, I will say that for Macherey, the *effect of presence*[14] is the production of the fact that all ideologically produced meaning can only lie in absence. But the presence of this absence, for its part, can be pinpointed as something alien at the heart of whatever this absence itself renders present. It is its *material*.

I propose to show, on the contrary, that the autonomy of the aesthetic process blocks us from conceiving it as

---

12 Ibid., p. 127.
13 Ibid., p. 128 (translation modified).
14 See the discussion below. For me, the aesthetic effect is the *presence* of a signification.

relation. In this process, the effect of presence is not added
on to an effect of meaning produced outside of it, or, so
to speak, injected as the witness of difference. Indeed, no
element of the process is *by itself* ideological or aesthetic.
The problem of the *passage* from ideology to art cannot
be posed as such. An element is *produced* as ideological in
the structure of the aesthetic mode of production. Reversal
[*retournement*], rigorously speaking, does not mean that
the aesthetic process produces an effect of the presence
of signification (the process, in this case, would work on
ideological materials). Reversal means that the process
produces an effect of signification of presence, with presence itself being an effect of the process. This is why the
mode of production of reversal is *doubly* articulated: the
effect of signification is produced just as much as the effect
of presence.

In fact, I myself for a long time committed the same
mistake as Macherey. And I believe it consists in a phenomenon that is all too obvious in literary production, which
is the existence, within the immediate object, of *separable*
ideological contents.

I will call a statement of the novelistic discourse that
fulfils the following three conditions a 'separable ideological statement':

1. It produces in and of itself a complete effect of signification, without any enclaves.
2. It has the logical structure of a universal proposition.
3. It is not tied contextually to any subjectivity.

Let us take some examples from Robert Musil's *The Man
Without Qualities*:

   a. A statement like 'I am convinced that it is the impen-
      etrable cloud of so-called progress that has brought it
      down from its arch' fulfils none of the three criteria. It
      is *absolutely* inseparable:
      • The 'I' is an enclave whose sense can only be

determined by the context. The statement produces no complete effect of signification.

- It is a singular proposition, with 'individual support'.
- It is a phrase pronounced by Ulrich: it is of the type X [d(Y)] (X says [or thinks] that Y has such a property).

b. A statement like 'Automobiles shot out of deep, narrow streets into the shallows of bright squares' or 'The man without qualities whose story is being told was called Ulrich' do not fulfil condition 2. They are inseparable statements. They are of the type d(A) or d(X) (an object, or a character, has such-and-such a property).

c. A statement like 'All the psychic disorder of humanity, with its questions always unanswered, attaches itself to each particular question in the most disgusting way' satisfies conditions 1 and 2, but not condition 3. It is, in effect, a statement 'in quotation marks', a phrase spoken by Ulrich. Statements of this type can be said to be obliquely inseparable. They are of the type X[S] (X thinks that such an affirmation is universally true).

d. Finally, a statement such as 'The voice of truth is always accompanied by fairly suspect parasites, but those who are most interested want to know nothing about it' fulfils all three conditions. It is absolutely separable. We will call it type S.[15]

The – frequent – existence of separable statements (of the type S) seems to introduce *within* the work certain

---

15 See Robert Musil, *The Man Without Qualities*, trans. Sophie Wilkins (New York: Alfred A. Knopf, 1995). Elsewhere I will try to show that the specific efficacy of novelistic subjectivity, conceived as an aesthetic mode of production, is attached to obliquely inseparable statements, of the type X [S]. In this case, indeed, the inseparability of the ideological statement S is not automatic; it is a result that depends on a complex series of conditions. In other words, it is possible for the statement S actually to function as separable, if it falls within the domain of a subjectivity.

ideological witnesses of the difference produced by the work. Such statements indeed owe nothing to the structure of the work. They function in isolation. They thus bear witness, within the literary structure, to that which it is not. Hence, the work appears as the internal indication of its scission, and the essence of its power may well be, as Jacques-Alain Miller indicates in an unpublished text, the fissure it opens in wanting to close itself. Or rather: the fissure that it *operates* in transgressing towards the presence of its own text that which the text signifies anyhow. Indeed, let us compare the status of a statement of type S and a statement of type X[S] – that is, in the examples from Musil:

1. 'The voice of truth is always accompanied by rather suspect parasites' (S).
2. 'All the disorder of humanity attaches itself to each particular question in the most disgusting fashion' (X [S], thought by Ulrich).

Nothing separates them in their logical structure. But their *position* in the structure of novelistic discourse assigns to them two different functions, so that this difference exhibits what separates novelistic enunciation, in its specific efficacy, from ideological enunciation. In the first case, S is validated as such. It is not accompanied by any outside, except its negation. It is thus produced as *truth*, and requires an evaluation. In the second case, S is *reversed*, since it is differentiated: it is indeed a phrase pronounced by Ulrich. In other words, this time the statement is affected with an outside, which is the system of conditions that render possible this enunciation rather than any other *for Ulrich*. The discrimination between the statement and its negation here is not a question of evaluation; it is a question of subjective coherence, which requires the exteriority of the *formula of coherence* proper to the system of novelistic subjectivity. This outside is also, for S, the assignation of a *presence*. This statement is indeed present inasmuch as it draws its legitimacy from the novelistic system of 'someone speaks'. This system is the fundamental backdrop of its presence.

The gap between S and X[S] in this case would be the product of the novelistic structure. And this gap is attested in the novel itself, by the mention of an S that is not transformed: S ↔ X[S] would be the space traversed by the process, the space *figured* in the work itself.

But in reality, I think that this is not the way we must present things. For if S functions entirely in an ideological way, then it cannot indicate from within the process the effect of this process. Indeed, it is wholly exterior to it. Here again we must avoid confusing the object as given (the novel) with the aesthetic process. An absolutely separable statement figures empirically in the object. But it is in principle excluded from what guarantees the intelligibility of this object, since the effect of signification that it produces owes nothing to the law proper to the aesthetic process. In reality, such a statement is *ideologically* produced, and refers us back to the theory of ideologies. To take seriously the autonomy of the aesthetic process means first of all to reject from this process itself any element of which the theory of ideologies by itself produces the knowledge. And such is, by definition, the case of separable statements.

More generally, we must clearly understand that what the aesthetic practice 'belabours' – the generalities that it transforms – cannot be heterogeneous elements: the 'raw material' of the process of production is itself 'already' aesthetic. The aesthetic practice is incapable of aestheticizing ideological elements (for example); on the contrary, it knows how to ideologically signify certain 'perceptible' elements, certain specific presences produced according to determinate modes of production. We will make these remarks the object of a fourth dogmatic statement.

STATEMENT 4

What the aesthetic process transforms is *differentially homogeneous* to that which does the transforming. The 'raw material' of aesthetic production is already in itself aesthetically produced. The history of art thus possesses a regional autonomy. But this history by no means corresponds to the history of creators or their works. It is the theory of the *formation* and *deformation* of aesthetic generalities.

In order to fix the ideas, let us call E ( ) the function of aesthetic transformation applied to an element (which amounts to saying that the element takes place in a structure and is submitted to the efficacy of structural causality).[16] Let us call *i* a 'pure' ideological element (for example, an absolutely separable statement), *e* an aesthetic element, *s* the effect of signification, and *p* the effect of presence. I consider inadequate the following schema:

$$E\,(i) \to s, p$$

Heterogeneous elements cannot 'enter' as such into the aesthetic process so as to be reversed therein into presence. Or again: *i* cannot 'enter' into the process unless it is first assigned as aesthetic by the structure. In this way the schema would be that illustrated in Figure 2 (with the reservation that we distinguish two operations that in reality are only one).

$$E\,(i) \to e$$
$$\diagup$$
$$E\,(e) \to p, s$$

Figure 2

---

16   The theory of structural causality is still very obscure. My impression is that such a theory is impossible, if one sets out to provide it with formal models. It is to be feared that only *regional* theories are possible. From this point of view, and unlike Althusser, I fear grave difficulties in the 'passage' from historical materialism to dialectical materialism.

I will give an example from Fyodor Dostoevsky, a scene from *Demons*, in which Varvara Petrovna chases away the sweet liberal she protects, Stepan Trofimovich:

> this is what amazed me at the time: that he stood up with remarkable dignity ... under Varvara Petrovna's 'curse.' Where did he get so much spirit? ... This was a deep, *real* grief, at least in his eyes, for his heart. He had yet another grief at that moment, namely, his own morbid awareness that he had acted basely: this he confessed to me later in all frankness. And *a real, undoubted grief is sometimes capable of making a solid and steadfast man even out of a phenomenally lightminded one, if only for a short time; moreover, real and true grief has sometimes even made fools more intelligent, also only for a time, of course; grief has this property.* And, if so, then what might transpire with a man like Stepan Trofimovich? A whole revolution – also, of course, only for a time.
>
> He made a dignified bow to Varvara Petrovna without uttering a word.[17]

It is clear that the italicized passage is a separable segment, a statement of the type S. By this we understand that it could figure as such in a collection of maxims, since it states the general properties of grief; and that nothing *in it* announces the singularity, the presence of the novelistic effect: it is an abstract proposition.

Under what conditions, though, does this segment figure in a scene from a novel? What is the rule of possibility for its novelistic pertinence? It is clear that at the end of the paragraph the ideological universality of the statement appears as the means for a determinate gesture on behalf of Stepan Trofimovich, as a condition for the plausibility of this gesture. But precisely the presentification of the ideological universal in the 'exit' of the character requires a pre-transformation: the 'primary' aestheticization of this element is assured by the syntactical anchorings that free it from its ideological self-sufficiency: the initial 'And' and

---

17 Fyodor Dostoevsky, *Demons*, trans. Richard Pevear and Larissa Volokhonsky (New York: Alfred A. Knopf, 1994), p. 201.

the final 'And, if so' are what transforms the ideological
closure of the separable statement into an opening for presenting itself in the process as being *already* transformed.
We have – in a linear fashion – the following mode of
occurrence:

$$X\,[d(X)] - And \dots S - Thus - d(X)$$

The marginal anchorings of S do not affect its separability
as far as the content is concerned. But, *by opening it up to
inseparable statements, they produce a formal effacement
of this separability.* We could make use of a topological
comparison.[18] One and the 'same' interval can be considered either as open $]a,b[$ or as closed $[a,b]$. A closed
interval is, so to speak, signed by its borders and contained
by them. By contrast, an open one plunged into a straight
line no longer has anything to distinguish it. We will say
that a separable statement enters into the homogeneity of
the aesthetic process only if it is open, in the sense that it
is certainly closed but *no longer contains its closure.* In the
example above, the element *i*, delivered from its closure by

---

18 I say: a comparison. The epistemological status of topology in
psychoanalysis and in the theory of the signifier is, according to Jacques
Lacan, much more ambitious: it is 'really', and not as a figure, that the relation of signifier/signified can be seen as presentified in the Möbius strip.
Allow me to find this affirmation adventurous. For if it is a matter of a real
identity, we will have to announce clearly that henceforth the theory of the
signifier is a branch of topology, a special mathematics. Conversely, if what
is at stake is a resemblance, a metaphor, this should not make one think
that this theory has been furnished with the slightest bit of supplementary
scientificity. Gaston Bachelard, whose teaching remains unknown in spite
of all the hat-tipping to which he is subject, has shown that the relation of
mathematics to the sciences that rely on it was neither a relation of identity,
nor a relation of analogy, nor finally an instrumental one. Between the
Möbius strip and Saussure's doctrine, between the signifying chain and the
algorithm with which Gottlob Frege tries – moreover in vain – to construct
number, we are far from tying together the specific relations that would
guarantee the rigour of a new object-of-knowledge. For in each case, either
what is operating is merely an impotent *image*, or else what we find, not as
produced but as unsuccessfully *translated* – that is, repeated – is only the
rigour of the first object: the mathematical object.

syntactical anchors, is an element *e*. It can thus function in turn in the production of the scene's effect of presence: in fact, in its open form, it is entirely *reversed* in the end in the dignity with which Stepan makes a bow. This gesture contains in its presence the implication of the intelligence of grief. It is the presence of the opened-up generality.

You can see how I seek to preserve the autonomy of the aesthetic process. No doubt, presence is a reality effect. No doubt, too, signification refers in the final instance (at the level of its 'reception') to the ideological series. But the *double effect* is articulated in a way that is homogeneous within the aesthetic process, without allowing generalities of another order to enter and remain in it. Thus, we should replace Macherey's schema in Z with the problematic schema represented in Figure 3.

On this basis we could develop the theory of aesthetic modes of production, or simply: theoretical aesthetics. Here it is not possible to give an idea of the problems that would be raised in still so evanescent a discipline. But since I started with dogmatic statements, I will end in the same way, conscious though I am of having opened up many more enigmas than I have tried to solve.

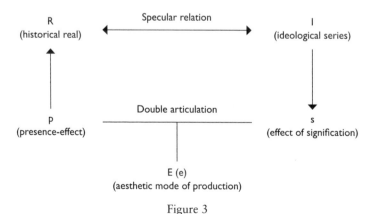

Figure 3

STATEMENT 5

By 'aesthetic mode of production', we understand the combination of factors whose effect is to operate the reversal. To operate the reversal means to give an ideological function to certain real-imaginary elements that are regionally produced by a historically determined state of the aesthetic process.

STATEMENT 6

To be more precise: an aesthetic mode of production is an invariant and invisible structure that distributes ways of linking real elements in such a way that these elements can *function* as ideological.

Remark: an aesthetic mode of production is by no means an art, like music or painting. Modes of production are transversal to the classification of the arts. Figurative space, for which Pierre Francastel in *Peinture et société* (*Painting and Society*) seeks to establish the genealogy, is a mode of production, not painting in general. Similarly, the tonal system, the metric system of Greek verse, and the system of novelistic subjectivity are, no doubt, modes of production.

STATEMENT 7

An aesthetic mode of production is manifested in a double articulation:

- that which assembles the operators of transformation (presence-effect).
- that which concerns elements transformed by the place prescribed to them by the operators (effect of signification).

But the structural reality of the mode of production lies in the mechanism by which the first 'encounter' the second.

Indeed, the operators are nowhere given other than in the elements, since the structure as such is invisible. There is thus a vectoral, or oriented, reality to the process of production: one can figure it as a 'field' in which are *distinguished* two hierarchical regions. One is the region of the operators, the other the region of the thematic elements. But the operators are themselves thematic so that their presence in the structured field is simply given as the encounter, or *double function*, with the characteristic asymmetry that makes it such that the first function renders possible the second, according to a rule (the visible *i*) that is the structure itself.

STATEMENT 8

The theory of an aesthetic mode of production supposes:

I) The definition of its elementary articulation.
II) The synchronic law of its effect (production of a new reality as ideological).
III) The diachronic law of the conditions for the *conservation* of its efficacy. (A real element that is 'ideologized' indeed risks henceforth becoming ideologically repeated, that is, *non-transformed*. In that case, it remains undoubtedly ideological, but the process that integrates it into 'the work of art' is itself ideological and not aesthetic. Or again, within the aesthetic process itself, the ideological element functions as such *on its own*).

STATEMENT 9

The complete intelligibility of an aesthetic mode of production presupposes that one conceives of its *genealogy*, that is to say, the process of the dissolution of the mode, anterior or contemporary to it, whose elements are rearticulated in the mode under investigation.

11

WHAT DOES LITERATURE THINK?

It would not be hard to say what literature knows. It knows the generic human subject. It knows its failings and its weaknesses and, on the basis of that knowledge, transforms the inevitability of resignation. Resignation to the fact that, as in one of the very first examples of the *Bildungsroman*, *Wilhelm Meister's Apprenticeship*, the world never lives up to the Idea; or, as in the earliest naturalist novels, by Émile Zola, resignation in the face of ignominious social conditions. In its lowest form, this is knowledge of a sort of dismal moderation of the real, compared with the wild assertions of theory – and of philosophy, in particular. Literature knows inside out the workings of deceit, ungratefulness, selfishness and stupidity. Literature serves as a 'critique'; it is often praised for its aggressive or morose insights, or congratulated on its 'lucidity' when, like Louis-Ferdinand Céline, it aspires to make 'little music' of our wretchedness.

Even Marcel Proust, as fine a writer as he may be, spends a very long time, and a great many volumes, exploring the interminable web of degradation and vanity, cruelty and resentment, absurdity, smugness and murky innermost sentiments, before finding salvation in the Second Coming

of writing; before discovering the only thing that matters –
and which marks the transition from knowledge to thought:
the victories of which humanity is capable. The 'supra-sen-
sual hour' that Henry James describes in connection with
the hero of *The Ambassadors*; Samuel Beckett's 'blessed
times of blue' in *How It Is*; the enchanted death of Prince
Andrei in *War and Peace*; Julie's testament in *The New
Heloise*; the peasants' procession around the wounded
airmen in Malraux's *Man's Hope* ... or Conrad's novel,
entitled simply *Victory*.

The idea that literature thinks, and that writers might
be thinkers, as Natacha Michel argues in an essay on contemporary prose, can only mean that it opens up the realm
of the particular – subtle psychological insights, social
differences and cultural specificities – to the field of knowledge.[1] For that must mean, as we know from experience
when a novel secures a victory in our own minds, that
literature's effect takes place at the level of thought.

What should the word 'thought' be taken to mean in
this instance? First of all, that there is an encounter with
a real, beyond the fictional world, which is its triumph,
and at the peril of language, which is its Assumption.
Beyond the fictional world, literature that thinks emerges
in the cracks in the story [*la fable*]. It has no interest in
wrecking the story, in contradicting it or pulling it to
pieces. It accepts the story and settles down in the spaces
it leaves.

I will turn briefly to my own work as a novelist. In
Calme bloc ici-bas (1997), I borrowed the form and characters for the story, as well as the relation between story
and History, from Victor Hugo's novel, *Les Misérables*. But
I pulled apart the building blocks of the narrative, rear-
ranged the spaces, and allowed my prose to explore areas
outside its initial scope.

I employed language in three distinct registers – narrative, rhetoric and shorthand – in the hope that a few

---

1 *Translator's note*: See Natacha Michel, *L'écrivain pensif* (Paris:
Verdier, 1998).

grains of the real would emerge from this clash of styles.[2]

In the essay to which I referred earlier, Natacha Michel proposes another method: that of allowing an 'other' language to take root in the language itself, with the reader witnessing the birth of a unique language.

In any case, the complicity between fiction and language aims to mark the real with the seal of the unique, of the One, of that which has never taken place prior to this complicity (this work) and will never appear again.

Literature thinks insofar as it brands a real pursued by fiction with the symbolic scar of the One. This gives rise to an essentially finite quality – common, in fact, to all artistic procedures – encapsulated in the word 'work' (of art). There is the 'unique language' of the writer; the binding of every work in the form of a Book, even if, as Mallarmé preferred, it is in 'several volumes'; the double meaning of the word 'end' – that signified by the word at the bottom of the last page, and that which the literary enterprise is compelled to bring to any sequence, whether we like it or not; and, last but not least, the standard of perfection. A work of literature is such – must, indivisibly, be such – that nothing in it can be changed. Each and every word of its prose is irreplaceable.

In stark contrast to the infinite variety of experience (which is perfectly obvious), the work of art or literature is the difficult, unlikely production of the finite. And it is precisely this production that constitutes thought.

The maxim of art-thought is simple: to produce something finite (artificial) to rival the infinite (natural).

I used the words 'work of art or literature', but what does 'literature' actually mean? Literature is a singular configuration which, unlike poetry, tends not to appear in the ranking of fine arts. In his analysis of categories of nineteenth-century aesthetics, Jacques Rancière makes some striking observations on the genealogy of modern

---

2   Alain Badiou, *Calme bloc ici-bas* (Paris: P.O.L., 1997).

meanings of the word 'literature'.[3] Not only does it fail to obtain the patronage of any of the Muses of classicism, but it cuts across literary genres: clearly, 'literature' cannot be confined to poetry, but neither is it restricted to the novel, the story or the essay. It refers to the development of a sort of literary exception in the field of art. The concept of this exception gradually takes shape in France, from Baudelaire to Blanchot, with contributions from Flaubert and Proust, although Lacoue-Labarthe and Nancy, in a book entitled, significantly, *The Literary Absolute*, have shown that it originated in Germany or, more precisely, in German romanticism.[4] Writing is granted absolute status by the exception, which not only raises it above classical genres, but puts it entirely beyond the scope of the empirical world. Thus, literature is an immanent reference to itself, a mark of its own self-sufficiency. It comprises Flaubert's prose, which, thanks to its style (a crucial operator in literature), the author intended to exist in its own right, with no imaginary referent in the world. It might equally be one of Mallarmé's sonnets, which he described as 'finished, existing, it takes place all by itself', or conceiving perfectly of itself.[5]

Of course, the advent of literature also corresponds to the emergence of a literary conscience, a conscience not exactly comparable to artistic judgment, since it relates not to rules of taste but to the conviction of the existence of an entirely separate phenomenon: the literary fact, as compact and distinct as an Idea.

---

3 *Translator's note*: See Jacques Rancière, *The Flesh of Words: The Politics of Writing*, trans. Charlotte Mandell (Stanford: Stanford University Press, 2004); and *Mute Speech: Literature, Critical Theory, and Politics*, trans. James Swenson (New York: Columbia University Press, 2011).

4 *Translator's note*: See Philippe Lacoue-Labarthe and Jean-Luc Nancy, *The Literary Absolute: The Theory of Literature in German Romanticism*, trans. Philip Barnard and Cheryl Lester (Albany, NY: SUNY Press, 1988).

5 *Translator's note*: See Stéphane Mallarmé, 'Restricted Action', in *Divagations*, trans. Barbara Johnson (Cambridge: Harvard University Press, 2007), p. 190 (translation modified).

But does this Ideal separation, obtained through stylistic density alone, not require the Idea to be fully self-conscious? In other words, if literature is a form of thought, must it not be the thought of that thought? We know about Mallarmé's revelation, or the crucial experience that inspires his poetry: 'My thought has thought itself, and I am utterly dead.'[6] This means that the poem as absolute requires it to be the thought of the thought that it is, and that the author should be excluded, since the author merely imagines the basic Idea, leaving it to deploy the various facets of its self-reflection, since the 'Master has gone to draw tears from the Styx'.[7]

But if literature's role is to allow fulfilment of the Idea as thought of thought, the author's task must not only be to marry his or her style with the initial production of the basic Idea, but also to ensure, explain, and stage the coming-into-being of the Idea as thought.

Thus, literature is always accompanied by successive manifestos of its becoming-absolute. The age of literature is also the age of literary manifestos, combining a diagnosis of the time (from Mallarmé's 'Crisis of Verse' to Natacha Michel's 'second modernity', not forgetting Breton's prophecy ['Beauty shall be convulsive or shall not be at all']) with a preferred procedure (hermeticism, self-reflexive writing, metaphor ...) which, at any one time, contains the essence of the literary phenomenon.

We can therefore make the following assertion: that what literature thinks is both a real marked in language with the seal of the One, and the conditions governing the way that real is marked. The thought process of writing is the conjunction, under the finite sign of the One, of the

---

6   *Translator's note*: See Stéphane Mallarmé, 'Letter to Henri Cazalis (14 May 1867)', in *Selected Letters of Stéphane Mallarmé*, ed. and trans. Rosemary Lloyd (Chicago: The University of Chicago Press, 1988), p. 74.

7   *Translator's note*: See Stéphane Mallarmé, '(With her pure nails offering their onyx high)', in *Collected Poems and Other Verse*, trans. E. H. Blackmore and A. M. Blackmore (Oxford: Oxford University Press, 2006), p. 69.

autonomous forces of language and the immanent occurrence of a real.

There are two questions to be asked about literature:

1. With regard to the real: what takes place, which is not from the empirical world, which is 'anywhere outside the world', and which is worth organizing into thought so that it can be encountered beyond the fictional world?
2. With regard to language: what takes place in the language, which might be equivalent to the real that-which-has-taken-place?

Literature can be represented as a graph with two axes, neither of which is literary per se. The first axis corresponds to the real as that-which-has-taken-place, or the non-empirical essence of all reality. Although it is left out of any ordinary story or prefabricated narrative, this is the real of which literature must speak. I do not believe, as Blanchot sometimes suggests, that this is the original silence with which all language draws strength from the infinite. The point is to open up to the realm of thought the singularity of whatever takes place outside that realm. Literature is a direct contradiction of Wittgenstein's axiom ('Whereof one cannot speak, thereof one must be silent'), since its first, essentially non-literary axis is the imperative to speak of the unspeakable of that-which-has-taken-place.

The second axis is language, as a flexible resource with infinite power, by all means – but not, in this case, employed for what it is capable of saying, rather exploited mercilessly for what it has not yet said, or what it has always been reluctant or unable to say. Writers are the torturers of language; they extract confessions and even, perhaps – and therein comes the danger – lies.

The literary act – sometimes called 'writing' – is like plotting a graph along these two axes. It can be drawn as in Figure 4.

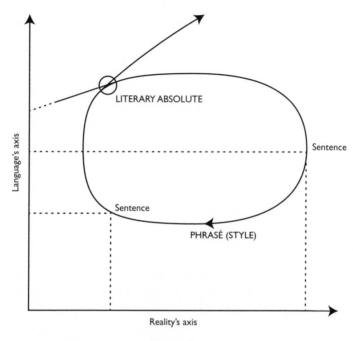

Figure 4

Every point along the graph can be called a 'sentence' [*phrasé*]. Each sentence indexes a real against a break in language. The active movement that joins two sentences together (with other sentences) can be called 'phrasing' [*phrasé*]. The laws that govern phrasing, which only become discernible afterwards, can be called the 'style'. The truly remarkable thing is that the graph of the literary act is always closed in certain places: a closed area (or areas) exist(s) because certain points are always drawn twice, becoming double points. If no such points exist, then the literary act constitutes a failure: the infinite dissemination of its linear emptiness; the total absence of the real; boring prose and conventional style.

The double point means three things. It repeats language, at a particular point in its own expression. Let us say that it produces knowledge of its creative innocence and, in so doing, puts an end to that innocence. For the perverse aspect of the double point is that literary desire is always, at least at some point, knowledge of its own form – a kind of calculated self-interest inflicted upon innocence. It asserts that thought is also thought of thought, turning its own thinking, at least in certain places, into a closed area, and a glimpse of the gap between inside and outside. The literary act commemorates its journey with a monument.

Lastly, it shows the same real point twice, making it impossible to discern from that point the beginning of the movement and the point that is ultimately reached. Like Proust's madeleine, the real point becomes an absolute, in which it is impossible to distinguish origin from destination. It escapes being situated in time. It is, in the literary work itself, the scar of its eternity.

In fact, this point is what we encounter in a work of literature, far beyond what we read there. It is the literary act itself, transmitted, and submitted, to us (for in this case transmission and submission are one and the same). It fulfils the pre-Socratic maxim: 'It is all the same to me from what point I begin; for I shall return again to this same point.' This double point is the symbolic seal of the One, the real of the real, which is also, to use Henry James's lovely expression, 'the figure in the carpet'. It was to this figure that the Romantics gave the most appropriate, and extravagant, of names: the literary absolute, which belongs to all eternal writing.

First translated by Alistair Clarke,
revised by Bruno Bosteels

12

A REQUIEM FOR THE FACTORY: ON FRANÇOIS BON'S *SORTIE D'USINE*

Everything hinges upon a point that François Bon, the author of *Sortie d'usine*, makes just before he finishes: 'That which could be different has not yet begun.'[1]

The factory is here the metaphor of the tomb of time. Its unspeakable self-sameness is divided in the book into four 'weeks', but one week here is only the name of one chapter, and one chapter in turn is only a unity of indifference. Whatever functions as event, even the strike, cannot make it into a chapter, since it repeats that which already, as always in the past, is part of the rule. The factory is only the social name of Kafka's Castle, whose reading meant for François Bon the discovery of the links between writing and truth.

We have already been able to read in *Le Perroquet* that the factory, for those authors who make it into their running theme, belongs to the metaphysics of the place.[2] The factory both prescribes and annuls the workers,

---

1 François Bon, *Sortie d'usine* (Paris: Minuit, 1982), p. 167.

2 See the article by Natacha Michel on Leslie Kaplan's *L'excès-l'usine*, 'Rien n'aura eu lieu que le lieu', in *Le Perroquet: Quinzomadaire d'opinion* 8 (8–22 April 1982), pp. 1, 12.

insofar as their substance, trapped in its rule, excludes their thinking. François Bon reorients this theme from the side of death. The central ritual, called 'The Passage', is the one in which whoever dies in the factory – and there are many people who die – is transported on a pallet through the workshops in the midst of a special racket in which everyone participates, even the boss who has come down for the occasion and who thus greets in the worker only his cadaver.

Wounds and death are the only punctuations in this abstract uniformity of gestures. But these representations merely concentrate what is the case: in truth, whoever is in the factory is already dead. The factory is, in the strict sense, the beyond of society. Not its hell, but rather its limbo. The few 'characters' that can be found there are myths of sorts, since always integrated into the architecture of the place, like this father figure, Thomas, surrounded by bizarre butterflies, in whom we recognize – since he pushes the cart with the dead – the Passer, the Charon of the factory-Styx.

Since the author tackles the social place of death, he knows that, because he himself has left this place, whatever truth he delivers is susceptible of being misrecognized. The factory is that place one does not exit: 'They [the workers] would not recognize themselves in his saying.' The fact of there being an 'exit from the factory' attests to the fact that one writes only from the outer edges of the truth. Its immanence excludes its utterance.

In order to come as close as possible to the truth in one's approach, however, a fairly neutral technique is needed, a special touch that respects 'the factory as an evidence closed in on itself'.[3] The author borrows from the toolbox of the *nouveau roman*: 'Then another corridor, to the right the escalator, which is working today, pure chance, down to the big room, the vast underground chamber where the long lines come across a printing press'.[4] The underlying philosophy of this descriptive apparatus consists in

3 Bon, *Sortie d'usine*, p. 162.
4 Ibid., p. 7.

guaranteeing the dominant grip of space over time. The factory, so to speak, is anti-Hegelian. If for Hegel time is the presence of the concept, here time, devoid of all meaning, succumbs to exteriority. We also note the ellipsis, in the phrasing of the sentences, of most syntactic connections that would clarify the subordinate clauses (circumstances, causes, concessions). The flattening out of meaning juxtaposes mere observations of fact, and whether they are subjective ought not to have any effect. For example: 'Less in any case than for cigarettes, the line that he had to go through, he does not smoke'.[5]

The text drops the 'buts', the 'becauses', the 'ifs', the 'at leasts' and the 'whos', 'thats', 'whoses' and 'wheres' – shavings thrown here and there in the sharpening of the sentences. The book itself is worked like a factory – compact, gathered up in a block of time without incidents or scoria. I see in this the tracking down and elimination of all subject effects for the integral service of the place. What matters is that nothing be an exception.

Someone might object that there are also long explanations – either technical, as in the bravura piece on the transpallet,[6] or genealogical, as in the hypotheses on the origin of the rite of passage,[7] or symbolic, as in the gloss on the pornographic pictures taped on the workbenches, or on the role of obscenity in the workers' speech.[8] However, insofar as an interpretation marks a break, we cannot say that François Bon is interpreting here. On the contrary, starting from an object that is supposed to be unknown to the reader (the transpallet), or from the workers' rituals, the explanation is meant to smoothen the rough edges off the obstacle, to eliminate the effect of the bizarre, and slowly to lead back to the neutral confirmation of the law. Thus with regard to the workers' language: 'As if these games of transvestism, this pornographic façade, prolonged the

---

5   Ibid.
6   Ibid., pp. 42–6.
7   Ibid., pp. 91–8.
8   Ibid., pp. 51–61.

order that they pretended to mock and were invested with the same indigence as the hierarchy that subdued them'.[9]

The second literary technique is essential, insofar as it confronts the abject temptation of any worker's prose: populism, the paternal gaze upon extant miseries, the self-satisfied gap between the narrative dignity and the vulgar human materials. The bravura of the book lies in not seeking to sidestep this risk. François Bon restores the spontaneous speech of the workers, but not in the form of dialogue (though it does so, for example, on page 87) but in a procedure of integration-reconstruction in which this language comes to glue itself onto the general neutrality, like gravel stuck in the cement of the text. If I read: 'He didn't like it when they came to bug him in his corner, sure thing. Elderly as in old-style, certainly, but nothing supernatural', I observe that the adjective 'supernatural' by itself reduces the interpolations from the spontaneous lexicon ('bug', 'sure thing') back to their status of ordinary materials, without any vocation for imitative restitution, but in line with the style's objective logic. There is no talking 'like workers' in this book. Rather, we should say that the worker's speech – equivalent to the transpallet, the strike, the clocking in, or the machine grease ('The grease is worse than gangrene')[10] – is one element of the factory-tomb, of the headstone erected by production in honour of the thousands of dead hours of the dead. The full form of these epitaph-like functions of language can be found in the capitalized version of a worker's aphorism, like those of a deaf co-worker ('It's not worth it to hear the shit that people tell'), set off from the main text, as proverbs rather than quotations, as harsh and solitary as the machines.

And yet, will there be poetry? Yes, sometimes – 'The sky is really transparent now, inside the light bulbs would not have been clearer than daylight, but in the grey zones some heavy dark clouds lingered on, torn apart by the wind

9   Ibid., p. 57.
10   Ibid., p. 47.

that made the rain hit them in the face'[11] – except that
poetry is the general envelope of closure, the open site of
the closed, while at the same time it fixates the distinction
of the seasons, which is useless for the thickened time of
the factory.

In short, this book has great quality. Speaking for myself,
I would say that the effect that is most external to its intent
is one of nostalgia. We might imagine that the factory is the
most astonishing novelty for prose, or for art in general. In
ten years, even though there has been May '68 and thousands of intellectuals established in the factory, how many
attempts have there been so far? Four, if we limit ourselves
to the worthy ones.[12] However, the impression is that of
a very old thing, always named, always taken up again.
By themselves, these four books define the stable law of
a genre. One senses that this genre pre-exists the books
themselves and will henceforth prosper all by itself, based
on a supposed essence of the factory, of which it suffices to
realize the different manifestations. Rather than a beyond,
the factory here marks a beneath. It has always been caught
in writing – albeit in the void. François Bon bears witness
to this perennial nature of the factory: 'Yes the reversal
was accomplished that in the end tilted the writing of the
factory over into the factory as writing'.[13] This 'reversal'
exhibits a pre-fixed written structure, an eternal inscription of the place. In whatever way you produce prose from
the factory, you will only nostalgically bear witness to this
inscription. We therefore must invert Godard's statement in
'Passion': the factory or work cannot be shown or filmed.
But no! The opposite is true! Factory-work has always
been shown, exhibited, written out. There is no need to do
so, since this only produces the retroactive conviction of

---

11   Ibid., p. 111.

12   Bruno Barth, *Les dos ronds; ou, Le retour en esclavage* (Paris:
Gallimard, 1973); Robert Linhart, *L'établi* (Paris: Minuit, 1978); Leslie
Kaplan, *L'excès-l'usine* (Paris: P.O.L., 1994); and the novel that is the
subject of these pages.

13   Bon, *Sortie d'usine*, p. 164.

something that is always already done. Capital has always written the factory.

Thus, Godard was also right. If this showing has always already been done, this is because there remains a leftover, which is unrepresented. François Bon arrives at the same conclusion: 'Such was the sought-after truth. But from this truth he remained desperately isolated'.[14]

Let us move beyond the metaphysics of the tomb of time. If the factory oscillates between pre-inscription and the unsayable, this is because it is caught in the trappings of its function as a machine and subtracted from its true essence, which is to be a political place, a production of truths. In the book-factories of our time we can see the ravages of an old mode of thinking – the one for which the prescription of the factory takes place on the basis of the productive economy, to which can then be opposed only the social (the strike). François Bon excels in showing that the strike is part of one and the same body together with the machinic place, of which it is the provisory inversion – just as reading *L'Humanité*, for that matter, is no different from the pornographic gloss. François Bon, the metaphysician descended from Kafka, just like Linhart, the Leninist, is to the same degree a victim of the old Marxism. Because if it is true that the factory structures the opposition between the constraints of capital and the social consciousness of labour, it does not follow that its active essence, its Marxist signification, can be resolved into these two terms. This is true only for the old Marxism and the workers' movement that is dead today. If you want to write the prose of the factory, you must – except if you opt for the figure of repetition – begin from that which constitutes an immanent exception: the new forms, punctual and scattered, of political consciousness. It is moreover from there that repetition itself becomes readable.

Old Marxism, old factory. François Bon's book assembles a metaphor that it cannot govern. Its factory, with its

---

14   Ibid., p. 163.

separated machines and French professionals, is part of an industrial past that the crisis is slowly annihilating. It is true that these factories of 600 workers on their work-benches are opaque and funerary places. It should not come as a surprise that death is present in them: it is a place that historically has been defeated and destroyed in terms of what interests us – that is, the innovations of worker consciousness, the labour of the subjective. If you want to know what is being said today about the factory, starting from the factory, go and look for it in those work-shops of special workers, in which a mass of immigrants are contradictorily being integrated into society.

François Bon's headstone is that of the old workers' movement in France.

The factory-genre is literally stillborn, even in its best products. We must pass from the abstract theme, eaten by the causality of lack, of 'the truth of the factory', to the active theme, which is in excess over the place, of the factory as a space for the production of the political truths of the moment.

We need a Marxist art, and not a metaphysical ode to the old Marxism.

13

ON THE PROSE OF
NATACHA MICHEL

War displaces the parts of the world, rather than annihilating its totality; you obtain some deported borders and
fragments, some places reserved for nothingness and others
for the troops, shadowplay and usual customs – though
different from what they once were and stirring up a dislocated geography. Such is the great organic metaphor with
which Natacha Michel designates the war to come, that of
the great powers, as an experiment for the whole human
earth to slide over itself, so that the end of stable references
and familiar connections may lay bare the essence of what
once was, of which the old order carried the effect only so
as to better hide its aim.

War is here the real of dispersion in which is inaugurated the licit narration of the subject of passions.

Previously unmarked, the frontier that separates and
conjoins men and women is all too often crossed in

---

1 Natacha Michel, *Le Repos de Penthésilée* (Paris: Gallimard,
1980).

everyday life for us to know where to find its riverbed or its beacon. But here this frontier is fixed by the revelation of catastrophe and provisionally assigned the bitter law of the duality of worlds.

Wanderers united among themselves, the women – the Amazons – rise up in arms and traverse the mutilated earth according to a nomadic principle in which each halting point reconstitutes the rightful usages in the service of life, nourishment, children, beauty. Without making concessions to the languid togetherness among women that was prevalent some time ago, Natacha Michel displays the productive firmness and radiant consistency of that which offers itself no longer as before in the invisible pores of duration, of the day or the week, but in its unified principle and its self-sufficiency.

To be sure, these women mean politics and war; they are a helping hand, whether fair or violent, against the fascists and the barbarians of the great powers. The foundations of several possible centuries are here laid down, albeit in the sombre respite of a disaster. The women here constitute a complete civilization, which authorizes the writer to adopt a particular tone in the book – one instituted by narrative brevity, like someone who would find certainty in the imminence, both calm and perpetual, of a departure that was formerly impeded.

The name of this dissolved state, its reflection, is: *Penthesilea*.

The society of men is named after Achilles; it is also built on the resistance against the worst. Achilles, for his part, claims that he has always thought that woman does not exist. This conviction confers upon him the tranquillity of someone who is pleased with himself, at the cost paid by all opaque persons: an exaggerated clarity in his speech. He is thus divided from those (Ulysses, for example) who still hold woman in the myth of restlessness and excess, and who are eaten up by aggressiveness for not knowing whether their barrack-room habits, or their nascent bureaucracy, may rightfully claim to present a total picture of life.

However, these men have the advantage over Achilles of a tortuous sense of the charade and a violent sense of reality, which they want to believe to be real.

Notice how you will not obtain all this until the end of the book, in the precipitation of an attempt at establishing an elective affinity – of Achilles with Penthesilea – wherein love, revoked by the fiction of the world in tatters, comes back just in time to die. And thus love is seized, not so much in its heritage and its self-evidence of 'that goes without saying', as in its founding ellipsis.

Natacha Michel's book obeys the rule of truth's retroactive movement. For the intermediate path is entirely made up of suspended memory. In the museum of the Amazons is kept, for the purposes of inquiry and assessment, the last love story of the world, that of Pierre and Urania, itself invented in the midst of past politics, the politics of an organization in which women and men could still recognize themselves in the identity of a place and let themselves be governed by the same cause.

This museum, which thus summons in its silent and multiple details both the point of weakness, onto which the separating fracture will graft itself, and the vague nostalgia of that eternal provisional solution in which both love and work, with the aid of the revolution, still had the power to constitute a link, whereas we know that any link is so revocable that nothing less than God was needed to name the irrevocable.

If love no longer can count on the Church, it draws its transparency in the world from being nothing more than the promise of a promise.

Besides, the temporal operator of the museum also solves a technical problem of modern prose, which is in conflict, as we all know, with linear storytelling. What this museum arranges is already staged and concentrated in the enigma of its sense and caught in the void by whatever the Amazons, regents and guardians of a memory which is not theirs either, would like the museum to represent, other than the separation of the present. We are told of the love

between Pierre and Urania as the legend of a legend, put
into a perspective of flight and indecision that the prose,
this time attentive and ramified to the extreme, keeps in
a changing and always amicable light, protected from all
anxiety and even from all tension.

The reader is thus recompensed for following the astonishing portrait of this Pierre, the man who loves a woman
like a woman may dream that the Other loves her according to her own rule of love. I say the reader, but I should
rather refer to the walker of prose who no longer holds on
to the guardrail of an anecdote but rather sticks to the interior sculptures, the ornamented paving stones, on which
her patience recognizes the oblique arrival of the sun.

And the suppleness of the metaphoric chains, this suc-
culent art in which Natacha Michel excels, results in a style
in which the advance of History – as in the surprising scene
in which Pierre and Urania, both militants in the revolutionary organization, we should recall, receive the order
to gather and disband in the midst of the crowd, which in
turn fashions itself into the subject confronting the fascist
gangs – instead of posing behind the characters of a love
story like the usual heavy trappings of a décor, seems to
burst forth from within the same whirling necessity.

In doing this, Michel's prose, as was already evident in
her 1975 novel *La Chine européenne* (*Europe's China*),
is particularly modern, seeking out a mode of caesura
between History and histories so that they would be
neither alternating slices nor painted stage settings, nor
'Fabrice at Waterloo'[2] – but something that is both ductile
and structured at the same time: the replacement of the
before-and-after with the spiral in which, without our
noticing it, the analytical drift of the slightest behaviour
leads us to the local riot and on to world war, from where a
set of subtle counter-effects, focalizing metaphorically on a

---

2 *Translator's note*: A reference to the grandiose realist style of the
famous scene that puts Fabrizio del Dongo in Napoleon's army during the
battle of Waterloo, in Stendhal's *The Charterhouse of Parma*, trans. John
Sturrock (New York: Penguin, 2006).

single detail, bring us back to the meaning of, say, a particularly masculine way of shaving, and so on and so forth.[3]

The spiralling prose of Natacha Michel, constantly composed of a telescope and a microscope, is put to major uses of which she herself is just beginning to perceive the full extent and foresee the principal consequence.

Taken as a whole, the book is a mirror of utopias.

The 'last love', Pierre's for Urania, other than the temporal limbo in which the museum presentation of the pre-war era leaves it, explicitly ends in failure and an element of undecipherability. Back in Paris, or rather showing up in a bachelor's room with more precision than a Platonic Idea, Urania is petrified by a sorrow that we guess, almost in between the lines, is due to the death of her mother, or the death of the archetypal Mother, as if the imminent war had produced, on the eve of the historic wipe-out, the necessary end of feminine filiations so that the Amazons, though mothers, would be the daughters only to themselves. Pierre, leaning over with the intelligent and maximal tenderness that a wave of fine writing bestows upon him all along, nonetheless finds no means to measure in knowledge whatever is found there that is incommensurable. Love is no more than the gaze, without concept, which is valid only for the moment, without duration.

As for the elective alliance, at the harshest point of the battle, with which Penthesilea aims at Achilles, and which applies to the singular but not to the multiple, it ends in the very cruel image of the devoured heart – the only point where Natacha Michel crosses paths with Heinrich von Kleist, to whom she has left the totality of the myth of Penthesilea.[4] Such a fusion in death would bequeath to us, in terms of the origin of love, only the repetition of Wagner's Tristan, were it not precisely for the fact that, at

---

3 See Natacha Michel, *La Chine européenne* (Paris: Gallimard, 1975).

4 *Translator's note*: A reference to Heinrich von Kleist's 1808 *Trauerspiel* rendered as *Penthesilea: A Tragic Drama*, trans. Joel Agee (New York: Michael di Capua Books, 1988).

this point of the story, the balanced retroaction sends us back to Pierre and Urania, as the future anterior of that for which the fury of love is only the initial energy. Theirs is the *coup de grâce* which we already know before, and thus afterwards, develops into the divisible becoming of losses and encounters.

Would it be reductive then to suggest that Pierre loves Urania as a woman loves, and that Penthesilea loves Achilles like a man? And that thus the double intrigue permutates the places just as war does? And that therefore these modern 'elective affinities' – more Goethe than Kleist – pronounce the law whose point of the real is love, thanks to the relief provided by an inversion of positions?

Now, in other words, the technique would be that of the stroboscope.

Perhaps it is the half-lost path opened up in *La Chine européenne* that we must follow to circumvent the mirror game of utopias and its outcome. Because, in the end, this final devouring of the heart, never mind the violent change of rhythm – the effect of a finale as with an acceleration of the orchestra, which one would have thought, really, to be reserved for music – has us in its grip and leaves us aghast!

Natacha Michel's instruments in *Le Repos de Penthésilée* are exploited to their fullest effect. It seems to me that they are adjusted above all to capturing the air that circulates between things and persons, but in such a way that a powerful collective aspiration, which here finds its expression as the site of History and revocation of the past, produces their universal dispersion, of which the 'characters', like those of May '68 in *La Chine européenne*, are no more than the captors, the relays, or the reference points.

If one agrees with me that Marxism is a civilization that is just beginning, a language to come for the centuries, already dragging along with it the totality of truth and falsity, of splendour and horror, arranged on a planetary scale for an adventure whose retreats and reflections can hide only provincially (I mean in Paris) their gigantic extension, then one will admit that this Marxism is a promise of art, not as already kept but still to keep, enjoining us to keep it: 'Marxist art' like we needed to say 'Christian art', and of which 'socialist realism' has only been the imitative barbarism of infamous beginnings.

I argue that, in the arcana of love which invents the networking of actions and subjects, it is in the blind service of such an art that Natacha Michel is at work, enjoining us to follow her in the formal innovation demanded by the representation of that which, according to the arrangements of the old writing, remains unrepresentable: politics.

Not History, nor the people, nor the revolution: politics.

This takes us back (via Penthesilea, Achilles, Ulysses ...) to the Greeks. For when it comes to the representation of politics, we always have this unsurpassed model: the tragedies of Aeschylus.

This is what a woman who is a contemporary writer announces to us: in order to be 'resolutely modern', we must know how to be Aeschylean.[5]

TESTIMONY TO A SINGULAR ACT: ON *IMPOSTURES AND SEPARATIONS*[6]

A book by Natacha Michel is immediately recognizable by the speed of its opening, which obeys the principle that the world is neither interrupted nor assembled by prose, but will already have been made as soon as the first sentence starts. This world, which is suspended from the future anterior, is immediately written, without the need to invoke either a referent in reality or a blank kind of writing that revokes its presence. Writing induces without delay a world that is both familiar and unprecedented. Its

---

5 *Translator's note*: For Badiou's take on what it means to be Aeschylean (as opposed to Sophoclean), see Part III in his *Theory of the Subject*, trans. Bruno Bosteels (London: Continuum, 2009).

6 Natacha Michel, *Impostures et séparations: 9 courts romans* (Paris: Seuil, 1986).

familiarity is what makes it anterior; its unprecedented nature defines the future.

In *Impostures et séparations* (*Impostures and Separations*), the book begins nine times ('9 courts romans', the subtitle indicates), but the speed proper to these beginnings is already the guarantee that this *neuf*, in the sense of both 'nine' and 'new', promises some One. Let us recall nevertheless that *Ici commence* (*Here Begins*) was the title of Natacha Michel's first novel.[7] Now each of the nine stories is the 'here begins' of a decision, as if deciding to write called for writing to be affected by the decision itself.

Redone (the first story) begins with 'The day when she left him'; *The Encounter on the Bus* with 'Camille meets Véronique ...'; *The Garden* with 'In Paris which is no longer one, declared Semper ...'; *General Strike in Poland* with 'On the eve of the general strike, Félicité crossed the city ...'; *The Waiting Room* with 'Esther was surprised to hear the name of Bonaparte ...'; *The Alley* with 'Before taking the road of the train station, as one puts on one's hat, Aunt R ...'; *The 'No' of Charles Scépante* with 'When Margot Scépante came from the specialist ...'. Declarations, temporal indications, gestures, walks: prose itself embarking upon the world.

For reasons that have to do with the architecture of the novel – the novel of these nine novels – only two stories, like the book's interior wings, the third and the eighth, begin with a descriptive stop: 'Betsy Vidalq belonged to this genre of woman ...' (*Life of an Illustrious Man*) and 'This afternoon was very sunny' (*The Triumph of Love*). What is marked thereby, by a singular kind of initial punctuation, is the fact that one of these stories is the absolute imposture, without charm or sublation, not even a dark one; and the other, by contrast, is the creative imposture, the one that calls up the love whose fable it had started by mimicking. One is indeed subject to the 'genre', which is a key word at the start of the story; and the other to the 'full

---

7   Natacha Michel, *Ici commence* (Paris: Gallimard, 1973).

sun'. Here we can observe not only that the promptitude of writing, for Natacha Michel, creates the future of a world but also that the choice of words, by an assured calculation, becomes the bearer, for whoever is capable of seeing, of meaning.

Meaning, precisely. What is a novel if not the adventure of a meaning which is such that a world struggling with a singular language proposes its question? This in any case is Natacha Michel's doctrine. *Impostures et séparations* is a novel because it unveils a meaning, of which the nine stories are the arrangement, sensible and formal at the same time, which we could compare to a philosophical tale if it were not rather the case here that the charm of the tale bewitches philosophy to the point where meaning is capable of doing without the concept. Which is, after all, the Kantian notion of beauty. In this regard, Natacha Michel goes against a tendency which holds that the world's relative lack of meaning can be answered with an academic or Flaubertian concept of the novel, and which thus believes, or feigns to believe, that for each era whatever the artist is capable of is dictated by the colour of his or her time (grey upon grey would thus be the current culmination of art). Natacha Michel opposes this tendency with the idea that the form of the novel practises an incision in its own time so that, in the prescription of a commencement, the brilliance or shine of meaning is independent of the general colour of the era. Because the real world is devoid of history and grace, today we witness an insidious apology of stories as reflections of the world. Natacha Michel, for her part, holds fast to the literary montage of machines, or even of machinations, whose formal autonomy is apt to open up and capture – without submitting to – the source of some meaning.

At issue in this book is nothing less than the question of truth, such as it is capable of circulating amid the arcane powers of love – but under what conditions? 'Impostures' is the name of that which interrupts the truth-effect of love. 'Separations' is the name of the realm in the midst of which

this truth can circulate. The meaning, which holds together
the novelistic unity of the book, is roughly as follows: it
is fatal for love to generate truth, and this is why, finally,
between men and women there are so many impostures
and separations.

Love is at the peril of truth. By naming the culminat-
ing point of this peril, Natacha Michel's book enunciates
the fatality of truth. In this sense, the book's thesis, as anti-
thesis, says about love the opposite of what Marcel Proust
says. For *In Search of Lost Time,* it is the imposture and its
correlate, jealousy, that are the ultimate truths. There is a
fatality of error ('This woman who was not my type', thinks
Swann, exactly in the way Natacha Michel places the word
'type' (*genre*) as an exergue to her only complete imposture[8]). Proust thinks that the art of the novel is the holy
sublation of this dereliction. For Natacha Michel, who does
not shy away from any sense of darkness and who practises
the most painful incisions in order for meaning to arrive,
it turns out in the end that imposture is only the fiction
of some truth. This is also why her whole art in this book
consists in inventing the machinery for the fiction of this
fiction. The impostures and separations that she narrates,
in the very precision, humour, and sometimes detectivesque
complexity of their intrigue and their ending, are formal
machines in which truth is circumscribed and ordered in
the fictive form conferred by what we might call the other
side of love, that dark obverse which is not the obverse of
a décor, but rather one of the threads of this depthless link
that, in duration, causes a woman and a man, or a child and
its family, to compose the history of a truth.

The major difference between Natacha Michel's novel
and, let us say, an allegory or an ornamental exposition of

---

8 *Translator's note*: A reference to the famous last lines in 'Swann
in Love' when Swann exclaims: 'To think that I have wasted years of my
life, that I wanted to die, that I felt my deepest love, for a woman who did
not appeal to me, who was not my type!' See Marcel Proust, *Swann's Way,*
vol. 1 of *In Search of Lost Time*, trans. Lydia Davis (New York: Viking,
2002), p. 396.

thoughts, resides in the fact that it is precisely not a matter of exposing the meaning mentioned above but of letting a sensible and complete world produce it. Hence the intensity of her prose, and the fact that the stories she tells are so marvellous, surprising, with a strange mix of something both fleshy and auroral – especially in *The Alley*, where a childhood garden is inhabited by the language that creates it like a paradise with its birds – and something absent and spectral, in which the form deliberately shows its teeth, as in *The Waiting Room*, where in an inversion of certain stories by Henry James, one might say that it is love that engenders ghosts. Indeed, the unity of the book, like that of a painting, is made up of the variety of its colourings, because the trappings of meaning suppose that the narration must unfold the full extent of its multiple capacities to make an impact.

Natacha Michel has always been an especially masterful writer of variations in tempo, as in the brilliant and harsh orchestral acceleration at the end of *Le Repos de Penthésilée* (*Penthesilea's Repose*). This time, she proves herself equally knowledgeable about the plasticity of great masses and capable of arranging, by contrast or by shading, in bas relief, sequences that are both independent and bound to the whole solely by the effect of their intrinsic tonality. There is delight in comparing these sequences from a distance, as an eye takes pleasure in the left corner of a pale sky because at the bottom there is a purple and gold mantle. Thus, also, we can compare the airy allure and the incomparable velocity of a 'small' story of separation, which is moreover justly named an encounter (*The Encounter on the Bus*), to the progressively Stoic gravitas of the final story (*The 'No' of Charles Scépante*), which voids and annuls, sentence by sentence, the reactive theme of adultery so as to show – ending the book on a kind of slowness and ceremoniousness of the decision – that it is by the truths it dispenses that love vanquishes death (in which sense Natacha Michel is opposed to the idea of love as mortal fusion à la Tristan).

This also shows that if the beginning of these nine short novels or novellas activates the world, their ending activates meaning. Here one rushes towards truth, since to the future anterior of the world, produced by writing, responds the future present of meaning, produced by the novel. 'She runs, she reaches back ...' (*The Alley*); 'But for Maryse, it [the truth] is always before her. Always before her' (*The Triumph of Love*)'; 'The separation that was not' (*The Encounter on the Bus*). There is no punch line at the end of these tales, as there is in short stories, whose technique is similar to that of the sonnet. There is a denouement ('I love denouements', says the author), because the interlacing of the story, its obliqueness – that innovative way in which Natacha Michel manages to shatter her characters on the basis of secondary characters or objects, as if one reached back to them by following the markers of the image – have the function of tying together the meaning. Consider for example – I do not wish to give away any of the plots that Natacha Michel draws from the endless arsenal of her taste for situations – at the beginning of *The Waiting Room*, how the name 'Bonaparte' harbours, in a very tight grip, the strange game played between Esther and Germain, which is indeed a game of strategy, errancy and dislocated repetition, so much so that when in the end we believe we understand what happens, it amounts only to the following: the word 'Bonaparte' has been opened up and elaborated by the story's intrigue until its primary operation – tightening or tying together – is undone and inverted, so that there may arrive the offering of a meaning.

Furthermore, between the opening attack, which situates the world, and the ending, which activates the meaning, Natacha Michel makes great use of the interlude, wherein we have the pleasure of not knowing how the story will continue. The narration's formal rigour and (in this book) the supple precision of the metaphors nevertheless make room for what is almost always lacking in the 'modern' novel, which is – even if it prides itself on the opposite – the multiplicity of possibilities (the genius proper to Balzac, and the reason why he is held to be the very type of the 'ancient'). Who can believe in a meaning engendered by a world of prose, if it is led from the outside towards its completion? This is the great defect of Flaubert's novels, which are always retrospective, closed off, directed. A novel by Flaubert is the murder of its own possibilities. Each paragraph leads towards its ternary cadence and symbolizes, on page after page, that nothing happens that has not happened. The peril is great of repeating this stagnant form when one tells a love story, for it appears to be obligatory, after all, to tell – eternally – its birth, its ecstasy, and its end.

I admire above all else that Natacha Michel does something completely different, precisely because it is her vital conviction that the future of love lies in the truth it engenders, of which love's 'end' is but the revelatory torment. As interludes, the function of the blanks separating two blocks of prose within one and the same story consists in maintaining the suspense of the possible. Randomly: in *The 'No' of Charles Scépante*, one paragraph ends with the phone call from Charles's unknown mistress, and his wife, Margot, overhears the conversation. This marks a stopping point: 'They are there, all three of them, the voice that speaks, Margot who listens, Charles who keeps silent.' Here the stopping point marks the imposture. Then, a blank. The sequence that begins right afterwards is in the form of a question: 'Why does Charles deny it?' Between the stopping point and the question, quite a number of things are possible and probable. The blank space is neither a separation nor, as in the *nouveau roman*, the introduction of a variant of what has already happened. It is the place of virtualities, of the pressure of anticipation. It is also what makes the prose of Natacha Michel into a prose of the decision, which contains a whole doctrine of the time of the novel: seeking neither the cohesiveness, without any glaring fissure, of the linear novel, nor its – always atemporal – shattering, but the logic of beginnings, of the orientation by which the world, at the same time as it is being constructed, is also wagered upon.

And the most surprising aspect is that this sense of the openness extends to what in general is the most compact and continuous of the component parts of prose – namely, description. For Natacha Michel, indeed, description is less a question of giving visibility to a consistency than of traversing an emotion by scaling it according to its objects. *The Alley*, the book's central masterpiece which ultimately tells of the – abstract – arrival of the Evil One in the paradise of Eve (the arrival of the lie in the garden of infancy), pushes descriptive suspense to extremes. There is for example the long sentence that ends with '... this source from where the sea came and which Noémie was looking for, without seeing it anywhere'. Then, a blank. Then: 'It was paradise as soon as one passed Marseille, as soon as on the quay the people who separated seemed to fulfil the ablutions of some religion of departure ...' We can see how, in the absence of spectacle, the rhythm decides that any place, no matter how stable it may be, no matter how anchored in ritual and childhood, is never anything but the occasion for a journey of thought and, in this sense, takes place only once.

Every book by Natacha Michel, at the same time as it builds up an oeuvre – and the periods during which she does not publish are, like the blanks of her prose, the opening of a decision – takes a stance with regard to the state of literature. *La Chine européenne* stated that a certain metaphorical regime of prose was in accord with May '68 and its aftermaths. Not to concern oneself with these events in literature would have been at the time a choice in favour of the ephemeral and the frivolous, for it is the accord with the new depth of its time that dedicates a book to its posterity. This agreement was the result of the fact that Natacha Michel's use of metaphor authorizes a 'collectivization' of the characters, in the sentiment of a general force of which they constitute points of intensity. In *Le Repos de Penthésilée*, where it was a question of war and the meaning of existence among women, Natacha Michel invented a communication between the minuscule and the gigantic for which the operator was the matrix of myth – myth is always the aggrandizement of a recognizable given. In so doing she took a stance against literary scepticism and the return to pallid introspections. *Impostures et séparations* combats the idea of a 'return of the novel', which is rather, like any 'return to', a renunciation and a speculation. A renunciation of literature as effect of language and rupture of forms; and a speculation, induced by the massive effect of that venerated pulp fiction novel that is Madame Duras's *The Lover*, on the benefits to be expected from a label of 'high literature', as one says 'high technology', bestowed upon academic productions whose only recourse lies in throwing wide open the register of petty miseries. This combat is all the more energetic and conclusive in that Natacha Michel proves that it is not a question of the subject-matter of the stories being told, since she accepts the challenge of dealing now with love and couples, which are the unaltered support for the dominant commodity-form all around us.

But we would be mistaken to believe that the heights she introduces, the subtlety of her arrangements, the tempo of her language, all this elegance with which she installs fiction on the border of the void – a bit like Henry James – in order to obtain a surplus of intensity, all this would amount to changing the ordinary into the extraordinary, redeeming the banal, or transmuting, with the resource of form, the vileness of the days of lead into the pure gold of the Idea.

No, from the very beginning we find ourselves on different territories. In the very movement that carries them and grounds them, Natacha Michel's couples stubbornly bear witness – beyond their torments and their fables – to a truth. The point is not to bedeck a degraded world with the borrowed brilliance of style. Besides, Natacha Michel is right to claim that, more than a 'style', there is a unique language, which is spoken in this world – the world of the novel – by everyone and understood by the author alone, even though it is understood by all of humanity – that of the real world. In fact, for her the point is to operate in literature, as Joseph Conrad wanted, the administration of a bit of justice throughout the visible universe.[9]

To read *Impostures et séparations* is to learn that nobody is ever summoned to forfeit, because even the worst that can happen, just because it happens, bears witness to the fact that there is meaning and that art, in any case, can capture and offer it. It is bestowed upon us to come about, and not to come back. Yes, that is it: in these nine short novels, apparently dominated by the confusion of the false and the pain of the separated, the recourse of writing, of speed, of the interlude, of suspense, and of the narrative machination fills us with a sense of advent. To love is to arrive-at or come-to.

This book is often written in the present indicative. This present is that of the race, of the coming-to-truth: 'She descends in turn, walks in the street ...'; 'She enters the garden.' But also, plain and simple: 'There lies of salvation.'

TRUTH IN THE GEOGRAPHY OF ITS PROSE:
ON *EAST-WEST COUCH*[10]

So we have proof of the fact that the paradox of a work of prose, brought to its culmination, captures long before its official date the thoughtful movement of a world that is everywhere declared to be immobile. Natacha Michel's new book, *Canapé Est-Ouest* (*East-West Couch*), is indeed less the inscription of the planetary division of an East and a West according to the milestones and zigzags of a journey than the elaboration in the patience of language of its traversing, or of its transversal, which is perpendicular to the accepted sense of sense. Its maxim can be found on page 150: 'Because now the world again is no longer

---

9   *Translator's note*: An allusion to Joseph Conrad, *The Nigger of the 'Narcissus'* (New York: Norton, 1979), p. 145. See also Badiou, *Theory of the Subject*, pp. 159–60.

10   Natacha Michel, *Canapé Est-Ouest* (Paris: Seuil, 1989).

round.' To detach ourselves from the worn-out roundness of this century: such is the task for which these encounters and discussions prepare us, long before Gorbachev or the demonstrations in Leipzig.

So what? People will say, she took the easy route with Poland, where everything began. To which I reply: Poland is not at issue here, but truth is. Second maxim, all the way at the end: 'The word conscience ... gives way to the word truth'.[11] East and West, which do not mark the cardinal points of any world, are the markers of an unprecedented orientation of the true. 'In Paris, too, the old truth is no longer true, but unfortunately the new one is not a truth'.[12] This is a book for the torsion of an undisclosed truth.

Of course! People will say, the West here refers to America, about which it is customary to affirm that truth is barely its concern. I say: Natacha Michel does not talk about such an America reduced to opinions, but about an America, both massive and dissolved, for which her guide is a disoriented friend, the woman called Patricia whom we now know as well as she does, even better than she, instructed as we are as readers by everything we take away from what the work of prose does not know. Patricia is the one who probes all kinds of risk and disaster, so much so that she keeps 'an appearance of being intact in the midst of life, with nothing being able to trouble or nourish her'.[13] Only a desire authorizes a truth: it is because Patricia does not come back with her to France – and Natacha Michel says: 'My educational novel was France, and staying there'[14] – that the narrator can conclude, regarding America, on a superb note: 'this country from which, in spite of its appearances, nothing comes forth'.[15] For nothing comes forth from where no One returns.

---

11   Ibid., p. 204.
12   Ibid.
13   Ibid., p. 93.
14   Ibid., p. 18.
15   Ibid., p. 99.

But what matters is the power of prose. It alone disjoins what it assembles – namely, the leaflets of time. Prose here circulates in the contrast between the writers from America – subtracted, indolent and delinked – and the militants from Poland – projected, open to lack of meaning, concerned with the invention of a collective. Such is Natacha Michel's prose: the highly combustible metaphorical link between that which has withdrawn and that which is just on the verge of its presence. A form of prose that, in order to preserve what happens, would like to be able to surprise itself.

What should I do, for example, if I wish to preserve San Francisco forever? Yes, forever, and insofar as its appearance contains for me an element of truth? In this regard, let us observe that Patricia and Natacha quarrel fiercely over the subject of Plato, from page 46 onwards. This is a capital opening: the work of prose aims at the idea, and this is precisely why it mobilizes such a heavy charge of the sensible. Patricia cloaks herself in 'I believe only in what I see', and Natacha retorts: 'I believe only in what I think.' Prose is neither emotion nor sensation; these are merely the singular means of art to provoke thought. So what is to be done, then, to make the reader *think* San Francisco, in the medium of a visibility without vision? Look at the solution:

> San Francisco is one of the most beautiful provincial cities in the world. City of slopes, rearing up. This city of earthquakes and tidal waves ironically has given itself the shape of a cold volcanic eruption. From high up on the hill, the immobile crater of Telegraph Hill indefinitely spits out the slopes like pieces of rock. At the bottom, the fertile plain of Chinatown. Even the sea, when it is not immense, resembles one of those icy lakes that constitute the secret of volcanoes.[16]

We see one of the technical virtuosities of Natacha Michel in the clarity of the opening, which is, however, discarded

---

16   Ibid., p. 75.

as soon as it is thrown on the page, because it is a wrong track to prepare the metaphor: no further use will be made of the idea of the 'province', even though it persists *underneath* the volcanic metaphor like a kind of tender restriction.

And in the same vein, this writer who does not spare us in the least – this is her highest virtue – in sentence after sentence likes to leave traces of an attempt, or of an image which is not quite unfinished but lacunary, as if the metaphorical plant had to be made to grow in the shards of an amphora. Thus, we will obtain the city 'rearing up' on its hind legs without being delivered the equestrian statue of itself that this city *perhaps* could also be – the 'horse' here rejoining the 'province' in the unvisited caverns of the final image, the only one to which will be confided the Idea.

Every true metaphor is induced from a denaturalization of its ideal issue. Often Natacha Michel constructs this indirect value explicitly: the volcano is 'ironic', it denies the seismic realism of the city, it is like a voluminous *reversal* of a fault line, or of a fold. From there, manipulating the metaphor as axiom, we must draw all the consequences without wavering: spat-out slopes, fertile plain, sea changed into lake. The punch line seals the idea, if it is capable of *redescending* towards the initial reversal: this redescent alone does honour to the name *chute* in French for 'fall' or 'punch line'. And, indeed, just as the volcano is the irony of the seism, the ice of the lakes is the secret of the fire of volcanoes. This way of rounding off *completes* San Francisco, henceforth immobile in its elementary idea-like composition, decomposed and recomposed all along its streets as the assemblage, in prose, of Fire and Water.

Now let us assume that a 'character' must be presented. Please note that we are not in a fiction; said 'character' exists: Natacha Michel has met him. How should he be put down into prose so that this pre-existence may be attested in a second immortality? How to mutate the absolute singularity of a man into an Idea? Here prose is what alone is capable – as Plato demanded – of making an Idea out of mud or a piece of hair. Or out of Bialecki, a militant of Solidarity:

> What is common in all activists in the world is something
> I see in Bialecki: the red circles around the eyes because of
> insomnia, a certain paleness of the skin, the cheeks like a
> pair of suede gloves that have been washed in water, the
> small rough points of the budding beard's wool, the torso
> bent forward in the listening attitude of someone waiting
> for the quick rubber-band snap of a response, the agitation
> taking the place of a secretary, an air of youthful fatigue, of
> exhaustion kept up with the discipline of a pianist, a sense
> of silence which is not that of the politicians in power, and
> the amicable alarm before the surfeit of questions as he
> rummages through his memory as in a drawer overflowing
> with papers.[17]

In Natacha Michel's book, the prose of the East is not that of the West. She keeps in mind the fact that 'the East is lacking for us'.[18] With regard to the East she approaches people and their words with a softness that is sometimes almost passive, a friendship that becomes instructive, whereas America is captured with the native power of the image, taken over by force, subjected. There is a flamboyant part and a delicate part, with the delicacy devoted to the novelty and density of meaning and a flamboyance that takes hold of a situation that is too-little too-real. Meagre America crackles like fireworks; inventive Poland walks on the tips of its toes.

The portrait of Bialecki thus begins with descriptive prudence and generic comparison. It is a tranquil beginning, without paradox or lacuna. One is tempted to say that we are moving towards a type in a repertoire, an idea that is *readymade*: the militant in periods of movement – harassed, supercharged, badly shaven.

However, in the aftermath of the passage above, we are astounded to see that the metaphorical materials are

---

17   Ibid., p. 173.
18   Ibid., p. 204.

much more scattered about, paradoxical, and heterogeneous than they were in the putting-into-an-Idea of San
Francisco. Before, from the volcano, writing *drew out all
the consequences*. Here, there is nothing axiomatic, but
rather a kind of acrobatic trajectory *between* disparate
poles. How in the world can a simple portrait of a militant
link together a pair of suede gloves, a rubber band, a secretary, a pianist and a drawer? And how to reach this end,
which is the opposite of an exquisite cadaver and rather
seeks out a precise living being? This is the other disposition of Natacha Michel's style – the one that compensates
for the danger of leaving a *great gap* among the images
by way of the pure speed of the intermediary terms. Here,
the dominant grouping of features will range from the
proximity to animal life, which is what is so striking upon
first impression (suede, wool), to a repertoire of jobs that
behind this accessible surface organizes a more essential
discipline (secretary, pianist). This is because, contrary to
San Francisco, which is a place, Bialecki is the subject-point
from which to capture a situation. The metaphorical system
of the location demands the continuity of the derivations,
whereas the metaphoric logic of the situations, which seeks
to make an Idea out of a dialectic, demands that one passes
through all the intricate turns of the multiple.

Besides, the technical resources of Natacha Michel's
prose are as multiple as is required by the world which it is
a question of raising up to the Idea. And if metaphor is the
principle of organization of these resources, they nevertheless cannot be reduced to it.

Sometimes it is the tonal rumour of language that satu-
rates the image, when it takes hold of something devoid of
any sweetness. Consider, for instance, the interior rumble
of the 'r's' as the local truth of an infernal subway ride:
'Down below, it is the great dark hangar of iron pillars, a
sort of sonorous entrepot under the sea, which the train
traverses with a thundering roar.'[19]

---

19   Ibid., p. 11.

But, at the opposite extreme of prose, on its French side, when one takes the shortest route to inhabit one's language, in the simple flash of the passage of an idea, we will also find a series of formulae, or maxims, in which the image is abolished without remainder in the fullness of the saying and the said. Thus: 'The ransom of any utopia is that it is executed';[20] or, in a dense resolution of what ordinarily drags with it a whole dialectic: 'Solidarity is a movement that confects an element of organization.'[21]

Perhaps most surprising, in a book whose modesty (that of a few truth-sightings) is fulfilled as virtuosity, is to see conjoined such transparent analyses and such sharp poems; and, above all, the fact that the reader at one and the same time may slide unjolted from the former to the latter and realize that this sliding announces a gap, a break, which is both intimate and historic, superimposing the balance sheet of a whole European century upon the stealthy desire of a friendly face. Thus, it is surprising to read the following, arranged into verse:

> The great cargo ships are only tiny stools, that is how big
>   the river is.
> The bridge is a bird that flies off into the far distance
> On the banks of the Mississippi some enormous blocks of
>   stone,
> Wooden staircases descend into the water
> People sitting on the stones, on the steps,
> Come and watch
> The water that flows,
> Attracts those who go slower than it.
> The spectacle takes place at two different speeds.
> It is also because the Mississippi is a free beast and
>   unconfined.
> In the river bend it seems to flex the muscles of its neck.[22]

---

20   Ibid., p. 20.
21   Ibid., p. 144.
22   Ibid., p. 40.

But one should also read, coming from the mouth of the Polish woman Barbara, with that astonishing capacity of Natacha Michel's to restore *exactly* the words of the interlocutor, so that it is this exactitude which makes up the singularity of her prose and style, the following: 'The economic situation, the small modifications in the state, the party changed and identical, the politics of regular crises that bear witness to instability but are also a method for negotiation: all this is where we're at.'

These are the two operations of Natacha Michel: to sweep the work of prose, to seduce the entirety of language *and* to hold steady in the most rigorous divisions and distributions. Speed of the continuous and stupor of the indiscernible. Recitation without story, and metaphor without repertoire.

In any genuine writer the flow of the prose pieces, more so than their insistence, is what constitutes style. Natacha Michel posits that, contrary to what was being said twenty or thirty years ago, the Idea fights on an equal footing against the obscene pressure of realism only if all the shades and colours are at its disposal. For the Idea is born from the *detour* of their consecution, from their interlacing or their mixture. 'Blank prose' is an abdication of thought; and from the notion that art – the art of prose – is precisely the thought of the sensible as such, it follows that in order to produce the Idea of blank, as well as blankness itself, we need the *total* spectrum of colours in between.

I would say that *Canapé Est-Ouest* is a luminous and blank thought, in the arc of forms, of whatever element of the sensible there is in the geographical distribution of thoughts.

A VISITATION:

ON *THE DAY WHEN TIME WAITED FOR ITS HOUR*[23]

Henri Bergson considered waiting to be the experience of qualitative duration, subtracted from the practical and spatial contents that most often divert us – in the Pascalian sense of *divertissement* – from such experience.[24] But here it so happens that Natacha Michel's title lets us know that the work of prose (that prose about which she says that it is the 'constitutive category' of the novelistic regime) is going to install time itself in the dimension of the wait. What experience, then, does her book propose to us?

When she speaks of 'the persuasive instant of the novel', Natacha Michel immediately indicates that it is a matter of a tension, immanent to the novel, between *operators of finitude* (stories, characters, imaginary worlds) and an *effect of infinity* detained by 'salvation in prose'.[25] The philosopher may be allowed to say a bit more about this and, as is to be expected, more heavy-handedly. The novel, if indeed one thinks of it – like any operation of art – in the dimension of the truth that it plots, possesses the singular quality that it establishes a 'world' only under the perilous law of a scission of time. Indeed, the intimate time of the subject is the refraction therein of a historic or 'worldly' time, without ever allowing us to say whether one includes the other, or represents it. It is in the delinking of these two temporalities that the novelistic *scene* is established. And it is true that this scene has the power of the infinite, or rather that of eternity, not because of the archetypal action of the epic but due to the temporal machination of a disjunction. The novel creates a truth not out of time as

---

23 Natacha Michel, *Le jour où le temps a attendu son heure* (Paris: Seuil, 1990).

24 *Translator's note*: See for example Henri Bergson, *The Creative Mind: A Study in Metaphysics*, trans. Mabelle J. Andison (New York: The Philosophical Library, 1946), p. 13.

25 Natacha Michel, *L'instant persuasif du roman* (Paris: Conférences du Perroquet, 1987); also included in *L'écrivain pensif* (Paris: Verdier, 1998), pp. 47–68.

such, but out of the disparate nature of multiple times, so that one or more subjects come to experience therein that eternity is the invisible material of life itself.

In this sense the time of waiting in Natacha Michel's latest book proposes a meditation on the novelistic effect, on its *experience*: what is the price of prose that we must pay so that at the unmarked crossroads of multiple times, our life, ordinary and precious, may be its own eternal Constellation? What 'supreme conjunction with probability' is needed to guarantee, in the absence of any soul, the salvation *in truth* of our loves, our capacities, and everything that Samuel Beckett used to call our 'company'?[26]

To reflect upon this problem in an act of prose, Natacha Michel, since at least *Le Repos de Penthésilée* (*Penthesilea's Repose*), has set up a refined system of experimental arrangements. Worlds exposed to conflict, hypothetical separation of the sexes, lives with a false bottom, ubiquitous immobilities: in order to enter this prodigiously diverse and metaphorical form of prose (who will account for the *comic* resource of her language, or the musical science of the velocities of her phrasing, or the abrupt epic interruption of kindness?), we must pass through *fictional axioms* that are indicative of its modernity. Indeed, today we know that no truth can be obtained except at the cost of *explicit* decisions. And what I like above all else is that Natacha Michel's novels are organized by anecdotal conventions that are as recognizable as was, for Henry James, what he called the 'idea' of the novel.

The founding axioms of *Le jour où le temps a attendu son heure* (*The Day When Time Waited for Its Hour*) seem to me to mark a turning point in Natacha Michel's oeuvre, simply because of their being so appropriate for the task at hand. Since what is at stake resides entirely in the infinite power of the finite plurality of times, one will assume the pure and simple encounter of two temporalities. There is first of all the time that opens the novel. This is the daytime,

---

26 *Translator's note*: See Samuel Beckett, 'Company', in *Nohow On* (New York: Grove Press, 1980).

the presentation of a paradise getting ready, a summer
house, porous to the beauty of the world and populated
by a loyal 'company', in which the central subject, Odile,
is going through old age with the serenity bestowed upon
those who have a sense of continuity. Indeed, this first temporality, gathered up in its auroral daybreak, stands for the
continuous itself, the sweet continuation of living, which
the prose here enumerates – even though it is innumerable –
by the grace of a style capable of turning its selections into
the vector of a deportment that is as uncontrived as the
surrounding sea. And the second modality of time is a past
that all of a sudden is made *present*: a young man, Charles
Saugueuse, arrives just as ten years before he had already
arrived, seduced Odile, married her, and lived with her in
the same house of the daytime to which he now returns.
Whereby we see that the two times are also distributed into
two characters, who are 'the same', the daytime Charles
and the Charles of the other time, the Charles who comes
to meet up with what his own life has become, that is to
say, to meet up with Odile, whom he must seduce a second
time. Such is the imperative of eternity in the conceptless
contrast of different times. The waiting for time during the
day is the waiting for the hour at which the One of love
will have to pass the tempting test of its double. Double,
doubling, redoubling of ecstasy: will there be victory? Of
what? Of the possibility that the paradisiacal One opens
itself up to the Two of a spectral event?

But within this first scission – of which Odile will
endure the enigma, since she must return to the time that
is foundational for her – there operates the essential scission of the time of the novel in general. Because Charles
Saugueuse as a young man carries with him the vivid time
of militant commitments, of the aftermath of 1968, of
strikes and acts of violence, of adventurist thoughts, the
novel is also the *forced* balance sheet of this era, taking
the constant measure of what remains thereof, not as
memory, but as historicity kept in the vivaciousness of its
second life. The work of eternity operates simultaneously

on the gap of passion, the painful truth caught in the nets of desire, and on that which represents the eclipse of grand History. Odile is thus *defined* by the superimposition, upon the continuum by which life generates the calm of which it is capable, of a discontinuity we must come to understand as that which also *will have instituted* the continuous itself, henceforth guaranteed by the stable presence of the Charles Saugueuse whom she has married. It is a miracle to see how Natacha Michel thus manages to fictionalize what I call the future anterior of truth: a time rebellious to the novel, it would seem, but which here is supported by the vital relation between the founding discontinuities (encounters, revolts ...) and the paradisiac continuities. This relation is in turn exhibited and tensed by the figure of the event, given to it by the sudden upsurge, in the midst of the blissful day, of the time that this day both realized and obliterated. The hour is the moment when time brings into the light of day a severe *summons*.

At this point, everything seems to be in place for Natacha Michel's novel to adopt, with regard to the question of the eternity of the visible, the classic solution of the *return*: for Odile to run off with the second Saugueuse, precisely because he is the first, and the abolition of time operates by way of the reiteration of the origin.

However, such is precisely not the solution that Natacha Michel proposes. She thinks – the novel thinks – rightly, that the return of origin and the reappropriation of the native element are mortiferous figures. These are figures that certainly abolish time, but in the night of nostalgia, instead of carrying it all the way to the radiance of its eternity. Thus, Odile, with the last word of the book, will say 'no' to the one whom she nevertheless will have loved, when he begs her to leave with him, to rejoin forever the time, both intimate and historic, of their youth. And this 'no' – symmetrical to the one that provides the title for one of the 'short novels' in *Impostures et séparations, The 'no' of Charles Scépante*, by which a man affirmed his transtemporal fidelity to a woman – contains all the torn optimism that is Natacha Michel's: the function of prose is not to save us at the cost of time, nor is nostalgia its vocation. Prose seizes on to the encounter of multiple times in order to magnify the *unrepeatable*. From an axiom of repetition, no matter how tempting its consolatory interpretations may be (nothing has disappeared, all comes back), prose draws only the rigorous consequences of a *fidelity*: the truth of what has taken place is delivered within the world, such as this world will have been according to this having taken place, without return or memory.

There is nothing eternal except time. There is no Charles Saugueuse except the one who was faithful to what he was no longer. There is no salvation of her own youth for Odile except in the age in which this youth *becomes*. The radiance of what is will always carry the day, in the contrast of multiple times, against the creative abolition of what once was.

Natacha Michel's novel proposes to us in fiction the courage to hold firm to that which Plato called 'the always of time', which is the point where, forever incomplete, breaking with all repetition, a truth proceeds, to infinity. The instant of prose persuades us that the secret from beyond the grave of time consists in never having to come back. History is perhaps, as Michelet claimed, the integral resurrection of the past; but the novel is the metaphorical surrection of the infinite power of the present.

HARVESTS OF THE NIGHT:
ON *MEMORANDUM TO MY ENTIRE HUMAN LIFE*[27]

We are familiar with Kant's famous question: what does it mean to orient oneself in thinking?[28] Natacha Michel, for a long time now, has been asking a closely related but very

---

27 Natacha Michel, *Circulaire à toute ma vie humaine* (Paris: Seuil, 2004).

28 *Translator's note*: See Immanuel Kant, 'What is Orientation in Thinking?', in *Political Writings*, ed. Hans Reiss (Cambridge: Cambridge University Press, 1991), pp. 237–49.

different question: what does it mean to orient oneself in prose? But let us beware! Prose is not the poem, so that the question ought not to resonate with that of Martin Heidegger, for whom the question of what the poem orients – given that the poem is the guardian of the retreat of being – is internal to that other question of the historical destiny of thinking. For Natacha Michel, to orient oneself in prose is by no means a question of destiny. But prose is also not writing. This time the question must be separated from that of Maurice Blanchot. If writing is, structurally, the infinite deferral of silence in which death remains, then to orient oneself in prose is by no means structural in this sense.

Neither structural nor destined, the notion of 'prose' is the combat that Natacha Michel intends to engage in and win. Prose is like an irreducible art of thought – thought activating the effect of its prose-bound orientation.

As to the nature of prose, we can find two inaugural reference points in the essay *L'écrivain pensif* (*The Pensive Writer*). First, at the very start of this essay, we can read the following, which is something like a wish: 'To write these thoughts of prose.'[29] To orient oneself in prose thus means to answer the question: what does prose think, for us to be able to think in such a way so that this thinking can be written into thoughts? Then, this observation: 'The novel ... is exceeded by its language, which I call prose.'[30] Prose, no doubt, is novelistic, but in the sense of what in the novel exceeds or overflows it – not ontologically but locally. In the novelistic regime in which it operates, the language said to be prose is the excessive destination of whatever it carries along – which will also be said as follows, rendering indistinguishable poetry and prose in the act of writing: 'Novelistic prose encompasses poetry and prose in the des-

---

29   Natacha Michel, *L'écrivain pensif* (Paris: Verdier, 1998), p. 7.

30   Ibid., p. 44. *Translator's note*: The ellipsis marks the point where Badiou skips the qualification 'of the second modernity', with which Natacha Michel proposes the renewal of novelistic prose after the closure of the 'first modernity' with Proust and Joyce.

tination of a particular poetics of prose.'[31] To orient oneself in prose thus means: to orient oneself according to whatever this destination produces in terms of thought.

What does Natacha Michel do when she writes not an essay, but a novel? She occupies the destination. She invests or besieges it from some place that is other than itself. Because she affirms that prose cannot be – in order for us to orient ourselves in it, or for it to orient us – the prose of prose, or blank writing. Let us say that, when one orients oneself in prose, one orients the possible thought of politics, of love, and of their aleatory crossing. To orient then becomes: to endow the contrasting path of truths with an unpredictable Orient. The point is for prose to endow the incision of love in politics, or vice-versa, with a new Orient. Thus reoriented through prose, a political sequence is eternal, something for which the purely political language in which it is immediately stated does not suffice.

The topic is an ancient one, people will say. What would the Peloponnesian war be for us without the ellipses of Thucydides? Or the Napoleonic war in Russia without the inexhaustible opacity of Tolstoy? The Spanish civil war without the figurative anxiety of Malraux?

Let us argue that the topic, in the case of Natacha Michel, belongs to our actuality. She has charged two of her books with producing the prose-thought of what was rather meagerly called leftism and which is much rather, using the name given by Sylvain Lazarus, the *militant* sequence of politics, unfolded between 1967 and 1976 – the nine red years. These books are *La Chine européenne* (1975) and *Le jour où le temps a attendu son heure* (1990). A third book must produce the prose-thought of the negative interval (the 1980s and 1990s), in which the central subjective figure is no longer at all that of the militant, but its shadowy obverse: the figure of the renegade of leftism. *Circulaire à toute ma vie humaine (Memorandum to My Entire Human Life)* is this book.

---

31   Michel, *L'écrivain pensif*, p. 44.

These two sets propose two strongly separate styles. Why? That is what we must find out. To anticipate, not without mystery: the first two books metaphorize a beginning or commencement; the third problematizes the transmission of this beginning, as a beginning or commencement that has been put under erasure.

In the first two novels, metaphor is Natacha Michel's major prose instrument, which fixates the orientation in whatever the present contains in terms of the future. In this sense, metaphor emerges immediately – I mean: without mediation, against the destined nature of the poem, which advances entirely according to the (re)turn to an original unconcealment or disclosure. But prose fights no less against the primordial silence of which writing would be the infinite recovery. Prose orients itself according to that which it orients: the new time of which the militant of the red years bears the indistinction that is to come.

'Metaphor', in Natacha Michel's case, means that which in prose overcomes all nostalgia in the direction of a beginning. Every metaphor makes what it names into a new dawn.

I take an example from *Le jour où le temps a attendu son heure* (from this title you can guess the play of the present-future, the exquisite hour, against the benevolent perpetuity of the daytime). Odile, the female hero, guides a young man, Charles, one evening, to the terrace of her house. The atmosphere is one of well-nigh mythical amorous tension. But consider the phrase: 'Under their naked feet, the terrace is a great vat of sandstone, exactly covering the house, one tramples the grapes of obscurity, they are intoxicating.' You have nudity, as sensation and not as a state of being; the inversion of the spaces – the vat is a hollow space and not the raised roof, so that this hollowness, combined with the stone felt by the naked foot, provokes a nightly harvest, the obscure grapes being trampled, whence proceeds the drunkenness, that of love, which is unnamed. We thus pass from the walk of the characters to the intoxication, following the rigorous as well as inventive order of metaphorical prose, by the intermediary of the stone and the night. All this in the end forces us to think the following: a single step onto the terrace and the world of love begins.

All this had been deployed magnificently in what we might call the first 'amorous cycle' of Natacha Michel. *Ici commence* (1973), *Le Repos de Penthésilée* (1980), and *Impostures et séparations* (1986), with the combined resources of the finite narrative élan and the infinity of the metamorphoses in language, treat of the principal enigmas of love, that secret truth whose intensity often dissimulates its exactness – its beginning which is always anterior to the circumstance in which it is coiled up; its 'end' always being later than the scene in which it is pronounced.

But in *Circulaire à toute ma vie humaine*, in which what is at issue is politics as *subjective illumination*, the prose takes on neither a beginning nor an end. We might say that it is a matter of (re)commencement, but this would mean missing the real linkage. Indeed, the problem is that of transmission – the transmission of the militant experience of the red years, such that the renegacy of a few known and well-placed leftists renders it apparently impossible. The result of this problem is a language more inclined to offer itself in its satirical dimension. Certainly, this dimension has always been present in Natacha Michel's oeuvre. Its prose cannot deliver the past to the intoxication of the beginning without in some subtle way making the hindrances and burdens of the simple state of affairs seem laughable. However, in *Circulaire*, the satirical impulse is given completely free rein. As a result, language becomes more concerned with speed than with the need to stop. The equilibrium between the two has always been a major concern for Natacha Michel. How should one make the prose flow, keep the narrative cadence going, sealing off, concluding, and at the same time enabling the advent of the ecstasy of the present? Let us say that this last aspect, in *Circulaire*, is more parsimoniously distributed.

Just as *La Chine européenne* was the first and perhaps only witness in prose of the sequence that we can call that of Maoist politics, both in terms of the radiance of its present and its possible failure, similarly *Circulaire* is the first and perhaps only novel of post-leftist renegacy, of the comic misery of its present, and of the possible victory, against this misery, of transmission.

The list of characters alone already sets this singular scene in which the extreme seriousness of what is at stake (to wit, can a radical beginning be vanquished by an organized forgetfulness?) traverses moments of great comedy – that of the characters, portraits, consensual speeches and farcical actions. There are first the organic renegades, those who form the self-satisfied society of the salesmen of regrets: Thomas Féroé, Claude Waterman, Simon Jude, Paul Braille ... All different, like so many shadowy or hilarious Tartuffes; and all alike, like so many petty Marquises of cultural consumption. They celebrate one another in comical seminars, and secretly are moved only by what they share: the foreclosure of their militant past, the intimate burial of the revolutionaries they once were – which is a negation that can be handsomely rewarding in the vicinity of the unchanged powers that be. Facing them are three characters who mobilize action with a revelatory force. There is the bearer of the future, Nour, the Young Girl, who is the equal of what the great novelists, from Jane Austen to Jean Giraudoux, made in their own time of this young age when one decides one's fate with the sovereignty of a storm. Then there is the subject of movement, Sébastien Lechevalier, the one who will transition almost blindly from the renegade's imposture to the illuminated return of what once was; the one in whom the resurrection of a transmissible beginning will take place, to the benefit of Nour. Finally, there is the narrator's 'I', Bella, Sébastien's first wife, who spins the thread of writing all along the process of this temporal comeback.

But this is a novel of large numbers, too disciplined to be picaresque, but still at all times more numerous than its apparent count suggests – a number exceeded by comic loquacity. A host of delightful and bitter characters swirl around the complacent renegades. They gather blissfully, scream, sing at the top of their voices, and mill about in a big scene in which a kind of conference of these renegades becomes an awful mess because of the total amnesia that reaches all the way to the present, to the recognition of all those present, including Sébastien, who is supposed to be one of the big shots of the whole affair. The latter provokes a scandal by calling the chief big shot, the head renegade, a 'misrecognized nonentity'.

The thesis that unfolds in the twists and turns of this novel, be they solemn or preposterous, can be recapitulated as follows: *if a present is amputated from the intensity of its past, it has no future.*

The decisive novelistic instance of this thesis comes in Chapter 5, 'Sébastien's Solitude', in which the character is literally invaded by his militant past. His amnesia of the present has prepared the return of the past. This proves that it is in the present that one decides to make use or not of the intensity of what has taken place. For their fragmented present as social climbers, the renegades need to reduce their intense past to nothingness. In order for this past to return in full force, Sébastien must first forget the present of forgetfulness. Let us speak for a moment like Heidegger, but against the grain of his intention: in order to restore the original mission (in this case, the subjective passion of the red years), we need – this is the amnesia of the renegade years – the *oblivion of oblivion.*

Sébastien can then dedicate to Nour what he did, thirty years earlier, with the Portuguese peasants who occupied and organized their lands in the face of the police squads; with the rebel inhabitants of a provincial town; at the gates of a factory in times of strikes and storms. In short: what matters is there, as such.

What Sébastien understands, and we after him as we are carried away by the subtlety of the prose, is that the renegacy of 'leftism' has been the instrument of a reintegration into ordinary history of whatever exceeded it. At this point the text raises its tone and paradoxically commemorates oblivion as a sign of intensity: 'Honour to the renegades who, in spite of themselves, showed that May '68 did not belong in history. And this is not its indignity but its force, since what had been called History was no longer active. The trend of renegacy at its most blatant tried by force to make May '68 enter into it.'

This is what prose gives us to think as enveloped in what it thinks: today, the task of transmission can no longer call upon the aid of History. It is no longer simply a matter of continuing to give the present the backing of the past. Transmission belongs to another regime of intensity. And what does this new regime of intensity presuppose, which decides what can and must be transmitted? It presupposes the *undoing of a certain form of acceptance, which itself is new*. Because we must always reach the affirmative kernel of a given figure – all the more so when this figure is seized and thought in its metamorphosis in novelistic prose. If the renegade is essential, it is not only, nor even primarily, because of the negative operations that he boasts about: to spit on what one once adored, to repress any memory of revolutionary exaltation, to deny the facts, to suppress in oneself any trace of militant subjectivity, to see in this past only totalitarianism and stupidity, and so on. Rather, it is because the renegade clears the path for a new form of acceptance of what is, a new form of guilty resignation, servitude, and fear. This new form of acceptance states the following: no experience is legitimate unless it is of low intensity. All true conviction is exaggerated. Natacha Michel offers us a fable of the consequences – both comic and sterile – of such a principle. But she also gives us the miracle of its abolition, the miracle of the fate of the young girl, who from now on will look in the world for the wherewithal to restore a political experience that would escape the norm of minimal intensity because, at last, the possibility of such an experience has been transmitted to her.

All true transmission of the intensity of the past is a victory over the new modes of acceptance.

This explains the language adopted by Natacha Michel, with its customary virtuosity. Since we can no longer rely on the help of History, let us wrest the story from the simplicity of narration, from the uniformity of register, from the modesty of flat or restorative literary intensities. Let us spin the metaphor of a connection between oblivion and intensity, via the oblivion of oblivion. Let us show in all its radiance, of laughter or imagery, that the future of a young girl will vanquish the present without past or future of the renegades who are currently in place.

In this astonishing book, the poetic destination of language permits the narration of the unnarratable: what happens to politics and to its decisive continuation when History no longer exists.

VOID, SERIES, CLEARING:
ESSAY ON THE PROSE OF
SEVERO SARDUY

Pier Paolo Pasolini said that what is proper to cinema is the authorization to construct a language of reality with the means of reality itself.[1] Everything therefore depends on the gap between, on one hand, the fragments of reality summoned – by surprise, montage or cutting – to install themselves in the discontinuity of a language and, on the other, the reality of which this language allows the capture, and which it is not exaggerated to call rather a point of the real.

Severo Sarduy's linguistic cinematography draws a major part of its repertoire from a heavy tropicalism, so that one might cry out from all quarters that rootedness, or nostalgia, is essential; that childhood sets the law for the ornaments of desire; that the author brings to his formal modernity that great current which has connected the Spanish language to a legendary Amazon and erected – for the glory of its rivers, forests, indigenous inhabitants,

---

1 *Translator's note*: See, for example, Pier Paolo Pasolini, 'The Written Language of Reality' and other essays in *Heretical Empiricism*, trans. Ben Lawton and Louise K. Barnett (Bloomington: Indiana University Press, 1988).

murderous caciques and vanished cults, sexual despots and scrawny black nurses – the unfinished monument where what enters literature is something like a cosmos in which human desire is indistinguishable from the teeming of plants.

Nothing of the kind is true. The word 'baroque', which Sarduy makes great use of even in his titles, should not be mistaken to mean here a category in which the absolute singularity of his texts would be dissolved. For what strikes me, without denying the comparative and metaphorical exuberance of Sarduy's prose, is the extraordinary *discipline* of his project. This is a discipline that we can rightfully compare to that of children, when they agree on a game's rules. As a matter of fact, to change everything sordid into a superior game is certainly one of Sarduy's ambitions. And it is to the abstract complexity of the rules of composition of this game that we should assign the word 'baroque', certainly not to the proliferation of images.

In a supposed 'Editor's Note' that one finds on page 68 of *Colibri* (*Hummingbird*, which I will take to be a metonymy of Severo Sarduy), we can read about the author that he is 'attentive to formal values and indifferent to the laws of narration'.[2] But it is not only to narrative laws that Sarduy's prose, apparently overladen, is indifferent. It is to everything that could be recognized as agreeable form, or as form whose labour of recognition we could do without so as to go straight to whatever sensible signification it organizes. A novel by Sarduy requires us to *pause* on the forms, and their colourful proliferation is like an ambush prepared for us, an insidious triage between those who will take great delight therein, without any malice, and those who will adopt an attitude of slight coldness

---

2 *Translator's note*: See Severo Sarduy, *Colibri*, trans. Aline Schulman and Severo Sarduy (Paris: Seuil, 1986), p. 68. All subsequent references will be to this French edition, after all co-translated by Sarduy himself. But references have been cross-checked against the Spanish original, *Colibrí* (Barcelona: Argos Vergara, 1984).

which authorizes a time to halt, preparing the necessary moment to conclude with regard to the *veritable* assemblage of forms.

Let us say that the colouring of prose is a feint so that the reader, in a kind of secondary indifference, may gain access to the depth of the stakes involved in the game. As a volatile Carmelite nun proclaims, between two levitations: 'To those who feign belongs the kingdom of heaven.'[3] To read Severo Sarduy is always at the same time (in a duplicitous or split reading) to let oneself be caught in the feint and evade its pitfall.

From time to time, Sarduy is kind enough to alert us. Speaking for example of a 'summary soliciting' whose cause (object-cause), as is only proper, is 'the bird's swollen crotch' that distracts its victim, the writer notes in a parenthesis: 'Just as mine distracts you, reader, or at least so I hope.' One could not be better forewarned that we had best show some distrust before getting too distracted by the eroticized frills of the surface of phrases. Otherwise it could well happen to us, as it did to an all-too-distracted Colibri, that someone sticks us 'there, in the arm, with a full syringe of Seconal'.[4] Reader! If you do not want to be put to sleep, be wary of your own labour, do not let yourself be charmed too much!

How should we receive, for example, a notation of this genre: 'First of all because it is true and second because the laws of this story – already burdened to an extreme with lianas, tangles of all kinds, vegetable curlicues and flourishes – demand it, I will say that the river was not far'[5]? Especially if we are warned that the 'laws of narration' are of no concern to the author. This certainly amounts to telling us that the tangles and curlicues are only apparently an ornamental excess, or the restoration of a baroquism of the visible, and that what is demanded of us is to know, at each instant, which real river traverses and animates,

---

3 Sarduy, *Colibri*, p. 77.
4 Ibid., p. 79.
5 Ibid., pp. 162–3.

though it is almost inaccessible, the phenomenal agitation of the writing.

This is because in the background of whatever proliferation is instituted in the phrasing, there is only emptiness, meagreness, and nonsense. There is 'the mute incoherence of the landscape, the unreality of the accomplished physical effort, the false presence of things'.[6] There is 'a universe reduced to the infamous thickness of representation'.[7] There is 'the jumble of a strident and monotonous actuality'.[8] Sarduy's strategy, starting from this incoherence, or this primordial vacuity, consists in saturating it by disciplined semantic fields, by an entirely *phrased* cosmology in which the flora and fauna, the stones and the rivers, the salons and the lampbearers, the filthy bistros and the mountain paths, gravitate around a primordial scene which concerns the attraction of bodies, the devotion of fat gents (the 'whales') all made up for turgidity and the sweat of the young bird-body. Then, in a second time, dissimulated by 'the unforgiving laws of narrative counterpoint',[9] it is a question of undoing this saturation, showing its underlying principles, and coming back, not at all to the adjacent proliferation, nor to the initial void, but to this state of affairs, which is the *serious* end of writing, in which one is 'peaceful like when one resists near the centre which gives everything its place and its name'.[10]

Sarduy proposes the construction of a centre of peace, from where names and places become visible, and where one can take a break, in a restricted action of sorts, to see to a kind of minor enchantment of life. Consider the storyline of *Colibri*: the hero, the young bird-body offered up to the desire of all, subjected in a tropical brothel to the Sadean law of the Regentess, does not stop fleeing and being pursued. The 'narrative' is nothing but a series of

6   Ibid., p. 113.
7   Ibid., p. 117.
8   Ibid., p. 64.
9   Ibid., p. 126.
10   Ibid., p. 148.

variations on flights, captures and returns; and it is this errancy that brings together fabricated landscapes, primitive scenes, and voluble ornamentations. But in the end, Colibri destroys the universe of sexual imprisonment in favour of what will be, always under the rule of desire and dance, the conquest of a universal calm, not unlike Rimbaud at the end of *A Season in Hell*: 'Colibri calmly examined the premises, as if penetrating the house for the first time: a good sweeping with the red broom would be needed. And putting back some lamps. If this was possible to find, he would bring up two or three tough guys from the estuary, in order to dance and bring a bit of fun to life.'[11]

To me there is something touching about this final existential modesty. It is something that is impossible to achieve unless one has first discerned the void of being, inscribed on this void the unlimited fury of representation, and undone this fury to install oneself calmly in a provisional centre, which itself is fictive but open to the gifts of chance: 'If this is possible to find ...' Severo Sarduy only displays the labyrinth of the infinite, the fractal space of his prose, in order to try to reach the point where peaceful thought may come to enjoy whatever comes. If this is possible to find.

The ternary and quasi-dialectical movement of Sarduy's desiring-writing (void, fractal, centre) demands that his style be like the lacing together of three threads – and not the inflation of images and rhythms as it is commonly seen.

Let us take the case of the bestiary, so crucial for the construction of an Amazonian *trompe l'oeil*. Contrary to Mallarmé, for whom the Swan alone is sufficient to name the absence of any bird, Sarduy engages in a kind of latent enumeration of the animal totality. At the farthest remove from any description, here we have an austere list, a dictionary, behind which there exists only the impossibility of naming 'in the real' any animal whatsoever. In *Colibri*

11   Ibid., p. 185.

alone, we find, in order of appearance: the 'whales', the jaguar, dolphins, sharks and sperm whales, coffer fish, dogs and cats, the crab, the antelope and the boa, the crane, the squid and the conger eel, the merian, the quail, the wolf, the squirrel and the falcon, the leopard and the snail, the sea urchin and the turtle, a lion and a colombe, the pig, the pigeon, the toucan, a rhesus monkey, some raptors, flies and scavengers, a rabbit, a cage of canaries, starlings, cardinals, nightingales, parrots, a robin, some fleas, a sparrow, pink flamingoes, an iguana, a magpie, some ostriches, catfish, grass snakes, a chamelion, some chestnut horses, a kangaroo, a bull, a lizard, an octopus, ducks and seagulls, tadpoles and chickens, several slugs, a cobra and some goats, a heron, some marmosets, a baby seal, a fat rat, an owl, a butterfly, a turtledove with a scorpion and an armadillo, some storks, an assortment of toads and dragonflies, a flock of vultures … It is at the centre of this nominal zoo that the proper name 'Colibri' takes flight.

To put into textual motion this inert and primordial list, flush with the void of all life, a first discrepancy consists in crossing it with another list, or another series, which is also appropriate for building up a whole fictive forest: the list of adjectives. This crossing is calculated according to varying degrees of probability, but tends towards a maximal gap, which subverts the zoological stability of the species and carries it away, around the bird-body of Colibri, towards a semantic zone of errancy and capture. For the antelope to be 'frightened' or the parrot 'boisterous' or the horse 'clumsy' is merely a convenient suture of the two lists, a reassurance of the multiple. Already it is more disconcerting to see a 'giant rabbit' pass by, or for an emaciated iguana to be 'transparent as a rock crystal'.[12] But certainly we enter into Leibnizian connections of everything with everything as soon as a 'multicoloured and tiny bird with a long and crooked beak' is 'violently nailed to the bluish wall and still breathes'; or when 'grey

---

12   Ibid., pp. 46, 93–4.

seagulls share an unstable square raft'; when storks become 'arrows of chalk'; or better yet, when a mollusc, which is obviously 'slimy' (normal suture), is 'opaque, as if in the lassitude of its passage it verified the rectangle's perimeter for eternity'.[13] By means of predicative corruption, Sarduy reaches the point where his bestiary comes to present, not a prelapsarian paradise populated by animals, but a series of detours and incongruences that are strictly parallel to the flights and returns of that central bird that is Colibri.

This still leaves us with the need to conquer the third moment, the one when this corruption itself comes undone in an image of peace and clearing, when the animal becomes the emblem of eternity. Take for instance the ending of Chapter 2, made up of silence and equilibrium, in which the powerful colour scheme (red, purple, bright yellow) welcomes the bird's flight: 'He rested against the trunk of a tree with its airy foliage, trembling, cut out of giant red and purple corollas. On the highest branch, like a slice of lemon on the rim of a daiquiri, a toucan came to settle down.'[14] Or, this magnificent and exemplary moment: 'There came, silent, without batting its wings, a heron, sharing the sky.'[15]

It is not only in the great series that the triplicity of movement organizes the text (we could repeat the same demonstration for the vegetable world, the human bodies or the figures of water as we showed for the bestiary: grand enumerating semantics, displacement towards improbable connections, restitution of an order). A great many passages that may appear purely ornamental are also local contractions of Sarduy's dialectic. Consider the following paragraph, which seems entirely 'descriptive':

> In bowls of terracotta, which seemed as if they had been placed there the night before as offerings for the gaze or voluptuous pleasure of a forest god, some pearly hibiscus floated, sprinkled with fine dew; everywhere, from the airy

---

13   Ibid., pp. 94, 101, 154, and 157.
14   Ibid., p. 35.
15   Ibid., p. 147.

metal of the scaffoldings, rusted and loose, threatening the
soldered joints of the assemblages, or breaking apart the
mouldy hinges with their thriving stalks, there sprouted
powerful flowers with multiple corollas and curved pistils,
like the antennae of nocturnal butterflies, at the tip of
which a drop of yellowish liquid pollen formed a pearl.[16]

The setting is that of a bourgeois house devoured by the
jungle, metaphor of the referral of all artifice to its basis
in nonsense, its cosmic vacuousness. The semantic population of this corruption crosses the plant series (always
indexed upon the series of colours) and the (for Sarduy's
prose also very important) series of the demolition sites,
the wastelands, and the ruins. But all this in the end serves
only as the polymorphous support for a concentration of
splendour; it is only the baroque vase in which, uniqueness
perched atop the interlacing, the drop of yellow pollen –
that glittering sperm – comes to flower.

Thus, locally and globally, in an internal reference that
makes every part the expression of the whole, Sarduy's
text constitutes a totality entirely given over to the outside
of prose, without depth or referent, but which, in twist-
ing the three threads of its dialectic in a kind of writerly
dance on the same spot, ends up acquiring the solidity of
a thing.

Indeed this is why that thing, such as a body or a bowl,
may be stolen or diverted from its regular use. This is what
we are told in the chapter 'The Theft of the Story', which
begins: 'When he came out, everything seemed changed to
him.'[17] Sarduy engages in the tortuous motif of a stolen
narrative (stolen by those who pursue Colibri), for which
is substituted another writing, about which the supposed
narrator will complain bitterly that it is like the mediocre
redoubling of his own style: '... these gangsters have stolen
my story, in order to fill it with pompoms, with archa-
isms and other affectations of the pastoral novel, useless

---

16   Ibid., p. 157.
17   Ibid., p. 101.

adjectives, synonyms and antonyms, gratuitous complications, repetitions.'[18] It is clear that the text's distance from itself authorizes the writer to express all the bad impressions he has of what might be (or are?) the defects that he attributes to himself: ornamental flourishes, homosexual stereotypes, adjectival inflation, and so on. However, we are not dealing with something like an internal confession. It is rather as if the central motif of the flight, of the wandering in the woods of a bird tracked down by its hunters, had to extend itself to the writer's own narration. Sarduy in the end tells us that this text, in which it is only in the baroque drift of a fugitive that one can gain, 'if this is possible to find', the modest peace of consistency, is bound to take flight from itself, so that the writer must always dislocate himself from the shelter he believes he can find in his own sentences. Sarduy moreover links this movement to a primitive scene, which he includes in the book: he is busy burning the bad pastiche that has been substituted for his stolen text, when suddenly his father appears, who enjoins him, while he's at it, to burn everything – namely, all that his father calls 'dirty hanky-panky'. Because, he says, 'Has one ever seen a man, a real man, amuse himself with the small fruits of glitter and glitz?'[19]

Therein lies the most profound problem of Severo Sarduy's prose, very different in this sense from Jean Genet, for whom the 'fruits of glitter and glitz' are prose's means of communication between abjection and sainthood, between the magnificent criminal and Our Lady of the Flowers. The figure of the saint is absent from Sarduy's novels, even though that of innocence is omnipresent. This is a delicate distinction, but one that has considerable artistic consequences. The link between abjection and sainthood, in its homosexual arrangement (which holds for Pasolini as well as for Genet), organizes a binary stylistic tension, which Jean-Paul Sartre, in his study of Genet, called a *tourniquet*

18 Ibid., p. 116.
19 Ibid., p. 133.

or 'whirligig': an extreme ornamental tendency, charged
with sublating impurity and giving it the figure of a rose,
or a diamond, must be able to find a sanctifying simplicity, a kind of naked prose, whose domination Genet will
assure through the use of metaphorical affectations.[20] For
Sarduy, there is no initial distinction between the desire of
bodies and the proliferation of semantic ornamentations
against the backdrop of the void. We might say that for
him, between the innocence of desire and the formal series,
there is neither whirligig nor dialectic, but a powerful unity
on the same plane, which he sometimes calls the cosmos.
Let us understand 'cosmos' as the complex name of the
void.

Besides, the motif of homosexuality is one series among
others, like that of the birds or the ruins. Here as elsewhere,
Sarduy gives his consent to the inertia of stereotypes, puts
them in motion by connecting everything with everything,
and finally sublates them by obtaining the peacefulness
of an amorous writing. These three temporal moments
correspond to:

1. The description of the libidinous 'whales' (the clients
   of the brothel in the forest) as well as the description of that which organizes the body-as-brothel of
   Colibri, its leather belt, its parts, the staging of 'the
   tortuous voluptuousness of obedience'.[21]
2. The constant connection between the sexual annotations and the disparate series, the fake leather beds,
   'white dressing gowns patched up with thick black
   stitching', urns and flaming roses, 'cigarette butts
   angrily crushed, subway stubs as lottery tickets,
   dented and empty shampoo bottles, leftovers of green
   bath soap and spit', everything that surrounds and

---

20 *Translator's note*: For the theory of 'whirligigs' or *tourniquets*
(referring to all the 'twists', 'reversals' or 'spinning sophisms' in Jean
Genet), see Jean-Paul Sartre, *Saint Genet: Actor and Martyr*, trans. Bernard
Frechtman (Minneapolis: University of Minnesota Press, 2012).

21 Sarduy, *Colibri*, p. 15.

composes what Sarduy, in a powerful formulation, calls 'the opaque archipelago of everyday screwing'.[22]

3. The amorous (but also violent) link between Colibri and the Japanese wrestler, his companion in misery and flight, the voluptuousness of the clearing: 'The Japanese licks his hands that are large, meaty and knotty at the same time; his fingers with their thick flat nails; the edge of his trembling eyelids. They roll onto one another in the humid grass, in the midst of sensitive plants that suddenly close their petals again.'[23]

But at no point is desire separated from the totality of the visible in the way that prose constitutes its superficial baroque, while both preserving and obliterating the initial void. Desire is carried away by the same fractal dialectic and, like everything else, seeks the central point at which to find a transitory peace. In this sense, the epic of flight and return, in the nominal appearances, is that of a radical innocence of desire. There is only the tension of its absorption into pure proliferation and the peacefulness of that which makes visible the nonsense beneath this proliferation and, beyond it, the repose. Hence an art which must not, like Genet's, gain a Greek simplicity against a labyrinth – or a mirror, like Proust. But rather an art of the cosmic distribution of intensities in which any poor desire whatsoever, if it can find the accord of its rhythm, is the equivalent of any living figure.

This is the art of Severo Sarduy: the innocence of desire, in the Leibnizian convolutedness of monads.

---

22 Ibid., pp. 83–4.
23 Ibid., p. 151.

PIERRE GUYOTAT,
PRINCE OF PROSE

I say that Pierre Guyotat is the prince of prose. What does
'prince' mean? It signals first of all Guyotat's nobility, the
extraordinary nobility of his prose: a nobility without prec-
edent since the speeches and sermons of Bossuet; and one
that is all the more striking in that it organizes, or enno-
bles, materials drawn from the base layers of our existence,
from the atoms of exposed flesh. Sex and cruelty, visible
and solar, hook up with being qua excremental being: the
word *putains*, 'whores', designates in prose the subsoil of
the sublime order established by the retreat of the gods.
This is the order according to which, covered by vomit and
come, I contemplate the void of which I am the sexuated
atom.

Completely given over to his own injunction, and to
his alone, this writer also stands unwaveringly under his
own law as unbeliever. 'Prince of prose' thus means, in the
second place, that Guyotat's prose is a prose of principles,
a prose of the principles of prose. Here I would name four
of these principles:

1. Never say anything except what *is*, insofar as what *is* never is what *just was*, nor what *soon will be*. Neither is memory useful nor the possible acceptable. Prose of total instantaneous oblivion and of the impossible.

2. Confer its full radiance on what ordinarily is only half-said or suspiciously left in the shadows. Reject all such precautions, which belong to the law of thuggery or to the servility of fear. Prose of the sonorous equality of its saying, without reticence or crazed rumours. Consequently, proceed to the declaration of all things as equal to the universe. This is a text that absolute egalitarianism forbids us from ever interrupting.

3. Reserve prose for the essential relations of the universe. The point is to inscribe the rhythm of what is, and never that – feeble and psychological – of the representation of what is. Direct and ecstatic inscription of constitutive collisions. Eradicate all psychology. Push to the extreme, within prose, Pascal's axiom: 'The self is odious.' Prefer the smallest drop of sperm, the tiniest tortured body, to the sophisticated arrogance of the self. Prose is the calm and at the same time violent declaration of what happens, or the illuminating description of what shows itself. It is never application, reflection or judgment. Yes, this is crucial: the ethics of prose exempts it from all judgment.

4. Like the universe, prose must pass from one thing to another without having to justify this passage. Or rather: in the retroaction of this passage, an evidence is created, which is that things are such and not otherwise. Prose transitions from act to image without the image being that of the act. And yet this image is eternally fixed, in the present, onto the act that it delinks. Principle of prose: schooled by the world, to create some eternal link by the effect in the present of a delinking.

And so, we have four principles: a principle of the pure present; a principle of the egalitarian radiance; a principle of non-judgment; a principle of the delinking of necessity.

Let us quote a passage in which all four are at work. Listen to the principles, because that too is the cadence of Guyotat's prose: a prose that makes us hear and see, in its own materiality as well as the spectral materiality of the world, the inflexible firmness of principles:

> I sit on the heaped-up corpses, blood wets my buttocks, a throat quivers under my cock, two breasts under my thighs and I tilt my head backwards, and my eyes become lost in the starlit sky; the breathing, under me, weakens, my hard-on points towards the stars, my chest moves up again towards my throat, the jackals' paws claw the flag-stones. At the bottom of the valley, the jeeps' and half-track vehicles' headlights dazzle the kingfishers mating on the reeds and on the pink shingles, the monkeys mating inside the ruins of the thermal power station, or playing on the motionless driving belts and gear wheels. At the noise of engines, breaths, moanings have started coming out of the pile of mingled bodies but, under me, the breathing has ceased and I lean back hands joined under the nape and I spread my thighs and I let my cock fall back on my belly and lift my belt. Headlights pierce the smoke, I spring up, I strike the comrades dozing in the vines, throat strangled by the grapes, and we run till morning towards the sea, to purify the harshness of our bodies and of our minds.[1]

You can clearly hear the pure present, and already the list of verbs alone is like the construction of this present that nothing precedes and which prepares nothing either. Watch the effect, which is immediately singular, of a small section of the verbal rainbow that is this passage: 'wet, quiver, breathe, having a hard-on, claw, dazzle, lean back, spread, pierce, spring up, strike, run, purify.' Look how, from this single sequence, we recognize the prose of Guyotat, because we recognize therein its principle, the prince's principle. And similarly the nouns stand implacably under the law of equality: whether in ordinary

---

1   Pierre Guyotat, *Tomb for 500,000 Soldiers*, trans. Romain Slocombe (Creation Books: 2002), pp. 105–6.

language they are trivial, obscene, magnificent, imaginative, drab or technical, the work of prose covers them with an egalitarian coat that arranges them like the atoms of the earth, or like the stars in the sky, so that their list is once again in principle recognizable as belonging to Guyotat: 'corpses, blood, buttocks, throat, cock, sky, chest, throat, jackals, flagstones, valley, jeeps, kingfishers, monkeys, thermal power station, moanings, breathing, thighs, belt, vines, grapes, morning, sea, minds'. As you can tell, this is already written in an absolute sense, already being the markings of the second principle, the egalitarian principle. But the movement of prose itself, its general tracing, obeys the third principle, that of non-judgment. Because the movement is always that of a raising, or a lifting up, of being, which carries with it all the useless hierarchies that judgment presupposes. In truth, there is no place for judgment because what is organizes the spiritual necessity of the pure present. The verbs, as we saw, are organized from 'wet' and 'pointing a hard-on' all the way to 'purify'. And the nouns are organized from 'corpses, blood and cock' all the way to 'minds'. Everything thus forms a trajectory that is traversed, linked, and sublated. Judgment is only the stupid delay with regard to the being of the present. And finally, the fourth principle: what is more paradoxically necessary, in the after-effect of prose, than the passage from a pile of corpses to some kingfishers on pink reeds? Or the passage that takes us from a pairing of monkeys in a thermal power station to the morning rush of men to the sea? Who fails to see and hear, in these passages, the very law of the universe, which at each instant engenders necessity with the materials of contingency and delinking?

However, ours is not just any universe. Guyotat has seen, no doubt before everyone else, at least with such opinionated force, that our universe is a prostituted universe. It is scientific, and by no means fantasmatic, to call *putains* the basic atoms of the world such as it presents itself today, and such as Guyotat has known that it was in the process of becoming almost half a century ago, unless something like communism happened to it. But communism did not happen to it, for the time being, so that the universe is in the process of becoming an integral regime of prostitution. Guyotat is also the prince of prose because in his prose he states the regime of prostitution as cosmology.

What does regime of prostitution mean? It means the reduction of every vital norm to the immediate mercantile potentialities of bodies; and, more generally, the transformation of the destitute, the weak, all those who compose the immutable bottom layer of the planet's popular human masses, into exchangeable bodies offered up to brute desire, cruelty, destruction, and consumption. Here is one example among thousands of the manner of this unlimited exposure of the general regime of prostitution in the prose of Guyotat. You will once again hear, in this prose, the tenacity of the prince's principles. But you will also hear a gripping truth about what constitutes the new planetary atrocity, which is the price to be paid by the people of gigantic flea-ridden cities for the deleterious enjoyment of a very small number:

> At the end of the room, on a battered paillasse, a young whore, legs joined under a large piece of linen bloody in places, moans: a sailor deflowered her too violently, she has been delirious and bleeding in the rags for three days; the shadows of the eucalypti shaken by the breeze pass on her cadaverous belly, blacken the hole of the navel, and the flows of blood; rats run along the pavement, whores scream; the men stopped in the middle of the street and embraced by the whores from below, pick up stones and throw them at the rats; children, out from the alleys, rush forward with sticks, club the rats still alive, pick them up by the tail and disappear again in the alleys screaming, fighting over the dead rats. Now and then a red sand wind rises beyond the city, comes out of some savage valley, covers the river then the corn fields; the whores, worked on, feel the sand coming, the clients give a start, their muscles snap slowly under the gleaming skin; their veins swell all along the whores' body; the red sand spatters the wall facing the open window, clings with its teeth and its claws to the

saltpeter, to the ivy. Far beyond the sea knives rise, in the white streets, pierce the hanging linen, men hand rifles to the children, put up in front of them some dummies to shoot at; the children, lying on their belly in the sand of the wash-houses, machine-gun those puppets, shoulders shaken by the shots.[2]

Such is the material substance, the atomic form, in the sense of Lucretius, of the regime of generalized prostitution. A key point therein is the requisitioning of children in the violent clash of exposed bodies, as well as in the armies of mercenaries that roam the territories – countless children, victims of rape or armed recruits, of which every day we are being told, or shown, the massive existence. Children to whom the prince of prose, haunted by this word, 'child', has also devoted himself from very early on.

Here we must evoke the question of paedophilia. Today we witness the forced incorporation of childhood in the spectacle of pornography, which is increasingly ubiquitous. We must hold that this incorporation is the correlate of the repressive obsession with paedophilia. It is because our planetary cosmology is the regime of prostitution that there is an obsessive repression of paedophilia, a relentless tracking down in the name of children's innocence. The general regime of prostitution, which is the exposure of any body, like anything else, to the shopping windows of the commodity, violently juxtaposes the pornographic ubiquity with the mythological innocence of the child, which people want to present to us, a century after Freud, as an asexual angel. If we think of the cruel and irrational nexus of the sale of pornographic images and the legal prosecution of paedophilia in the courts, of universal exposure and obsessive imprisonment, of the commercialization of false desire and the juridicalization of false innocence, who can fail to see that Pierre Guyotat is the great prose-writer of these phenomena, their great denouncer under the princely law of prose?

---

2   Ibid., p. 229.

That is because Guyotat has included all these arrangements in a grandiose cosmology. Carrying our world on
his shoulders as a writer, sublimating the obscenity of generalized exposure by way of inflexible principles, Guyotat
has invented the cosmology of the general regime of prostitution. For him, we will never fully come to understand
a world whose basic constituent is subsumed under the
word *putain*, *les putains*, with both masculine and feminine inflections being equally contained in this term.
Neither masturbatory fantasy, which is the instrument of
useful writing, nor *marxisant* anthropology, which also
amounts to useful good will, can fully grasp this. What is
needed is a theory of the world, of the universe: an atom-
istic theory of bodies. Between these bodies there exists a
force of attraction, or rather two forms of a single force:
sex and cruelty. That is what, without any morbidity, in a
cold and intense objectivity, conjoins the bodies. Or, rather,
as with Lucretius, that is what organizes their collision:
the collision of bodies exposed as a collision of whores,
these atoms of humanity in the universe of generalized
prostitution.

Consider a short example of the similarity between the
attraction of bodies reduced to sex and cruelty, on one
hand, and the collision of atoms, on the other; or else the
cloud of flies, or the settling of dust, or the call of the birds:

> he turns to the woman, seizes her by the shoulder, drags
> her towards his bed, knocks her down under him, tears
> her dress, bites her mouth, gives a broad hand signal; the
> other women come to lie by his side and begin stroking
> him again, and caress his hips, his back, his chest, his cock.
> Illiten bears heavily on the woman, rolls, writhes on her,
> groaning; the taut cock gets tangled in the torn dress; the
> woman's head rolls in the dust, flies gleam in the rays of
> light, run between the man's fingers, on the sweat running
> from the woman's breasts, settle under the eyebrows black
> with makeup and sweat. The two bodies glow in the dust,
> Illiten slides over the woman, his fingers claw the earth,
> raised dust falls back on the man's shoulders. The soldier
> now and then looks back, his heart beats inside his chest,

he leans against the wall, flattens his belly, the battledress
gets crumpled and white with the saltpeter; a cock at the
bottom end of the village, crows.[3]

You can hear, I think, what such a text contains in terms of
pure and abstract thought, but through a sensible or sensuous materiality chosen for its heaviness and its suffocating
insistence. It is with this gluey, sticky, mixed-up materiality
that the point is to create the pure fiction of the universal
attraction of bodies, which is our truth. To this very day
Guyotat insists on this point, that the world created by
his prose is a real world precisely insofar as it is not realistic, or referential. It is a double, a spectral world, which
is the truth of the given or visible world. We can conclude
as much from the fact that the cosmology of generalized
prostitution presupposes that, in order for it to be transmitted to us, the ordinary world must be transformed into
a non-world, or chaos. This is the function of the colonial
war, for example, in *Tomb for 500,000 Soldiers*. It is the
collapse of the world, bloody chaos, and rage. And then,
against the indifferent backdrop of nature's splendour, we
can see, I mean really see, the atomistics of bodies and their
law of prostitution, the agitated and senseless attraction of
the human atoms, of the whores, by sex and cruelty.

Thus, we can say that the principles of Guyotat's prose
enact the statement about the death of the gods. If there are
no more gods, then there is no more world. The cosmology of generalized prostitution must be thought of outside
the world, and thus according to a solitude in which only
the basic attractions rule. In this sense, Guyotat's courage
consists in uttering the death of God in the present. Let us
quote:

God, who has been at the point of death for three centuries, dies. His priests, in vain, strip the ritual service of his
worship, whiten the walls of his temples. God had hidden
the secret heart of man, man now sees his bestial heart, his

---

3   Ibid., pp. 133–4.

eyes are unsealed, the smell of the beast chokes him, God
dies at the moment of man's greatest solitude.[4]

In the humanist controversy – the controversy between
Sartre and Foucault, for instance – Guyotat clearly takes
the side of antihumanism. It is first of all to his own prose
that the observation he makes in the early 1960s applies:
'An art is born with no place for man, for safety.'[5] This is
what renders him so strange to our age of human rights,
hypocritical compassion and commercial pardons. It is
also what renders him so glorious. The death of God opens
up the possibility, not of the promotion of man, but of the
discovery by man himself of his beastly core. This beast is
the inclusion of man in the silent collision of bodies under
the control and influence of sex and cruelty. In the retreat
of God it is not man, nor meaning, nor peace that happens,
but a package of animal atoms. Man is thus asphyxiated
by his own drunkenness, becoming that beggar who pleads
to the dead God: '... in the intoxication of wine, you call
your god, the dumb god, whose absence and silence earn
the wrath of men'.[6]

Beyond the formal power of his sexual cosmology,
beyond the condition to which we are confined by the
death of the gods and the uncertainty of revolutions,
beyond generalized prostitution as the nakedness of the
absence of a world, Guyotat, it seems to me, proposes to us
a productive hesitation between two outcomes, or between
two stars.

The first outcome is that the only thing that survives
is the almost solar vigour of doubt. The question of life
and death is indeed radically posed by the dereliction of
meaning in the sexual cosmology. If there is no world, if
there is only sexual and murderous attraction of atoms,
or of whores, if the heart is silent, then love is probably
impossible. In that case, it is better to die. Whence the

4   Ibid., p. 43.
5   Ibid.
6   Ibid., p. 114.

call: 'Dispatch me; how can I live with a silent heart?'[7] Doubt, at least, remains for its part in agreement with the indifference of nature, with the sexual collision of human atoms, with the fictive character of all belief. There might be a joy in doubt, a kind of eternal joy. This is the truly beautiful and striking formula, in which Antoine Vitez saw concentrated the genius of Guyotat: 'I go in for disbelief, with a quivering of joy. My forehead, I want it crushed and squeezed by the bow of a litter, and my shoulders soiled by vomit. O doubt, only eternity.'[8]

In Guyotat we thus obtain an eternity of joy without belief, an eternity of doubt in which I discover at last the foul glory of matter. But the fabulous joy of eternal disbelief demands a firmness of all instants, because, before anything else, this disbelief is the disbelief in man. Yes: true joy, the joy that makes you tremble, is the pacifying certainty, whose form is doubt, that man does not exist. We then gain access to eternity, to which the principles of prose bear witness.

But a second outcome is sketched out. This would be the appearance of another world, a new world, beyond the sexual cosmology and the eradication of any true world by the unleashing of generalized prostitution. A new couple, an incalculable alliance with the feminine, perhaps? Or a kind of paganism revisited amid the fever over a dead world. Here and there, you find this sketch, even sometimes at the disciplined heart of chaos. It unfolds in the seventh and final song of *Tomb for 500,000 Soldiers*. Without deciding the matter in an abstract way, this song tells us that what is being invisibly prepared is perhaps the dawn of a recommencement of the world as a whole. In the couple of Kment and Giauhare, this song indeed presents us with a renewed figure of the original couple, Adam and Eve submerged in a disjointed nature after the disaster. The woman is expecting a child. It is a humanity under a completely new emblem. No doubt this is Guyotat's version

---

7   Ibid., p. 296.
8   Ibid., p. 44.

of the obscure formula of Heidegger's testament ('Only a
God can save us now'). Which God? No, not in the form of
the gods, but in the sense that a new humanity would come
from the depths of universal obscenity, with the mission of
restoring a world. The two survivors of sexuality as brute
attraction of bodies, which we cannot distinguish from
the cruelty of destruction – in short, survivors of the murderous atomistics – understand that they are alone. Some
emblems of the old deities still circulate: a goddess, a faun
with his mane, a Christ between dove and thorns. Then,
love is tenderly and powerfully restored. I read the very
end of *Tomb*:

> Kment and Giauhare, woken up, knees and fists in the
> thorns, push the hedge aside; a man bending over the stone,
> is mating with the goddess; a mane sticks out of his nape
> and of his back; on his head a dove and a crown of thorns;
> his bare legs are vibrating, incandescent; in the distance,
> on the sea, the sail scuds along towards the island and the
> fish shoot out, sparkle on the forge, strike the sides of the
> boat, play in the deep beneath the shadow of the hull; the
> boat is empty but a beam of light, the first one of dawn,
> watches and stands by, upon the sail. Kment kneels down
> before Giauhare, and Giauhare before Kment. Fists on the
> ground, they kiss each other on the knees, on the genitals,
> on the forehead.[9]

The prose principles of our prince have allowed him, with
a force that nothing can match since then, to fabulate the
following truth: we find ourselves in a worldless age, an
a-cosmic age, because we are bound to the generalized
figure of prostitution that is the commodified body, a figure
that properly speaking atomizes us. In that case, Guyotat
tells us, there are probably two hypotheses:

1. Doubt is the only attitude that has not been won over
   by the corruption of the world. This is the position of
   'Stoic' or 'superior nihilism'. One takes on board the

---

9   Ibid., p. 378.

knowledge of the absence of meaning, as well as the fact that one's self is naked in the sexual collision.

2. New love happens. Kment and Giauhare are face to face, on their knees; they have interrupted the chaos of cruel collisions. They can hug and create. The world will turn to the worst, but this worst is pregnant with a new dawn.

My conviction and my optimism certainly make me turn towards a third hypothesis, which would not be hanging in the balance between doubt and miracle and would not have to find support in any myth. I accept the contemporary absence of a world. But I hold that in the absence of a world there is the outline of a world, its drawing, its watermark, a kind of sketch on the walls of an underwater cathedral, a network of event-traces that are to be traversed and assembled. In this sense, I for my part desire to go in for belief, and not for disbelief, with a tremor of joy.

Nevertheless, I know the risk to which any belief is exposed, even if it visibly separates itself from all the saving gods, fables and totalities, as well as from meaning in general. It exposes itself to the fascination with what Guyotat superbly calls 'the melancholy of the perfect centuries'. It is true – even if we attempt to read the stigmata of a renaissance in the devastation, let us beware of the melancholic desire for the coming of perfect centuries. Perhaps we may be protected from this desire by a quality that Guyotat disparages, which is the Cartesian quality of common sense: the political good sense which preserves us from contemporary extravagances and unprecedented debasements, of which our current capitalo-parliamentarism offers us the ruinous spectacle. Of good common sense, to conclude, we will accept Guyotat's definition, which is truly instructive about our dubious paths: 'Common sense, weakened form of savage custom.'

A NOTE ON THE TEXTS

1. 'The Age of the Poets' was first published in French as part of the seminar at the Collège International de Philosophie organized and subsequently edited by Jacques Rancière under the title *La politique des poètes: Pourquoi des poètes en temps de détresse?* (Paris: Albin Michel, 1992), pp. 21–38.
2. 'What Does the Poem Think?' was first published in French as 'Que pense le poème?' in *L'art est-il une connaissance?* edited by Roger-Pol Droit (Paris: Le Monde Éditions, 1993), pp. 214–24.
3. 'The Philosophical Status of the Poem after Heidegger' was first published in French as 'Le statut philosophique du poème après Heidegger', in *Penser après Heidegger*, edited by Jacques Poulain and Wolfgang Schirmacher (Paris: L'Harmattan, 1992), pp. 263–8. A slightly different version of this text can be found in English in 'The Philosophical Recourse to the Poem', in Alain Badiou, *Conditions*, trans. Steven Corcoran (London: Continuum, 2008), pp. 35–48.
4. 'Philosophy and Poetry from the Vantage Point of the Unnameable' was first published in French in the journal *Po&sie* 64 (1993). A later version was published and translated as 'What Is a Poem? Or, Philosophy and Poetry at the Point of the Unnamable', in Alain Badiou, *Handbook of Inaesthetics*, trans. Alberto Toscano (Stanford: Stanford University Press, 2005), pp. 16–27.

5. 'One Must Descend into Love: On the Poetry of Henry Bauchau' was first published in French as the preface to Henry Bauchau, *Heureux les déliants: Poèmes 1950–1995* (Brussels: Labor, 1995), pp. 7–16.

6. 'The Unfolding of the Desert' was first published as the preface to Salam Al-Kindy, *Le Voyageur sans Orient: Poésie et philosophie des Arabes de l'ère préislamique* (Arles: Actes Sud, 1998), pp. 11–15.

7. 'Drawing: On Wallace Stevens' is the text of a talk first published in English in *lacanian ink* 28 (2006), pp. 42–9. Based on the author's unpublished typescript, 'Le dessin'.

8. 'Destruction, Negation, Subtraction: On Pier Paolo Pasolini' is the text of a talk presented in Los Angeles in February 2007, first published in English online at lacan.com. Based on the author's unpublished typescript, 'Destruction, négation, soustraction'.

9. 'Poetry and Communism', previously unpublished, is the text of a talk presented at the Sorbonne, in April 2014. Based on the author's typescript 'Poésie et communisme'.

10. 'The Autonomy of the Aesthetic Process' was first published in French as 'L'autonomie du processus esthétique', in the journal *Cahiers marxistes-léninistes* 12/13 (1966), pp. 77–89. The original text bears the composition date of June 1965. Previously it appeared in English in *Radical Philosophy* 178 (March/April 2013), pp. 32–9. The translator wishes to thank Peter Hallward and Peter Osborne for their help with this earlier version.

11. 'What Does Literature Think?' was first published in English as 'Qu'est-ce que la littérature pense? (Literary Thinking)', trans. Alistair Clarke, *Paragraph* 28:2 (July 2005), pp. 35–40.

12. 'A Requiem for the Factory: On François Bon's *Sortie d'usine*' was first published in French as 'Un requiem d'usine. François Bon : *Sortie d'usine*, roman', in the periodical *Le Perroquet: Quinzomadaire d'opinion* 16 (November 6–25, 1982), pp. 1, 4–5.

13. 'On the Prose of Natacha Michel' is a set of book reviews published in French over the course of two dozen years. In chronological order, the texts translated here were published as 'La prose et la spirale. Natacha Michel: *Le Repos de Penthésilée*', *Critique* 490–491 (1981); 'Témoignage d'un acte insigne, Natacha Michel: *Impostures et séparations*',

Le Perroquet: Quinzomadaire d'opinion 65 (November 1986); 'Le vrai dans la géographie de sa prose. Sur *Canapé Est-Ouest* de N. Michel', *Le Perroquet: Quinzomadaire d'opinion* 84–5 (January 1990); 'Une visitation. Sur *Le jour où le temps a attendu son heure*, roman de Natacha Michel', *Lettres sur tous les sujets* 3 (January 1992); and 'Vendanges de la nuit. *Circulaire à toute ma vie humaine*', *Critique* 707 (April 2006), pp. 362–8.

14. 'Void, Series, Clearing: Essay on the Prose of Severo Sarduy' was first published in French as 'Vide, série, clairière. Essai sur la prose de Severo Sarduy', in Severo Sarduy, *Obras completas*, edited by François Wahl (Paris: UNESCO, 2000), vol. 2, pp. 1619–25.

15. 'Pierre Guyotat, Prince of Prose', previously unpublished, is the text of a talk 'P. Guyotat, prince de la prose', presented at the Centre Pompidou in Paris in October 2005. Based on the author's typescript.

INDEX